CW01501141

FIGURES OF THE THINKABLE

MERIDIAN

Crossing Aesthetics

Werner Hamacher

Editor

Translated by Helen Arnold

Stanford
University
Press

Stanford
California
2007

FIGURES OF THE THINKABLE

Cornelius Castoriadis

Stanford University Press
Stanford, California

English translation © 2007 by the Board of Trustees of the
Leland Stanford Junior University. All rights reserved.

Figures of the Thinkable was originally published in French in
1999 under the title *Figures du Pensable: les carrefours du
labyrinthe VI* © 1999, Éditions du Seuil.

This book has been published with the assistance of the
French Ministry of Culture—National Center for the Book.

No part of this book may be reproduced or transmitted in any
form or by any means, electronic or mechanical, including
photocopying and recording, or in any information storage or
retrieval system without the prior written permission of
Stanford University Press.

Printed in the United States of America
on acid-free, archival-quality paper

Library of Congress Cataloging-in-Publication Data

Castoriadis, Cornelius, 1922–1997.
[Figures du pensable. English]
Figures of the thinkable / Cornelius Castoriadis ;
translated by Helen Arnold.
p. cm.—(Meridian: crossing aesthetics)
Includes bibliographical references.
ISBN 978-0-8047-4234-4 (cloth : alk. paper)
ISBN 978-0-8047-5618-1 (pbk. : alk. paper)
1. Philosophy.   2. Social sciences.   3. Psychoanalysis.
I. Title.
B22.C28513 1984
194—dc22
2006037118

Contents

Preface to the French Edition

The first volume of *Carrefours du Labyrinth* (in English, *Crossroads in the Labyrinth*)[1] appeared in French in 1978. Four other volumes of the series were published during Castoriadis's lifetime, between 1986 and 1997.[2] He presented the singularity of this experience of "entering the Labyrinth," the unique philosophical questioning he pursued over two decades, in the opening pages of the *Crossroads:* "To think is not to get out of the cave; it is not to replace the uncertainty of shadows by the clear-cut outlines of things themselves, the flame's flickering glow for the light of the true Sun. To think is to enter the Labyrinth. . . . It is to lose oneself amidst galleries which exist only because we never tire of digging them; to turn round and round at the end of a cul-de-sac whose entrance has been shut off behind us—until, inexplicably, this spinning around opens up in the surrounding wall's cracks which offer passage."[3]

In that first volume, Castoriadis reflected on the being of language, the anonymous creation of speaking subjects, on psychoanalysis, which he viewed as an essentially practicopoietic activity, and he scrutinized the enigma of the historical nature, in the fullest sense, of philosophy and science and the mode of being of the social-historical sphere. During that same period, he was also staking out what he considered one of the fundamental political questions of our time: will the project of autonomy be able to survive if the anthropological type consubstantial to its birth and development is threatened with extinction? Those queries, which received broader, deeper examination in the subsequent volumes, are broached in the texts contained in the present work.

Figures of the Thinkable: Cornelius Castoriadis did not choose the title, but the expression is his nonetheless. "This is not a question of literary style, or of the 'style' of thought—any more than it is a question simply of new 'ideas.' It is a question of new and other forms, types, figures/schemas/significations; and of other 'problems,' and a new sense of what is and is not problematic."[4] The reader will clearly realize that "what is and is not problematic" for Castoriadis sets him radically apart from the people in the forefront of the contemporary intellectual scene. These texts, his last, dig deeper into those "galleries" he so often haunted, be it on such themes as the limits of the "rationality" of capitalist society, democracy as explicit self-institution of society, literary creation as creation/positing of new types of *eidos,* a philosophical interrogation on science, or on the mode of being of the social-historical sphere and of the psyche. Whence some unavoidable repetitions, particularly because, as Castoriadis had already had the opportunity to write when publishing another of his collections of texts,[5] the presuppositions behind them are far from self-evident for all readers.

Under the heading "Poiēsis"—meaning poetic creation, definitely, but also institutional creation—we have placed two texts side by side, in which Castoriadis reflects on poetry, that which, within language, is creation par excellence, to show that "the poet is not simply *metropoios* [creator of meter, versifier] and *muthopoios* [creator of sense and meaning], she is also *eikonopoios,* creator of images, and *melopoios,* creator of music."[6] He also points to how the differing responses of the two great Greek tragic poets of the fifth century BCE already show the transition from the idea of a divine anthropogony to the notion of the self-creation of humans, aware of their own mortality. These two texts—"Notes on Some Poetic Resources" and "Aeschylean Anthropogony and Sophoclean Self-Creation of *Anthrōpos*"—shed light on some aspects of human creation that, although not entirely absent from Castoriadis's writings, have rarely been broached frontally by him, or from that angle.

Notice

Cornelius Castoriadis had planned to publish a sixth volume of the *Crossroads in the Labyrinth*. His papers include two tables of contents. One, undated, includes the following titles:

1. Space and Number
2. The Psychical and Social Roots of Hate
3. Aeschylean and Sophoclean Anthropogony
4. Notes on Some Poetic Resources
5. True and False Chaos
6. The Enigma of the Foundation of Politics
7. The Psyche and Society Anew
8. (Ardoino?)
9. Heritage and Revolution
10. The "Scientificness" of Psychoanalysis
11. The Historical Status of Meaning, the Psychical Status of Meaning

The other, no doubt later, carrying the date "18/06/96," is composed as follows:

1. False and True Chaos
2. Space and Number
3. Talk with Ardoino
4. The Aporias of Science
5. The Socialization of the Psyche
6. Psyche and History
7. Ontology and Anthropology
8. The Historical Status of Meaning

9. Aeschylus and Sophocles
10. Notes on Poetry
11. Hatred of the Other, Self-Hate
12. The "Rationality" of Capitalism

Neither of these lists of writings destined for publication was definitive, of course, if only because some texts only existed in draft form, or simply as projects. Moreover, he would certainly have considerably modified those that were completed or had already been published, as he usually did.

Some of the titles he projected had to be excluded because the state of the manuscript seemed to preclude any publication in the near future. Furthermore, it seemed appropriate to add some essays that had not been chosen for any earlier volumes for no obvious reason, as well as other more recent writings that we may reasonably surmise he would have selected when composing the final contents, and that offer greater detail, further developments or clarifications on some important points.

With the few exceptions duly noted in the text, editorial work on the manuscript was limited to the introduction of references when they seemed indispensable, the correction of *lapsus calami,* and a few minor stylistic modifications. With a single exception (the new heading, "Poiēsis"), the different headings ("Polis," "Psyche," and so on) have been carried over from the previous volumes of the *Carrefours,* but the ventilation of the texts was an editorial decision. All notes written by the editors, including footnotes, are placed between square brackets.

The texts contained in this volume were selected and copyedited by a collective composed of Cybèle, Sparta, and Zoe Castoriadis, Enrique Escobar, Olivier Fressard, Myrto Gondicas, Pascal Vernay, and Dominique Walter.

The French Editors

Addendum

Full references for the works of Castoriadis mentioned in notes are placed in the Appendix. My thanks to Sparta and Zoe Castoriadis, Enrique Escobar, Daniel Ferrand, and Myrto Gondicas for their invaluable help and advice.—Trans.

FIGURES OF THE THINKABLE

Poiēsis

§ 1 Aeschylean Anthropogony and Sophoclean Self-Creation of *Anthrōpos*

For Constantin Despotopoulos,
A gift, in return for everything . . .

What is *anthrōpos?* The question is always present in Greek[1] tragedy, whether in mediated or immediate fashion. It is posed—and given an answer—with specific intensity and clarity in two of the most significant and masterful tragedies: *Prometheus Bound* by Aeschylus (possibly one of the last works by this poet, dated circa 460 BCE) and *Antigone* by Sophocles (dated 442 or 443 BCE).

As I shall try to demonstrate, the answers the two tragedies provide to a question that is fundamental to the whole of Greek civilization stand perfectly opposed. This difference cannot be simply attributed to each poet's individual stance. In spite of the brief period separating the production of the two works—approximately twenty years—the difference expresses and is consubstantial with the extraordinary rhythm of intellectual creation in democratic Athens, the increasingly radical marginalization of traditional representations, and the expanding and deepening of human self-awareness. In a sense, this is analogous to the difference between Herodotus and Thucydides, which is thus previewed some twenty or thirty years in advance.

Constraints of time and space do not permit me to go into all the "hermeneutic" matters (in the contemporary sense of the term) that are necessarily raised by these extraordinary texts. I shall deliberately "extract" the passages of central concern to me, without addressing—apart from incidental allusions—the relation these passages entertain with the whole of the tragedy in which they are found, and even less with the entire oeuvre of the two poets. Nor will I refer to the wide-ranging network of anthropological attitudes appearing in Homer's and Hesiod's time and subsequently, up to the fifth century and even later.[2] All related questions are, of course, legitimate. But I also consider it legitimate to attempt to theorize in themselves and in their full potential certain spoken positions of the two poets (in full knowledge, naturally, of all that surrounds them, but without explicitly elaborating on this knowledge) and then, from that starting point, to attempt to elucidate the whole of the Greek landscape.

Our subject here is the question, what is said—thus, what is proposed to the attention of the Athenian audience—regarding *anthrōpos* and his essential attributes, alternately, in *Prometheus Bound* and in *Antigone?* It is of scant interest, then, whether Aeschylus and Sophocles "invented" their words or "borrowed" them, whether they conceived them in a perfectly lucid state or dreamed them or received them in a moment of divine madness. It hardly interests us, moreover, whether they "believed" them (although they did of course believe them). What matters, from this standpoint, is only that in 460–440 BCE Athens, someone could in fact conceive the matters we discuss here, that someone could express them, present them to the people, and, in the case of *Antigone* at least, be crowned with the laurel wreath for what he had conceived, expressed, and presented. In other words, what matters is the actual presence, in the Athenian social-historical space, of certain significational complexes, which have an intimate affinity with the overall imaginary institution of this space, as we well know. Aeschylus' relation with the roots of a mythical/religious tradition, upon which he imparts a decisive shift, and Sophocles' relation with the entire philosophical (and "sophistic") ferment and creation of his contemporaries are more or less known. I believe they will be elucidated further by the comparative analysis that follows.

In addition, I cannot address previous and more or less well-known interpretations of the two works.[3] I shall only recall two points, briefly. There is a "translation" and extensive "interpretation" by Heidegger of the one stasimon (choral ode) in *Antigone* we shall discuss below, beginning with the famous words *Polla ta deina*.[4] This "translation" is essentially a repulsive violation of the Sophoclean text. It supports—and is supported by—an "interpretation" that is, as is almost always the case, a simple projection of Heidegger's patterns of thought. True, these patterns in themselves may propel one toward thought and productively "incite" the usually indolent reader of ancient texts, but in this particular case they lead to an artificial and unsound construction, which (1) presents Sophoclean *anthrōpos* as a complete embodiment of Heideggerian *Dasein,* and (2) is characterized, incredibly and monstrously (like everything Heidegger has written about the ancient Greeks), by systematic disregard for the *polis,* for politics, for democracy, and for their central position in ancient Greek creation. The unavoidable result of this disregard is of course a wrong, biased "understanding" of ancient philosophy, which is indissolubly interwoven with democracy and the *polis,* even when it considers them enemies. Even Plato—indeed, particularly Plato—is not only inconceivable and impossible without the democratic *polis,* but is also incomprehensible as a philosopher without his persistent struggle against democracy. All this, the national-socialist Heidegger (1933–45) does not want and is not able to see. (One consequence of this blindness will be encountered below in my discussion of Sophocles' text.)

Heidegger's arbitrary practices go so far as to combine tampering with the text's evident punctuation with removal of those words that point to how out of place this tampering is. For example, he reads the stasimon's verses 360–61 in *Antigone* as *pantoporos aporos, ep' ouden erchetai* instead of *pantoporos: aporos ep' ouden erchetai to mellon,* "capable of going everywhere, of traversing everything, of finding answers to everything; he advances toward nothing that is in the future without having some resource,"[5] so as to translate as, "going everywhere and yet left behind, without experience and without a way out, he comes to nothing"[6]—a shameless violation of the text that, in order to achieve superficial plausibility, must covertly omit the words "the future" (*to mellon*).

Some of Heidegger's impudent and arbitrary interpretations have already been pointed out by Daniel Coppieters de Gibson (among others), and this brings me to my second introductory remark.[7] Against Heidegger, Coppieters de Gibson himself calls on the works and findings of the contemporary French "structuralist" Hellenists—Vernant, Detienne, Vidal-Naquet—according to whom "the figure of Greek man . . . determines the status of *anthrōpos,* placing him in a relation with the gods and, correspondingly, with animals."[8] And it is beyond any doubt that the Greek conception of *anthrōpos* is generally defined by the organizational structure animals/humans/gods, which, in a way, delineates the boundaries of this conception from the emergence of Greek civilization (at least since Hesiod) up to the classical years and even further (consider Aristotle's *either beast or god*—*thērion ē theos*). This structure, which seems self-evident to those of us who find ourselves in the continuum of its Greek formation, is not at all "self-evident." Let us consider, for example, the Jews, the Hindus, the Chinese, or the Indian tribes of America, where we often observe a "circulation" between the animal, human, and divine conditions—a circulation, not a rupture.

Yet this structure is simply the encasing, the shell, within which an enormous—and for us decisive—social-historical creation takes place that completely alters the signification of those terms or elements making up this structure. And this happens exclusively by the alteration of signification—of the significational magma—that concerns the central element of this structure, namely *anthrōpos*. This alteration is accomplished by the effort toward self-knowledge, which is, precisely, a crucial characteristic of this creation. If we retain this "structuralist" perception, we are in danger of repeating the critical misapprehension that has plagued the approach to the ancient Greek world for centuries. We are in danger of speaking of "the Greek *anthrōpos*," "the Greek *polis*," "the Greek conception of nature," etc., forgetting meanwhile that the basic characteristic of ancient Greek history is precisely that it is *history* in the most emphatic sense of the term, that the "spirit" of ancient Greeks is realized precisely as alteration, self-alteration, self-institution—all three notions interwoven with striving toward self-knowledge, which is continuous effort, work, and process, not a static result.

We can perceive a decisive moment in this alteration by analyzing and comparing the anthropologies of Aeschylus and Sophocles. The juxtaposition of the two poets stands witness to an ontological reversal of the utmost importance, which occurred over those twenty years.

$\sim$

The question, what is *anthrōpos?*, is not posed explicitly in the two tragedies in the manner of a philosophical text. It is contained within the tragedies and actually comes to be a question by the fact that it is given an extensive response. Aeschylus answers his own implicit question with an anthropogony. This anthropogony is mythical not simply in an external sense—insofar as it refers to a myth, the myth of Prometheus, which it redeploys. It is mythical in the deeper philosophical sense of the term: it answers the question concerning *anthrōpos* by turning to the source of his existence and by presenting a narrative—*anthrōpos* is whatever he is because at some point, long ago (beyond all possible empirical corroboration or disproof), something happened that surpasses our usual experience. Prometheus, a superhuman creature, gave human beings what made them truly human. Definition of a myth: the narrative of origin responds to the question of essence. However, in Sophocles, as we shall see, the presentation of this essence responds both to the question of essence and to the question of origin. The essence of *anthrōpos* (the fact of being *deinos*) is his self-creation.

Let us take a closer look at Aeschylus' text. The anthropogony is presented here as the work of Prometheus, as a consequence of his decision and his action. This decision emerges in turn from a conflict between superhuman powers—the conflict between Zeus and Prometheus. Zeus wanted to destroy the humans (lines 231–36) and Prometheus decided to save them—and he does save them by passing on to them a part of the potential *prattein/poiein*—acting/creating—which had been the exclusive property of the divine powers until then.

There is a point to underlining this desire for destruction of humankind, which Aeschylus emphatically attributes to Zeus. The reasons or motives of Zeus, in the mind of Aeschylus, remain unknown. The poet probably described them in his *Prometheus Fire-bearer,* a work that has not survived.

What was the condition of humanity before Prometheus' intervention? By elimination, the enumeration of all those elements that humans did not possess in their primitive existence (lines 248–54, 458–506) does of course yield an indirect answer, by contrast. But Aeschylus also gives a direct answer with an affirmative description of prehuman humanity (lines 248–54, 443–57). The description, particularly in verses 443–57, is extraordinary. The prehuman condition of humanity, as Aeschylus presents it, is literally incredible. It is entirely fantastic, without any apparent plausibility or even any effort toward such plausibility.

These "humans," if they can be called that at all, are like insubstantial shadows; they remind us of the zombies in contemporary gothic novels. They saw without seeing, without gaining any utility (*matēn*) from what they saw. They heard without hearing, and, "just as shapes in dreams" (*oneiratōn alinkioi morphaisi*), they passed their long life without any order, abandoned to chance (*eikēi*). They lived underground, inside sunless caves, unable to distinguish between winter, spring, and summer, and did everything without thought, without discernment (*ater gnōmēs to pan eprasson*). And they did not foresee—they did not know—death (line 248; I shall return to the interpretation of this verse). This condition is entirely unrealistic, for us as well as for Aeschylus' time. This is not an issue of superprimitive savages, nor of any other possible or conceivable zoological species. Neither apes nor even ants (referred to in line 453) can be said to resemble shapes in dreams who see without seeing. The prehuman condition of humanity is not, according to Aeschylus, a usual animal nature. From a biological standpoint, these creatures are monstrous and radically unfit for life. Had they ever appeared, they would not have been able to survive past the second generation; we do not need a Darwinian theory to come to this conclusion. Nonetheless, Aeschylus' description presents something more significant than reality: it presents the human condition "before" or "outside" the institution of social life—of the arts, of work, of speech. *Anthrōpos* is described here as he would have been if he had a body, of course, and a soul, but not discernment (*gnōmēs*). It is a description of what I would call the originary unconscious, the a-rationality and a-reality of the monadic psyche. This condition is conceivable only logically and hypothetically, one that resembles a dreamed shape—and it is full of dreamed shapes—in an abstract sense: it shows what and how *anthrōpos* would have been without thought and without art (*technē*). I consider this abstraction more significant than reality because only this enables us to conceive all those elements in humanity that derive from what is beyond humanity's primordial fact (the psyche)—elements that refer to humanity's social condition, to what for us is the institution of thought and art and, for Aeschylus, are Prometheus' gifts to humans: "they who were like babies before they speak, [I made them] full of thought and endowed with thought capable of imposing itself on what exists" (*nēpious ontas to prin, ennous ethēka kai phrenōn epēbolous,* lines 443–44).[9]

It would be rather ridiculous, a priori, to seek any systematic logical-philosophical order in the ensuing enumeration and description of Prometheus' gifts (lines 457–506). Yet the order of the exposition itself, as well as what it includes and what it leaves out, are certainly not fortuitous. Prometheus begins by talking of the risings of the stars and their settings, which are difficult to distinguish (*duskritous duseis*). The reference here must be to sunrise and sunset as everyday occurrences, but above all, to the *epitolai,* to the periodic appearances of stars in the sky by virtue of which the yearly seasons may be determined. The simple rising and setting of the sun or of any other star is not "difficult to discern," and the inability of the prehuman humans to discern the seasons was announced just before (lines 454–56). Thus, Prometheus gives humans the signs, the stable reference points through which the conception and measuring of time becomes possible. This measuring of time and of everything measurable comes immediately afterward: "[and] I invented for them number, the superlative 'sophism' [invention, discovery]" (*arithmon, exochon sophismatōn, exēuron autois,* lines 459–60).[10]

How can one not recall Aristotle, in this conjunction between time and number, "time is the numbering of movement according to a before and an afterward" (*chronos esti arithmos kinēseōs kata to proteron kai husteron*)?[11] For enumeration to exist, there must be first a definition and determination of divisible parts. And humanity without arithmetic is inconceivable. Immediately afterward come *grammatōn . . . suntheseis, mnēmēn hapantōn, mousomētor' erganēn* (line 461): the co-articulations or interweavings of engraved or drawn signs, which can embody any memory and can serve any work "that bears the Muses": what we call the arts and knowledge.

After this gift of time, numbers, and the (artificial) signs supporting and embodying memory come the arts of production, namely technique, in today's language. I shall not comment here on this enumeration (lines 462–69, 500–503). I draw attention only to the emphatic reference to medicine (*to megiston,* "the most important," lines 478–83) and to the exhaustive description of divination and the interpretation of dreams (lines 484–99), to which I shall return. The verse that brings the enumeration to a conclusion has a profound meaning: "all the arts [come] to the mortals by Prometheus" (*pasai technai brotoisin ek Promētheōs,* line 506). Our axiom in this analysis is that the poet must be taken seriously. *Pasai technai*—all arts—is equivalent to *pasa technē,* every technical ability. Prometheus did not grant humans certain elements out of which they in turn composed and assembled the rest; from him (*ek*) originate all arts, *pasai technai.* Surely Aeschylus cannot possibly be ignorant of the fact that in his day, the arts were constantly being perfected (and that he himself had decisively transformed his own art). What is at issue here is the total rupture with the prehuman condition and the sudden emergence of the arts as such. There cannot be a gradual, imperceptible passage from nontime to time, from nonnumber to number. Numbers either exist or they don't. The existence of half a number or a small part of number (and the "progress," for example, to three-quarters and then to the whole number) is inconceivable. Once number exists, we can then enumerate increasingly greater numbers—or even other kinds of numbers. The same is true of the arts (in the primal sense of the term): either they exist or they don't. The appearance of art cannot but be a passage from nonart to art, a rupture, a total otherness that has no room for degree. Suddenly and totally, we pass from one level to the other, no matter how primitive this other is. From the prehuman to the human condition there is no gradual transition (think about language!).[12] The transition either happens or doesn't; when it happens, it is a shift to total otherness—which is to say, creation. Aeschylus cannot think of this creation as self-creation as does Sophocles. He knows, however, that it cannot be the result of any kind of accumulation, and this is what he expresses with Prometheus' gift, from which "all the arts" are derived.

I return now to the extensive passage on divination and the interpretation of dreams (lines 484–99). It too deserves in-depth commentary, but I will confine myself to two remarks and questions. The first observation—which imposes itself, and I simply mention it here—is of enormous and amazing stature: Aeschylus speaks of divination, not religion, and he only refers to the gods in passing, and for utilitarian purposes. The entrails of animals slaughtered for the sake of divination must be examined in order to reveal whether they are suitable for "the pleasure of the gods": *daimosin pros hēdonēn* (line 494). Once again, I am not saying that Aeschylus "believed" this. I say that these *thoughts* (and their public expression)—as well as the depiction of Zeus' power as brutal tyranny and of Zeus himself as a momentary tyrant bound to fall, in turn—were indeed possible and conceivable for the Athenians of 460 BCE.

The other remark concerns the juncture, the length, and the necessity of this description. This passage is the most extensive in the anthropogony, numbering some sixteen lines. Why, and why here? And why was it necessary? I believe that the (surely incomplete) answer to this question resides in the relation between *anthrōpos* and time, particularly the relation with the future. Prometheus granted humans the apprehension and measuring of time. He also gave them the means to institute a relation with the past: combinations of letters (*grammatōn suntheseis*), which are the memory of everything (*mnēmēn hapantōn*). With divination and dream interpretation he allows them to relate to the future, guiding them to "this art, very difficult to penetrate" (*dustekmarton technēn*) and enabling them to understand "signs from the flames [of sacrifices]" (*phlogōpa sēmata:* lines 497–98).

From the moment a conception of time comes into existence, there also exists the horizon of the future and its basic determinations: uncertainty, expectation, hope. In order for humans to confront these characteristics of the future, Prometheus endows them with the arts of divination and dream interpretation.

This complex of ideas enables us—indeed, demands of us—to return to an earlier, fundamental passage which we have not yet addressed. It concerns lines 247–52, which contain the first reference (after lines 235–36, where Prometheus declares that he saved humanity from the annihilation that Zeus had planned for it) to everything that Prometheus did for the sake of humanity. This very first act—even before the gift of fire—is described in the exchange, on alternating lines (the stichomythy), in lines 248–51, which must be quoted here in full, both because of their great significance and also because I think their usual translation is perfectly absurd.

ΠΡΟΜΗΘΥΣ	Θνητούς γ ἔπαυσα μὴ προδέρκεσθαι μόρον.
ΧΟΡΟΣ	Τὸ ποῖον εὑρὼν τῆσδε φάρμακον νόσου;
ΠΡΟΜΗΘΥΣ	Τυφλὰς ἐν αὐτοῖς ἐλπίδας κατῴκισα.
ΧΟΡΟΣ	Μεγ' ὠφέλημα τοῦτ' ἐδωρήσω βροτοῖς.

[Prometheus:	I put an end, for mortals, to the non-foreseeing of death.
Chorus:	By having found what remedy for that illness?
Prometheus:	I have imbued them with blind hopes.
Chorus:	That is a most useful gift you gave to mortals.][13]

The first verse is usually translated as, "I emancipated humanity from the foreseeing of death."[14] First, this translation is straightforwardly contradictory with Prometheus' description of the prehuman condition (lines 447 ff.). The above lines definitely refer to the passage from a prehuman to a human condition. The gift of fire only occurs afterward (line 252). How could such creatures, who don't even have a sense of time, conceivably be able to "predict" their death? How can we impute Aeschylus with such inadmissible nonsense? Second, this translation violates the obvious meaning of the text. To perpetrate that violence, the word *mē* ("not") must be artificially viewed as a condensation of *hina mē* ("in order to avoid"). The text says, I put an end to the condition whereby mortals did not foresee their death (a self-evident fact, since they lived "without thought"—*ater gnōmēs*). This is not meant to say that I taught them to foresee or predict the hour and moment of their death but to have a sense (a foresight) of the event: that is, I taught them that they are mortal. Third, it is impossible to attribute to Prometheus the ridiculous idea of making those mortals (who foresaw their death, though they simultaneously "saw without seeing" and "in vain") no longer know that they are mortal. If there is something certain for humanity, and altogether certain for the ancient Greeks, it is their mortality. From Homer to the end of Athenian tragedy, the certitude of this fundamental characteristic of human existence is repeated at every opportunity.

Prometheus taught humanity the truth: that men are mortal and, according to the true ancient Greek conception, irrevocably and unavoidably mortal. But to be mortal and to know it is, as the chorus says in response, an affliction for which you need a remedy. This remedy was discovered and disseminated by Prometheus: he instilled in humans "blind hopes." Blind hopes, obscure expectations, vain longings: these are the weapons (futile, in the last instance) whereby *anthrōpos* fights his mortality, which would be unbearable otherwise. Thus, when the chorus responds, "You granted these mortals a most useful gift," the answer is *not* ironic. For human beings to emerge from a prehuman condition, they had to know the first and last truth: they are mortal. This truth could easily have crushed them, as it so often crushes us. The counterweight resides in the blind hopes. These hopes do not refer to some "positive" immortality (as we know from Ulysses' descent into the realm of the dead in the *Odyssey*). They are relative to what *anthrōpos* does and is able to do in this life. Naturally, they are blind, for the future is unknown and the gods envious. But these two elements constitute *anthrōpos,* or at least ancient Greek *anthrōpos:* the *knowledge* of death and the potential of a *prattein/poiein,* making-doing/creating, which this knowledge sharpens rather than stifles. Ancient Greece is the most brilliant demonstration of the possibility of transforming this antinomy into a source of creativity.

∿

Athens, 442 BCE. The thirty-year peace treaties with the Peloponnesians in 446–45 had officially consecrated Athenian superiority. In 450, the sculptor Phidias erected the colossal bronze statue of the goddess Athena on the Acropolis, where it could be seen, it was said, all the way from Cape Sounion. The construction of the Parthenon had begun in 447 and would be completed in 438. Pericles' Odeon was built during 443. The Long Walls, finished in 456, were partly renovated in 445. Herodotus has already visited Athens, where he probably read parts of his *Histories* in public; Sophocles will compose a poem about him in 441. Among other great figures visiting or inhabiting Athens, we should include Protagoras, known for his "*Anthrōpos* is the measure of all things." Protagoras himself had certainly composed an anthropogony, rather faithfully rendered by Plato, I think, in the dialogue of the same name, which describes humanity's successive invention of art and knowledge as well as the equitable distribution of political wisdom as the underpinnings of democracy. In 444/443, the Athenians, motivated certainly by "the instituting passions" (*astunomous orgas*, in *Antigone*, lines 354–55),[15] decided to found a Panhellenic colony in Thourioi, on the site of Sybaris in Italy. They chose a non-Athenian, Protagoras from Abdera, as legislator. Aeschylus had died in Sicily; Sophocles (born in Colonus in 496) had defeated him in the Dionysian competition in 468. In 443/442, Sophocles, who was then writing or completing *Antigone* (at the age of fifty-three), was named *hellēnotamias* by the Athenians.[16] Euripides had already been taking part in tragedy contests since 455 and would win for the first time in 441.

This is the people of which Pericles will say, twelve years later, "[We have] forced all earth and all sea to become accessible to our daring" (*pasan gēn kai pasan thalassan esbaton tēi hēmeterai tolmēi katanangasantes*). This is the creative social-historical space from within which emerges the verse, *polla ta deina kouden anthrōpou deinoteron pelei.*[17]

Twenty to twenty-five years earlier, Aeschylus had presented his anthropogony, not as a gradual process, but as a sudden passage from beforehand to afterward as the consequence of the decision and action of a rebel Titan, as if some superhuman force had snatched, indeed nearly stolen, abilities and potentialities belonging to other superhuman forces (and therefore, already in existence). Sophocles, on the other hand, presents an anthropology presupposing nothing and whereby these abilities and potentialities are created by humans themselves. He simply, clearly, and emphatically posits humanity as self-creation. Humans took nothing from the gods, and no god gave them anything. This is the spirit of the fifth century, and this is the tragedy that the Athenians chose to reward.

The stasimon on lines 332–75 must of course be interpreted in connection with its position in the overall economy of the work. It comes right after the new threats by Creon, who has just learned of the second attempt at the (symbolic) burial of Polyneices, and it immediately precedes the discovery and arrest of the guilty party (Antigone). Its meaning—in essence, the meaning of the entire play—resides in its concluding lines (364–75), which link the ode to the sublime significations that are at stake in this tragedy. In this *anthrōpos,* as described and praised in the previous and most extensive part of the choral ode (lines 332–63), creative *deinotēs*[18] is intertwined with an insurmountable division within his nature. His wisdom and his art surpass every expectation, but his double reality directs him sometimes to good, sometimes to evil (*technas huper elpid' echōn tote men kakon, allot' ep' esthlon herpei,* lines 365–66). The poet does not define this good and evil in a moralizing sense; he does so politically.

Anthrōpos proceeds toward the good when he succeeds in interweaving (*pareirōn*) the laws of his city (*nomous chthonos,* with the chthonic element referring here not to the Earth in the cosmological sense, but meaning the land of his ancestors, the *polis,* the political community) with the judgment/justice of the gods guaranteed by oaths (*theōn enorkon dikan*). In this case, *anthrōpos* becomes *hupsipolis*—a word whose polysemy makes its translation impossible. *Hupsipolis:* standing high within one's city, but even more, great (sublime, as in Longinus' treatise *On the Sublime*) as member of a city, of a political (hence, human) community. At once, an opposition is drawn; against *hupsipolis* emerges *apolis,* a man who, *tolmas charin,* because of reckless daring, impertinence, or impudence—in short, because of *hubris,* to use the proper term—becomes *apolis*—allows the *mē kalon,* the opposite of beautiful/good, to inhabit him. Whoever is possessed by *hubris* departs from the political society of humans and the concrete outcome cannot but be death, flight, or exile. He becomes, as the French say, *sans foi ni loi, sans feu ni lieu*[19] (with no faith or law, with no hearth or home). And the chorus concludes by declaring: I do not want this *apolis* to be *parestios,* to reside within my home or beside my hearth, nor do I want him as *ison phronounta,* endowed with the same wisdom—with equal wisdom, common to all citizens—hence justified to consider himself equal to the other citizens.

I am obliged to give a total interpretation of the tragedy here, in condensed terms.[20] The subject of the tragedy is neither the fight of an innocent victim, Antigone, against the tyrant Creon, nor the contradiction between ethics and *raison d'Etat,* the individual against the State (these are contemporary interpretations), or the antithesis between the family and both the Law and the Polity (the Hegelian version). Over and beyond all that, the subject of the tragedy is *hubris* itself: the act committed "because of reckless daring" (*tolmas charin*). Certainly, Antigone and Creon represent two conflicting authorities. The poet, however, does not consider these two authorities—the *nomous chthonos* and *theōn enorkon dikan*—absolutely incompatible, since *anthrōpos* can become *hupsipolis* by weaving them together (*pareirōn*). Both Antigone and Creon are incapable of this interweaving. Both of them, by equally blindly and absolutely defending one of the two principles, become *hubristēs* and *apolis*.

We have a superlative paradox here: by going beyond the limits of *phronein*[21] and wanting to be *monos phronein* (to be the only one who "thinks right"), Creon, the upholder of the city's laws, becomes *apolis*. But it is equally obvious that Antigone herself is *apolis*. Immediately after the choral ode in question, when the sentry brings in Antigone, having caught her as she attempted, for the third time, to throw some dust over the corpse of Polyneices, the chorus, expressing mournful sorrow, does not address Antigone as champion of piety and respect for divine laws, but characterizes her as insane (*en aphrosunēi kathelontes,* line 383). Antigone's senselessness resides in that she too is not only incapable of weaving together the two principles, but she also transgresses the limits, *tolmas charin*. No *polis* can exist without "its own laws" (*chthonos*). By transgressing those laws, Antigone too becomes *apolis* and is no longer *ison phronein*.

The poet says to the Athenian citizens: even when we are right, it is possible that we may be wrong—there is never a final *logical* reason. Indeed, the arguments of both Creon and Antigone, theorized as such, are impervious to each other and with no possible logical refutation. This is expressed clearly by Haemon, when he says to his father, "Neither do I want nor am I able to say (*out' an dunaimēn, met' epistaimēn legōn,*) that you are wrong" (line 686), but you are wrong for other reasons, because you insist on being right all by yourself, or on being the only one who is right. I must quote verses 707–9 here, for they are stunning:

ὅστις γάρ αὐτός ἢ φρονεῖν μόνος δοκεῖ
ἢ γλῶσσαν, ἥν οὐκ ἄλλος, ἢ ψυχὴν ἔχειν.
οὗτοι διαπτυχθέντες ὤφθησαν κενοί.

[For whoever believes he alone is capable of judgment, or whoever believes he has a soul or an eloquence that no one else has, when such people are opened up, they are seen to be empty.][22]

Creon is wrong, even though he is right, because he insists on being *monos phronein* (thinking alone). He is not within the realm of *ison phronein;* he does not and cannot listen to the discourse and the reasons of an other and of others. He is inhabited by *hubris* because he is incapable of "interweaving" the elements.

Much like the Funeral Oration for the Athenians in Thucydides, *Antigone* is a summit of democratic political thought and positioning. It excludes and condemns the notion of *monos phronein;* recognizes *hubris* as intrinsically human, responding to it with *phronēsis;* and confronts the ultimate problem of autonomous *anthrōpos:* the problem of the self-limitation of both the individual and the political community.

Self-limitation is necessary precisely because *anthrōpos* is terrifyingly formidable (*deinos*), a quality that can never be essentially restricted by something external, not even by the justice/judgment of the gods guaranteed by oaths. The oath is one of the principles that govern human life, but it is by no means enough. Were it enough, neither *Antigone* nor even tragedy would exist, just as no tragedy exists or can exist where *one* ultimate authority gives answers to all questions, as in both the Platonic and the Christian worlds.

Tragedy (and *Antigone* in particular) presupposes precisely the terrifying formidableness (*deinotēs*) of *anthrōpos,* which reaches its summit and self-destruction in *hubris* but may raise him to the summit embodied by *hupsipolis* man, provided it is "interwoven" with *ison phronein.* Herein lies the internal necessity that leads the chorus to describe and praise this terrifying formidableness for most of the stasimon (lines 334–63).

The central meaning of the choral ode is announced in the two first lines (*polla ta deina kouden anthrōpou deinoteron pelei*), which immediately open several questions. The critical word in these lines is of course that untranslatable *deinos.* Heidegger translates it with the terribly insufficient *unheimlich* (uncanny), which forgets several of the word's central significations. His French translator widens the gap by rendering *unheimlich* as *inquiétant* (disturbing). To condense the conclusion of another study[23] in one phrase, I would point to an essential element of ancient Greek poetry: not only is Sophocles not always obliged to choose among the different meanings of a word, but he clearly often makes no choice whatsoever. He can and wants to provide all significations at once. *Deinos:* whoever justifiably provokes awe, fear, terror—someone who is terrifying, horrifying, and dangerous. This leads us, thanks to one of the most beautiful creations of meaning in the Greek language, to: stunningly forceful, powerful, provoking wonder and admiration, probably even a sense of strangeness. Provoking wonder and admiration, why? Because of being capable to the highest degree, dexterous, wise, a supreme craftsman, one who always finds a solution, who is never without means, all-inventive (*polumēchanos*), and cognizant of many ways (*polutropos*), as Homer would say. Sophocles says just as much at the end of this passage: *aporos ep' ouden erchetai to mellon* (lines 360–61). Lexicographers and translators are forced to choose among these significations; not Sophocles, or those of us who are fortunate enough to understand a bit of Greek.

The significational complex of this word is elucidated and enriched by what follows it in the text. From *Antigone* onward, *deinos* means everything that Sophocles views as *deinon* in *anthrōpos*. And the first instance of elucidation is granted us by the repetition of the word in the rest of the phrase, constructed by the negation of comparison to connote a quasi-superlative degree: "nothing is more *deinon* than *anthrōpos*." *Deinos* defines *anthrōpos* and is defined by *anthrōpos*: it is the characteristic element that no creature achieves to a degree comparable to *anthrōpos*.

Ouden anthrōpou deinoteron. Nothing is more terrifying, formidable, amazing, achievement-capable than *anthrōpos*. I ask once more: Dare we take the poet seriously? Are we to suppose that the poet uses words haphazardly? Sophocles, the master of the precise and just word, says it clearly and forcefully: nothing. Not the "graying sea" (*polios pontos*), not "the southerly wind that blows in winter" (*cheimerios notos*), not "the races of wild beasts" (*thērōn agriōn ethnē*), nothing. Nothing in nature. But Sophocles does not confine himself to nature—he says it absolutely: nothing. Therefore, not even the gods.

This further elucidates the meaning of *deinos,* although it seems to make it more obscure. In what sense could *anthrōpos* be more *deinos* than nature—and more than the gods? The answer is nonetheless self-evident, presented, almost immediately, in the following lines of the stasimon. The *polios pontos* and the *cheimerios notos* are surely more powerful than *anthrōpos,* as are the *thērōn agriōn ethnē* and so many other creatures. But these creatures are—and are what they are—by virtue of their nature. They have always done, they do and will continue to do, the same things in whatever time frame. And they have their inherent powers because they have been granted them once and for all, with no possibility of ever changing them. Their *ti estin,* "what they are," as Aristotle would say, what defines them and develops their various attributes does not emerge from within them.

The exact same thing is true of the gods. Crushingly more powerful than *anthrōpos,* endowed with innumerable powers and potential—however, not omnipotent, let us recall; immortal, but not eternal or timeless—the gods are what they are by their "nature" without having done anything to this effect. Thus, for instance, they have no need to resort to art, to *technē*—to build ships in order to be mobile or to write something down so as not to forget. On the other hand, however, Hephaestus' art is surely superior to all human art, but it is an art not invented by Hephaestus; it is innate to him. Hephaestus is *technē,* like Ares is war and Athena is wisdom.

Anthrōpos is a being in comparison to whom nothing is more *deinon* because nothing he does—necessarily described in merely indicative and fragmentary fashion in lines 334–51—can be attributed to "natural" qualities. The *ti estin* of *anthrōpos,* which is expressed and expounded through various attributes, is his very own work. In philosophical terms: *anthrōpos* posits himself as *anthrōpos;* the essence of *anthrōpos* is self-creation. This phrase is to be understood in two senses: *anthrōpos* creates his essence, and this essence is itself creation and self-creation. *Anthrōpos* creates himself as creator, in a circle, whose apparently vicious logic reveals its ontological primacy.

That this is Sophocles' conception becomes apparent beyond any doubt with one word, which—along with *pantoporos: aporos ep' ouden erchetai to mellon* and *ouden anthrōpou deinoteron* ("capable of going everywhere, of traversing everything, of finding answers to everything; he advances toward nothing that is in the future without having some resource")—is the third pillar of this part of the choral ode: the word "self-taught" (*edidaxato,* line 354). As we know, the middle voice denotes reflexive action. No one has taught *anthrōpos* anything (not Prometheus, for example); *anthrōpos* is self-taught. When I am taught, someone who already possesses some specific knowledge gives it, offers it, imparts it to me. When I teach myself (the middle voice, in Greek), I give myself something I don't have (otherwise, why should I give it?), but also something I do have (otherwise, who gives it?). The apparent absurdity disappears once we understand that the reflexive action of the self-taught *anthrōpos* brings into existence both its "content" and its "subject," which define each other and exist through one another.

This third pillar is possibly the most important because the verb *edidaxato* redefines and repositions everything that was stated before: all the works and creations of *anthrōpos* that pertain to the specific arts (sailing, agriculture, hunting, and so forth). For the decisive factor underlying all these arts is what *anthrōpos* has taught himself:

καί φθέγμα καί άνεμόν
φρόνημα καί άστυνόμους
όργάς έδιδάξατο...

[He taught himself speech and wind-like thought, and the instituting passions] (lines 354–56)[24]

A century later, Aristotle was to define *anthrōpos* as a living being that possesses reason (*zōon logon echon*) and a political living being (*zōon politikon*). I dare say that the poet is more profound here, because he is more radical, than the very profound philosopher. *Anthrōpos* does not "have" *logos* as a "natural" faculty or as a gift—nor is his political substance simply given or acquired once and for all. *Anthrōpos* has taught—created for—himself speech (*phthegma*), thought (*phronēma*), and *astunomous orgas,* which Heiddeger translated, in explicitly Nazi fashion, as "the passion for dominating the cities" (*den Mut der Herrschaft über die Städte*). This translation is, moreover, aberrant. For there to be domination of the cities, there must first be cities. Sophocles does not speak of domination of allegedly already existing cities; his standpoint is the very "moment" (on the ontological stratum) when *anthrōpos* creates language and thought, as well as *astunomous orgas,* the instituting passions, the passionate temper, the dispositions and drives, that give laws to cities—that institute cities. Instituting passions—this is possibly the best way to render Sophocles' extraordinary and profoundly true idea: extraordinary because we usually think of law and institutions as something absolutely opposed to temper or passion, and profoundly true because there is a prelogical intention and "will" at the root of the primordial institution, and no institution can hold without passion.

The *deinotēs* [terrifying formidableness] of *anthrōpos* is summed up in the phrase that concludes this part of the stasimon: *pantoporos: aporos ep'ouden erchetai to mellon.* I would simply like to stress the fact that *pantoporos* refers not only to all-inventiveness (*polumēchania*), but also to human self-creation *in its totality.*

The poet knows one first limit to this *deinotēs,* death: "the only thing
he will not find is the means to flee Hades"[25] (*Aida monon pheuxin ouk ep-
axetai*). Hades the definitive—according to the conception of preclassical
and classical Greece, which refuses (until the end of the fifth century) to
be placated with stories about immortality and deluded hopes for a life after death—does not appear here merely as a reminder of the final truth. It
also serves to underline the *deinotēs* of this creature, which, although fully
aware of its mortality, does not cease nonetheless "to advance" (*chōrei*),
"to tire [the land for his benefit]" (*apotruetai*), "to make [birds] prisoners" (*agei*), "to become the master [of wild beasts]" (*kratei*), and "to teach
himself" (*didasketai*).

The second limit, which is, if I may say so, internal and intrinsic to
anthrōpos, is his double nature that directs him either to evil or to good.
This is a limit because Sophocles (like Thucydides twenty or thirty years
later), while describing a titanic process by which *anthrōpos* creates and
acquires ever-increasing power and faculties of all sorts, sees this process,
quite rightly, as achieving no "ethical progress." Good and evil have accompanied and will always accompany *anthrōpos;* they will always be the
two poles that alternately guide his steps. The twentieth-century reader
will easily accredit the poet's perception, given the experience of twenty-
five centuries worth of masterful achievements and monstrous crimes, the
worst of which were perpetrated in the name of noble ends and humanity's worldly felicity or otherworldly redemption.

The poet, however, does not see this double nature in fatalistic fashion.
He knows that *anthrōpos* has the potential to become *hupsipolis* by interweaving "the laws of the land" with "the justice of the gods." This justice
thus appears as a third limit to human practicopoietic activity. *Anthrōpos*
teaches himself his own laws; he posits and institutes them. However,
next to these laws exists the justice of the gods, which certainly does not
suffice (otherwise, there would be no need for the laws of the cities), but
which cannot be disregarded either.

In *Antigone,* the justice of the gods has a specific content that concerns
the established rites of burial. Already in *Antigone,* however, even this justice encounters its limit. Worshipping the gods without a *polis,* without a
lawful human community, is inconceivable. Yet it is just as inconceivable
for a city not to protect itself from the risk of having a person (Polyneices), whose sole motive is thirst for personal power, commit treason and
collaborate with the enemy. To let the behavior of Polyneices go without

sanction would, in the last instance, render any divine worship impossible. But punishment in the form decreed by Creon (forbidding burial) is also an affront to the gods. The justice of the gods does not have a single, unambiguous meaning, as we well know thanks both to Homer and to numerous other tragedies. The gods themselves are constantly warring among themselves; they themselves have no laws, and their relations are regulated by means of power, not law. Aeschylus' Orestes is one of the many victims of the battles among divinities. The commands of the gods are obscure and have many meanings; they may easily lead to catastrophe, as they do in the case of Antigone.

We don't know exactly what Sophocles thought about the gods, and it is very difficult to infer it. We do know that he belonged to the circle of Pericles, as did Protagoras, who said: "Concerning the gods, I can know nothing: neither what they are like, nor whether they exist or do not exist, nor what form they might have."[26] Nevertheless, *Antigone* allows us at least to say, unhesitatingly: just as the justice of the gods is insufficient, so are worldly laws. In obeying them, *anthrōpos* must know that these laws do not determine absolutely what is permitted any more than they exhaust the range of the forbidden. Another element must exist next to the law instituted on each occasion—affirmative law, necessarily limited by its precise location in space and time, therefore relative—an element that needs to be interwoven with the worldly law, without dictating its content or canceling it. It is this element that the poet, using the language and the representations of his city and his time, names *theōn enorkon dikan,* "the judgment/justice of the gods guaranteed by oaths."

~

In conclusion, let us briefly compare the anthropogony of the two poets. They obviously share the idea that thought and art are decisively significant. Beyond this, the differences are immense. Aeschylus does not mention the foundation and institution of political society, whereas Sophocles focuses the entire choral ode on the "instituting passions" (*astunomous orgas*), and the notions of *apolis* and *hupsipolis.* Aeschylus starts off from a dreamlike, nightmarish prehuman condition and presents the passage to the human condition as a gift, coming from the decision and action of a superhuman creature. There is nothing analogous in Sophocles, for whom there cannot be a prehuman condition as far as humans are concerned since from the moment *anthrōpos* exists he is defined by his own active self-creating practicopoietic activity, by his self-teaching. Prometheus taught the Aeschylean *anthrōpos* that he is mortal, and counterbalanced the unbearable weight of this knowledge with blind hopes. The Sophoclean *anthrōpos* knows that he is mortal and that this fundamental condition is insurmountable. Naturally, given the subject matter and context of *Prometheus Bound,* there is no reason, way, or place to describe the problems faced by *anthrōpos.* Sophocles' conception is radical: he views these problems as consubstantial with the double nature of *anthrōpos,* his inherent *hubris* (*tolmas charin*), and his tendency to want to be right all by himself.

In the course of a quarter of a century, Greek self-knowledge moved from the idea of a divine anthropogony to the idea of the self-creation of *anthrōpos.* The stasimon in *Antigone,* along with its inseparable, unsurpassable counterpart, Pericles' Funeral Oration in Thucydides, twelve years later, impart its most vivid forms to this self- knowledge.

§ 2   Notes on Some Poetic Resources

Some difficulties encountered by the translator lead to the conclusion that the ancient Greek poets often made use of a trait of the Greek language, one probably shared by other primary languages, which may be called the indivisible polysemy of words and grammatical cases. Modern European languages no longer possess this feature, and poets have used other means to achieve comparable expressive intensity.

These observations lead us to examine the pathways taken by poetic expressiveness, and its semantic musicality in particular.

I

Let us take four famous lines by Sappho (Bergk edition, 52):

δέδυκε μὲν ἀ σελάννα
καί πληΐαδες· μέσαι δὲ
νύκτες, παρά δ' ἔρχετ' ὤρα,
ἔγω δὲ μόνα κατεύδω.

Translated "literally," this would come out, approximately, as:

The Moon has gone down
and {so have} the Pleiades, it is the middle
of the night, the hours pass
and *I* sleep alone

Deduke, from the verb *duō,* means "has plunged." In Greece, with its two hundred inhabited islands and some ten thousand kilometers of coastline, the sun, moon, and stars do not go down; they plunge. *Se-lanna* is the moon, of course, and the word cannot be rendered otherwise. But to a Greek, *Selanna* immediately suggests *selas,* light: *Selanna* is the luminous one, the luminary. *Plēiades* are the Pleiades—plural—the Numerous ones. For a French—or European—person who is not particularly cultivated, the word is meaningless, and for a moderately cultivated French person it designates a famous group of sixteenth-century French poets and a Gallimard Publishing Company imprint. But for the peasants, craftspeople, and sailors of ancient Greece (and still recently, in fact), it evoked a cluster of stars—at least seven are visible to the naked eye—within what a contemporary astronomer would call a globular cluster of several million stars. This magnificent constellation belongs to the most beautiful nocturnal configuration of the sky, an immense curve arching over more than half the firmament, starting with the Pleiades, continuing with Orion, and ending with Sirius. In late summer, when Sirius appears just before sunrise, the fading Pleiades have passed the zenith on their westward march. When Sappho is speaking, the Pleiades have already plunged. This is a precise, precious piece of information, to which I shall return later.

Mesai de nuktes, literally: the nights are in their middle, it is the middle of the night. In the middle of that night, at midnight of that particular day, the moon and the Pleiades had already plunged. Let us suppose, for the time being, that the end of the poem may be rendered as:

. . . the hour passes,
and *I* lay in bed alone.

The speaker is Sappho, born in about 612 BCE on Lesbos. The poem was probably written around 580, perhaps earlier. It is what we call a lyric poem, one that expresses the poet's feelings and moods—and yet the *muthos,* the narrative, the story, is present in its nostalgic splendor. Effortlessly, we see the night sky revolving, the moon and the Pleiades already set, and that woman, perhaps in love with someone who is not there, or perhaps not in love but full of desires in any case, and who, in the middle of the night, unable to fall asleep, tells of her sadness at being alone in her bed.

To read a poem from ancient times is to rediscover a now-bygone world, one now shrouded in the indifference of "civilization" to what is elementary and fundamental. It is the middle of the night and the moon has already set. This is meaningless for our contemporaries. They have no realization that because the moon has gone down before midnight, it is somewhere between the beginning of the new moon and the first quarter, and therefore the beginning of the lunar month (the measure of time for all ancient peoples). But the Pleiades too have already set. Here we have a degree of precision typical of the ancient poets, rarely found in the moderns. This indication would almost suffice to date the writing of the poem.

It is springtime—and actually early springtime—for that is when the Pleiades set before midnight. As the year grows older, they go down later and later. Sappho is in bed, and the *ōra* passes.

What is the *hōra?*[1] The translator "naturally" renders *ōra* as hour, derived from that Greek root,[2] via the Latin. But in Greek, *hōra* also means the season (this is already so in Homer), and that sense persists through Alexandrian and Byzantine times: *hai hōrai tou etous,* the seasons of the year. It is also the hour in the usual sense, not the hour of our clock time, but the hour as subdivision of the length of the day. One of the most famous poems that late antiquity ascribed to the lyric poet Anacreon begins with the words: *mesonuktiois poth' ōrais,* in the hours of the middle of the night. But *hōra* is also the time when a thing has its hour, when a thing is truly fine and lovely, and therefore, for human beings, the height of youth. In *The Banquet,* Alcibiades tells how he tried to sleep with Socrates, but arose in the morning having been no more molested (*katadedarthēkōs*) than if he had slept with his father or his brother. He concludes: Socrates is a *hubristēs,* a man who insults others, to the point where he scorned (*katephronēsen*) my *hōra,* he spurned my youth, my beauty, the fact that I was ripe for the picking like a beautiful erotic fruit.

Last, I must simply mention the conjunction *de,* which might be "and" as well as "but." One is obliged to choose, and I simply translate it by "and." What, then, does Sappho say?

The Moon and the Pleiades
have plunged, it is the middle
of the night, season, hour, youth are departing
and *I* lay in bed alone

No modern translator, to my knowledge, has dared use three words for that single word, *ōra.* But the force of the poem peaks precisely in that word, which contains several meanings jointly without there being any desire or need to choose between them. It is the season of the year, springtime—the new departure of the year after the winter, the season of lovers—hours going by and Sappho's youth wasting away in vain because she has no one in her bed. It is her genius, too, to choose that word with its wide range of meanings, illuminated and enriched by the rest of the poem (the sense of season/springtime for *ōra* would not impose itself as much had she not mentioned the setting of the Pleiades).

The same indivisible polysemy is found in Aeschylus, in his *Prometheus*. When Prometheus, nailed to his rock, summons the Earth his mother, the divine ether, the sources of rivers and the breath of the winds to witness the suffering he is enduring unjustly (see verse 89 ff.), he also calls:

> [...] ποντίων τε κυμάτων
> ἀνήριθμον γέλασμα,

> [. . . of the waves of the sea
> {the} laughter countless]

Let us set aside the richness of the tropes (we have both prosopopoeia and hypallage here: what is countless is the waves, not their laughter) and concentrate on the word *gelasma*. The only possible translation is laughter, but an ancient Greek who read or heard that verse could not avoid perceiving the other meaning of the word *gelaō*, found in the epithet *Zeus geleōn*, Zeus of the light, or in the Ionian tribe of the *Geleontes*—the illustrious, the brilliant. *Gelasma* has very strong overtones, then, and probably an etymological kinship with *gelas*, brilliance, glittering. Even now, to say that a day is nice and cheerful, the French depict it as *riant*, laughing, because the sun is shining and the day is bright. When you are at sea, especially the Aegean sea, today exactly as in Aeschylus' times, you see that innumerable laughter with your own eyes: that endless sparkling of the waves under the midday sun.

The prose of Herodotus provides another example. In the first book of his *Histories*, Herodotus says that he is presenting his investigations so that what men have done does not disappear with time, and so that the great and admirable *erga*, some accomplished by the Greeks and others by barbarians, do not lose their renown, be they peaceful *erga* or *erga* in and by which they made war on each other. *Erga*, the plural of *ergon* (yielding *ergazomai*, to work, to accomplish), are acts and deeds as well as works, be they occupations or works of industry (see Hesiod, *Erga kai hēmerai*

[*Works and Days*]). In his excellent introduction to the French bilingual "Budé" edition[3] of Herodotus' book, Legrand says he hesitated between the two senses of *ergon,* a piece of work or work of industry (*ouvrage*), or a feat, a deed (*exploit*), and explains why he chose the latter. It is not up to us to discuss whether he was right or wrong. We simply observe that, as in the case of Sappho's use of *ōra,* the modern translator is obliged to choose and to prefer. In truth, however, one must not prefer. Herodotus is obviously speaking about pieces of work, works of industry—the walls of Babylon, the statues and consecrated objects at Delphi, the bridge over the Hellespont built by Xerxes—just as well as of deeds: the conquest of Asia by Cyrus, of Egypt by Cambyses, the wars waged by Darius, as well as Marathon, Salamis, and Plataea. He describes both and designates them as *erga megala kai thōmasta,* great and admirable works, accomplishments (*oeuvres*) and feats, some achieved by Greeks, others by barbarians. Actually, *erga* may be said to be "doings," "deeds," provided we consent to restore the double meaning of the word, both a noun and a participle, and reinstate the sense of *doing* as human activity in history, irrespective of whether the result produced is separate from the act (Aristotle's *poiēsis*) or not separate (a *praxis*), a beautiful act like the battle of Salamis. This is all making/doing (*faire*), and its description is the *ergon,* both the work and the feat, of Herodotus.

Let us now look at two examples from Sophocles, in the stasimon from *Antigone* that begins with the famous *polla ta deina kouden anthrōpou deinoteron pelei,*[4] "numerous are the *deina,* but nothing is more *deinon* than man." The modern translator is obliged to choose between the many meanings of *deinos* and usually settles on something like "wondrous" or "terrible," but the listener of ancient times was not forced to choose. He heard all that at once, just as the writer had thought it all in one. *Deinos* is certainly he who is terrifying, he who provokes terror (*deos*); it is also he who is very powerful, but also he who is wondrous, who excels in an occupation or an art—one may be *deinos* as a swimmer or an orator—who excels to the point of eliciting terror and wonder. The constellation of meanings that come under the word cannot be grasped without an elucidation of the main point of this chorus, to which we will now proceed. To begin with, let us simply say that the word *deinos* can no longer be understood in the same way once one has heard the chorus in *Antigone.*

The most important part of the explanation of the meaning of *deinon* begins with line 353. Speaking of man, of *anthrōpos,* Sophocles says that he has taught himself (*edidaxato,* a verb to which I shall return later) language (*phthegma*) and thought (*phronēma*), said to be *anemoen. Anemos* is the wind. The case here is the opposite of those encountered thus far: we must eliminate some of the word's many references and retain others. For example, Homer (in *The Iliad,* III, 305) says: *Ilion anemoessan,* Ilion the wind-swept. We picture the lofty walls of Troy perched on top of a hill, exposed to the winds. But Sophocles is obviously not talking about windy thought. Thought is extremely volatile, like the wind, first here then almost immediately far off; it too is powerful and violent, like that natural element, and again, it too is transparent most of the time but may also carry clouds and darken the sky. In French or in English we would have to weaken that imagery by writing: like the wind. *Ventée,* or "windy," obviously would not do at all.

Language and thought are not "natural," given attributes of mankind. Man *edidaxato,* he taught them to himself. The reflexive form of the simple verb *didaskō* contains an incomparably audacious philosophical idea, on which there has been no follow-up for twenty-five centuries. Man does not "have" language and thought: he gave them to himself, created them for himself and taught them to himself. Plato would have said: how can I teach myself something? If I know it I don't need to teach it to myself and if I don't know it I do not know what to teach myself. And that is indeed what he says: one can never learn what one does not already know in some way. Sophocles breaks that apparently irrefragable logic and clearly asserts what I have called the primitive circle of creation: the "results" are presupposed by the activity that brought them into existence; man teaches himself something he does not know, and in doing so he learns what he must teach himself.

Sophocles continues with the assertion that man *edidaxato,* "taught to himself" the *astunomous orgas.* I translate this immediately: the passions instituting cities. *Astunomous* comes from *astu,* which is generally the city (town), but here the accent is placed on both the law that posits the city and the law that governs it as a political unit. *Orgē* too has many meanings, and here again, translators are obliged to choose, or to invent something. In the "Budé" edition, Mazon writes "the aspirations from which cities are born." But the text does not mention birth. The Liddell-Scott dictionary, citing the verse (s.v. ἀστυνόμος), says "the feelings of law-abiding" or "social life" (but s.v. ὀργή, it translates *astunomoi orgai* by "social dispositions"). Like any dictionary, it must resort to division and univocal attribution. But it is important to know what a dictionary is, and to use it appropriately. A word is not a package of cookies of various kinds put side by side, of which we can always take one and leave the others. *Orgē* is the drive, the impulse, temperament, mood (and also anger). This is the word from which *orgaō* and *orgasmos*—orgasm—are derived. Here, *orgē* is the drive, the impulse, the spontaneous, irresistible thrust. Our first impression is that *astunomous orgas* is a contradiction in terms, or an oxymoron. How can drives and impulses lead to the institution of laws? But Sophocles says *edidaxato,* and thus adds another meaning to the verb. Those drives that gave impetus toward the constitution of societies, man educated them, he schooled them, shaped and transformed them, sub-jected them to laws, and thus constituted cities. All of this, potentially the contents of a philosophical treatise, is said by Sophocles in three words: *edidaxato . . . astunomous orgas.* Man educated himself by transforming his drives so that they would come to found and regulate cities.

A detailed discussion of *astunomous orgas* is also important for a his-torical reason. Here, for the first time, we find the explicit formulation of what will later be one of the major themes of classical political philosophy, from Plato up to and including Jean-Jacques Rousseau, to be forgotten thereafter in the deadening intellectualism of the last two centuries. That is, "to institute a people," as Rousseau says, one must first change its "mo-res," and mores come essentially from the schooling of passions, requiring at the least that the laws positively take them into account in the *paideia* of citizens. In his *Politics,* Aristotle speaks of *philia:* lawmakers, he says, must be concerned, above all, with establishing *philia* (which is no in-sipid "friendship" but affection in the strongest sense of the term) among citizens, for when there is *philia* there is no need for justice. In that same work, *Politics,* in which he condemns "communism," Aristotle goes on to say: the proverb is right when it says that friends' possessions are common property. When Sophocles speaks of *orgai* here, he is thinking about the passions and mutual affections of members of the community, that essen-tial cement of the life of cities—for better or for worse.

For these reasons, *deinos* is only comprehensible through this complex (incompletely explored here) of semantic potentialities that we have at-tempted to elucidate. To be *deinos* is to possess the effective conjunction of those attributes designated by the poet, all of which, in their essence, refer to a single central idea: that of the self-creation of man. This formu-lation may seem exorbitant. I believe it will find full justification if we consider the decisive characterization introduced by the poet from the start, in the same phrase in which he uses the term *deinos:*

πολλά τά δεινά κοὐδὲν ἀνθρώπου δεινότερον πέλει

[Numerous are the *deina,* and nothing is more *deinon* than man.]

The *deina,* the pedant would say, form a collection, and that collection contains a single, maximal element: man. About ten years ago, I attempted to sketch out the immense implications of that phrase.[5] I will summarize the main points of that discussion here. One objection to Sophocles' assertion comes to mind immediately: how can we claim that man is more *deinos* than the gods? Sophocles is not irreligious, as shown by the last lines of that same chorus, and an atheist text would certainly not have won the laurel wreath at the Dionysia. So Sophocles is not saying that man is better than the gods, nor that he is more powerful than them. But he is *deinoteros,* and we must discover the sense in which this may be so—provided we take the poet seriously, that is. And the answer, introduced by a *gar*—very precisely, "for," "since"—is given by all the rest of the chorus, enumerating and qualifying man's many achievements. It then becomes self-evident that man's *deinotēs* is characterized by that ongoing, immense transformation of his relations with nature, but also with his own "nature," as is clearly signified by the reflexive verb, *edidaxato.* His alterity with respect to the gods then becomes obvious. The gods did not teach themselves anything; they did not modify themselves. They are what they have always been since they came into existence, and what they will be forever. Athena will not become wiser, Hermès speedier, Hephaestus a better artisan. Their potency is an immutable attribute of their nature, and they did nothing to acquire or change it. They build and fabricate, but always by combining what is already present. But mortal man, infinitely weaker than the gods, is more *deinos* because he creates and creates himself. Man is more *deinos* than any natural thing, and more so than the gods, who are *natural,* because man is supernatural. He is the only creature, mortal or immortal, who modifies himself.

Anyone who contends that this elucidation of the text introduces contemporary notions foreign to fifth-century Greece should think back to the "anthropogonies" of Democritus and some great sophists, and to the potentialities to be found in Thucydides, both in his Archeology and in Pericles' Funeral Oration. Fifth-century Athens put its finger on the idea of human self-creation—and it took the defeat of Athens in the Peloponnesian war and the reactionary Platonic tradition to stifle and bury those seeds. That reaction was so powerful that it has almost completely dominated European interpretations of this fifth-century invention.

The second famous chorus in *Antigone,* devoted to love,[6] sheds light on some other aspects of the poetic creativity of indivisible polysemy. It arrives after the dispute between Creon and his son Haemon, who threatens him as he leaves the scene (he will commit suicide shortly thereafter). The chorus sings the power of Eros the invincible (*anikate machan*), Eros who is in ambush in the girl's tender, smooth cheeks (*en malakais pareiais neanidos ennucheueis*), and goes on to say:

νικᾷ δ' ἐναργὴς βλεφάρων
ἵμερος εὐλέκτρου νύμφας

In the "Budé" edition, Mazon translates this as, "Who triumphs here, then? Clearly, it is the desire of the eyes of the virgin promised to the bed of her spouse." This pusillanimous Victorian translation must be reworked from one end to the other, but I quote it as a further illustration of the ordeal of the good modern translator. Let us proceed word by word. *Nikai,* is victorious, gets the upper hand; *himeros,* desire; *enargēs,* in a philosophical paper this would be translated by evident, but it is much more here. *Enargēs* is derived from the same root as *argos,* which yields *arguros,* silvery (and *argentum,* silver, in Latin), indicating brightness, brilliance, light; *himeros enargēs* is therefore manifest desire, shining out. Whose desire? *Blepharōn eulektrou numphas.* This says nothing about a virgin promised to the bed of her spouse; it speaks of a young bride, or at any rate a young woman ripe for marriage, as shown by the epithet *eulektros.* There is no reason to beat about the bush: the ancients were not afraid to call a spade a spade. *Lektron* is the bed, and *eu* is good. A woman who is *eulektros* is a woman whose bed is good—that is, who is good in bed and for going to bed; in modern Greek, we would tend to say *kalokrevati,* a literal, exact translation of *eulektros.* There remains the genitive *blepharōn,* of the eyes. Whose eyes? Liddell Scott, quoting that line, translates it as "desire beaming from the eyes," indicating that the girl is the subject of the desire. Mazon retains the ambiguity, but it is important to make it explicit. There is both the desire "of" the young woman and the desire "for" (the eyes of) the young woman. The desire comes from the young woman's eyes and is directed to her eyes. A great modern poet in prose, Proust, expresses the same situation in a magnificent passage of *In Search of Lost Time*. During the evening party in the "gardens of avenue Gabriel," at the home of the Princess de Guermantes, the narrator is talking with Swann—a seriously ailing Swann, nearing the end of his life—about the Dreyfus Affair and the growing anti-Semitism with which Swann is obsessed, when the Baron de Charlus passes by, lavishing exaggerated praise on the Marquise de Surgis, his brother's mistress:

> the Marquise, turning around, addressed a smile and held out her hand to Swann, who had risen to greet her. But almost without concealment, because his advanced years had deprived him either of the will, from indifference to the opinion of others, or the physical power, from the intensity of his desire and the weakening of the controls that help to disguise it, as soon as Swann, on taking the Marquise's hand, had seen her bosom at close range and from above, he plunged an attentive, serious, absorbed, almost anxious gaze into the depths of her corsage, and his nostrils, drugged by her perfume, quivered like the wings of a butterfly about to alight upon a half-glimpsed flower. Abruptly he shook off the intoxication that had seized him, and Mme de Surgis herself, although embarrassed, stifled a deep sigh, so contagious can desire prove at times.[7]

Swann plunges his gaze into the corsage of the Marquise—probably low-cut for the evening party, we imagine—and although the Marquise doesn't have eyes on the tips of her breasts, she feels his gaze there and is troubled by it. Here we have the two-sided reality of desire. Notice the accuracy, originality, and subtlety of the adjectives used by Proust—attentive, serious, absorbed, almost anxious—but also the accumulation used to achieve the desired effect.

Parmenides gives us a different example of rich semantics. This time it is grammatical rather than lexical:

Λεῦσσε δ' ὅμως ἀπεόντα νόῳ παρεόντα βεβαίως

[Consider how the absent (neuter plural: absent things) are present with total certainty (*bebaiōs* = on unshakeable foundations) *noōi*.]

Noōi is the dative of *nous*. The word unquestionably means "thought" or "mind" here. This is one of the many sentences molested by Heidegger, who translates *noōi* as *Vernehmen*, "to perceive, perception." Translated this way, Parmenides' phrase immediately becomes absurd: how can things absent be present through perception, the object of which is, by definition, a thing simply and directly present?

To perceive is certainly one of the basic meanings of *noein,* but it is not by any means the only one. Heidegger is led astray by his furious desire to de-Platonize pre-Socratic terms. *Noos* definitely means thought, mind, from the first lines of the *Odyssey* on. Ulysses, says Homer, "far more than other men, has seen cities and known (understood) *noon,*" thought, the way of thinking. In Parmenides' verse, *noos* is the ability to make present to oneself with total certainty what is not there. *Apeon,* what is not there, may be a memory, the face of someone absent, a mathematical theorem, or the existence of people in bygone times. *Nous* can make all those objects present even when they are physically absent. It is evident, given this attribute, that the term must be understood as comprising both the imagination and memory. How can we translate this dative, *nooi,* into a modern language like English or French that does not decline nouns? Just about the entire catalog of uses of the dative known to grammarians is used here. To choose any one would represent a mutilating interpretation rather than a translation. This dative is instrumental: it is by means of the *nous* that the absent become present; it is locative: they become present in the *nous;* it is "ethic" ("for the sake of"): the absent become present "for" the *nous;* it is the dative of the object: the "make itself present" applies to the *nous;* and it is of course eminently subjective: things absent are present "to" the *nous,* not in the sense of a place, but of a subject before whom the absent become present.

II

I have attempted to highlight a specific feature of ancient Greek, and what poetry was able to achieve by using it. The semantic and expressive possibilities of a primary tongue such as Greek are not to be found in modern European languages. The great European poets have taken other paths to achieve effects of comparable intensity. To explore them at all systematically would be an enormous and most probably endless task. I will attempt to illustrate a single case here as an example—one I think has broader value. I am referring to Macbeth's famous monologue in act 5, scene 5 of the tragedy of the same name.

Let me briefly recall the place of the lines discussed here within the play as a whole: Macbeth, a Scottish general, returning from a victorious battle, meets three witches who predict that he will be king of Scotland. Shortly thereafter, King Duncan comes to stay in his home and at the instigation of his wife, whom he has informed of the witches' prophesy, and who, guiding his hand, damns her soul for him, Macbeth kills the king in his sleep and mounts the throne. Following many other "preventive" crimes, Scotland rebels against him, and an army led by a Scottish noble, Macduff, besieges him in his castle, Dunsinane. Just before the siege, Macbeth, tortured by the permanent sleeplessness to which he is condemned and by the madness to which Lady Macbeth, crushed by the weight of her crimes, has succumbed, returns to see the witches, who predict that he will not be overcome until the day when the forest of Birnam marches on Dunsinane, and that "none of woman born shall harm Macbeth"—"Fear not, till Birnam wood do come to Dunsinane" (5.5.44–45).

The witches' pronouncements match the Delphic oracles for ambiguity. At one point in the siege, Macduff orders his soldiers to cut branches from the trees of Birnam wood, and the men march on the castle in this camouflage. Macbeth is told that Birnam wood is marching against him. Later, in the final duel with Macduff, Macbeth calls out: "I bear a charmed life, which must not yield to one of woman born," to which he hears the reply: "Despair thy charm . . . Macduff was from his [dead] mother's womb untimely ripped."

Scene 5 is the midpoint of the fifth and last act of the tragedy. The act begins with the entrance of Lady Macbeth, holding a candle to the darkness. The lady is suffering from a delirium that makes perfect sense to the spectator because it is composed of broken, jumbled fragments of the story that has unfolded before the spectator's eyes during the previous acts. Lady Macbeth is trying to remove imaginary stains of King Duncan's blood from her hand: "Here's the smell of the blood still. All the perfumes of Arabia will not sweeten this little hand." She speaks to her husband, saying: "No more o' that, my lord, no more o' that. You mar all with this starting," and each sequence of her delirium ends with the same sinister refrain: "What's done cannot be undone." A waiting gentlewoman and a doctor of physic enter. The latter, after listening to Lady Macbeth, says, "This disease is beyond my practice." Three scenes later, scene 5 begins when one of Macbeth's first lieutenants, Seyton, comes to see him. Macbeth asks him, "What is that noise?" Seyton answers: "The queen, my lord, is dead." Then come the ten lines spoken by Macbeth that I am going to discuss. They begin by:

She should have died hereafter,
There would have been a time for such a word.

The lines that follow are of the improvised free-association kind typical of Shakespearian monologues and that, to my knowledge, did not exist before him—or at least not with comparable opulence and intensity:

Tomorrow and tomorrow and tomorrow
Creeps in this petty pace from day to day
To the last syllable of recorded time;
And all our yesterdays have lighted fools
The way to dusty death. Out, out, brief candle!

Next come those five famous lines to which I would like to give special attention:

Life's but a walking shadow; a poor player
that struts and frets his hour upon the stage,
And then is heard no more. It is a tale
told by an idiot, full of sound and fury,
Signifying nothing.

There are many other examples of this typically Shakespearian association process. One of the most beautiful is Richard II's monologue in act 3, scene 2 of the play of the same name. To illustrate what I mean by an association process, I will discuss Hamlet's universally known "To be or not to be" monologue. In each of these cases, what is important is not that the character talks freely and "naturally"; that is already perfectly true in Greek tragedy and in any worthwhile play. If a character does not talk spontaneously and "naturally," the play is simply bad. But Shakespeare's characters speak as though they were improvising in a way that is in appearance only very indirectly connected with the situation. They are carried away by a flood of ideas calling each other forth in ways that are far from evident until afterward, when they become compelling. Hamlet begins with an unexpected question—"to be or not to be, that is the question"—and goes on to ask: Is it nobler to suffer or else to take arms? He describes the woes of life, rather unrelated to his actual situation, and goes on to explore the other term of the alternative:

To be or not to be . . .
To die, to sleep,
To sleep, perchance to dream. Ay, there's the rub,

The rub—tragedy, anguish—seals the impasse of life. Who knows what dreams that sleep may hold, and whether they would not be worse than waking life? To be or not to be, to die, to sleep, to dream, dream, nightmare: this is the chain of associations.

To return to my quotation of *Macbeth:* the queen is dead. She should have died hereafter; there would perhaps have been a time for such a word, but not now, not when catastrophes are piling up. But Macbeth immediately gets a grip on himself and mocks his reaction: hereafter, that is to say, once again, and as for all the other fools, tomorrow and tomorrow and tomorrow. . . . We always say tomorrow, but that tomorrow, rather than embodying hope's accomplishment, is simply what keeps us in chains, forcing us to creep, from day to day, to the last syllable of recorded time. The syllable, maybe the last word of the dying man? Recorded where? By whom? Recorded in advance, like the time allotted us on our way to dusty death, like the short hour allotted to that poor player. And from tomorrow he moves to yesterday, for all those tomorrows, with their petty creeping pace, turn into yesterdays that turn out afterward to be traps that fooled us, fools as we are, by illuminating the only way we can ever tread, the way toward the dust of death. So, out, out, brief candle of life. Next come the three sublime metaphors, slipping one into the next and opening up, like venomous, deadly flowers, in a cinematographic movement. Life, our life, is a walking shadow; it is also a poor player who has his hour to appear on the stage, strutting and fretting, but his hour is soon over and we hear no more of him. What is this all? It is a tale told by an idiot, full of sound and fury, signifying nothing. We move from one metaphor to another in an ascending, expanding movement arriving at its acme with the tale told by an idiot.

Why brief candle? We have just learned of the death of Lady Macbeth, so that old poetic *topos,* the little candle of life, consumed or blown out by some *Moira,* reminds us of how Lady Macbeth made her last appearance in the play a few minutes ago, holding her candle, before her life was snuffed out. Another *topos:* life is a walking shadow. Pindar had already written a more forceful version, *"skias onar anthrōpos,"* "man is a dream of a shadow," but the clichéd metaphor is revivified here, and entirely refreshed by the context, with its harmonious melody; the leading melody that continues is in harmonic consonance with what goes before. For we have just seen a shadow walking on the stage; it was Lady Macbeth, she was there, she walked, delirious, before her life went out. But she, that walking shadow, was also life, Macbeth's life. Not only had she damned her soul for him, but she was his soul, purely and simply. It was she who encouraged him when his courage—his soul—failed him on the point of assassinating the king, she who made him return to the king's bedchamber and commit that hideous crime, she who pressed him to murder Banquo, she who supported him when the ghost of Banquo, killed by Macbeth's men, entered the banquet room to which he had been treacherously invited. She who had always put spirit into him—that was her, the shadow we saw a minute ago, walking, the delirious shadow of herself. This life, poor player, poor pitiful actor who has been given a scant hour on stage, once and for all, that scant hour of our life on the stage of the world, on which we strut and fret. Poor player, because regardless of what he does, the outcome will be poor, wretched, just as wretched as Lady Macbeth, whom we just saw, whose hour on stage has just ended. She will no longer be heard, we will no longer hear of her. But Macbeth himself is that poor player whose hour will soon be over. Within the play itself, the plot will succeed: he has withdrawn into Dunsinane castle, where he is surrounded by his enemies with no hope of getting out, and the first of the witches' prophesies has just come true by a sinister reversal of impossibility into reality. As for the spectacle, the spectator knows that the play is coming to a close; this is act 5. And he who says that life is a poor player who has his hour on stage is himself, not *in dicto* but *in re,* a player whose hour of fretting is just about over. Macbeth is speaking about himself, and the actor playing the part of Macbeth is speaking about himself.

All of that is a tale told by an idiot. The etymological kinship must be kept in mind: a tale told. Full of sound and fury. Sound, here, is not just sound, it is obviously noise. Shakespeare does not hear life as musical singing; he hears noise—as we ourselves do.

A tale told by an idiot. The chain of metaphors comes to a break, without demolishing the continuity. What makes for continuity is the referent, always the same: life. The break is the change of level. The first two metaphors—life as a walking shadow, life as the poor fretting player . . . —are external, so to speak; they are images or comparisons. Someone speaks from without, inspects, compares, and states. This externality is incorporated in the texture of the metaphor: for there to be shadow there must be light; for there to be a player there must be a theater and a spectator. The dereality of life is grasped in reference to an opposing reality, without which the metaphor would be meaningless. But when we arrive at the tale told by an idiot, everything is engulfed in the metaphor itself, there is no longer any external opposition, the metaphor has dilated to the point of absorbing the whole of reality. Life is a tale told by an idiot, full of sound and fury, signifying nothing: this encompasses everything—you, me, the author, the spectator, Macbeth, the player, the speaker, the listener, life, and the theater portraying life. Space closes in on itself, a black hole plunging into the abyss of itself.

If we resort to differentiation and opposition to understand the terms of that sentence, as we necessarily do for any sentence in any language, that is exclusively due to the needs of the very effort at understanding; they are not immanent to the metaphor. The first two metaphors situate life within something and by opposition to something else: shadow and light, the illusion of the poor player on stage and the reality outside the theater. Shakespeare's greatness resides in his making the nothingness that is everything explode in the third metaphor. This is the absolute metaphor. As a mathematician would say, it is algebraically closed. It does not speak of something about life relative to some other aspect of life; it takes life as a whole, and that life is absurd and speaks of itself as absurd. It is a tale told by an idiot; that is what is happening on the stage and between the stage and the spectators. Macbeth, the actor who plays his part, and the spectator watching are one and the same thing. It is the absurd tale speaking of itself as an absurd tale; the person who speaks is part of the absurd tale, and to understand, in this absurd tale, that one is in an absurd tale is part of that tale and of its absurdity, embracing everything and everyone. This statement eludes the Epimenidean dilemma. He does not say, I am lying; he does not say, what I say is absurd. The statement is true to the second power. The absurdity of life is not abolished if some living person observes that life is absurd. It is *reinforced*, for precisely, if life is absurd, what use is there in knowing it? That knowledge itself is absurd; it really signifies nothing. The statement is self-corroborating. Our knowledge of the absurdity of life reinforces that absurdity. From the humble, human viewpoint, life would certainly be less absurd if we were unaware of the fact. Religions are all there to testify to this—to assert that life is not absurd, or that if it is, there is also another life which, for mysterious (and in fact absurd) reasons, will not be absurd. The Greeks knew that absurdity well, and Aeschylus knew it, when he had Prometheus say that he had inspired mortal men with "blind hopes" (*tuphlas elpidas,* line 250).

Here, the magnificence of the poem is in the play of that unfolding, that dilation of the metaphor. There is also, of course, the constant *lexis*, the unexpected, brilliant precision of the words chosen—the player who struts and frets, who swaggers around the stage, the tale told by an idiot, immediately made concretely visible by its referral to the spectacle of Lady Macbeth, for her true life and the truth of her life have become delirious. What she says is a tissue of absurdities, and those absurdities are true for anyone who knows the story. She talks about spots of blood, a murdered king, and so on, but in the end, that reality itself is a tissue of absurdities, because all those crimes were committed in order to seize the crown and to enjoy its possession, and the final outcome is folly and death for Lady Macbeth and the impending destruction of Macbeth. Here again, there are three successive levels. The words are rich and perfectly apt, as in any of the great modern poets, but to weave that poetic sense, Shakespeare necessarily resorts to the unfolding metaphor. Unlike Sappho, Aeschylus, and Sophocles, he can no longer find it in a single, singular word and in the indivisible polysemy of what that word is able to convey.

Another related but profoundly different type of metaphor is what may be called the polysemous image or metaphor. Here the word is "univo-cal." It is not the word used that contains an indivisible polysemy, but rather, it immediately conjures up a multitude of references pregnant with meaning. In German, *Lider* means eyelids, and nothing else. But let us consider the depth of the word when Rilke uses it in the epitaph he wrote for himself:

Rose, oh reiner Widerspruch, Lust
Niemandes Schlaf zu sein unter soviel Lidern

[Rose, O pure contradiction,
joy of being no one's sleep under so many lids]

What lids are these? The dead man, who is no one, *Niemand, outis,* sleeps behind his own eyelids. He sleeps under the lids that are the shroud and the coffin, and also under the many layers of earth covering him. He sleeps under the countless lids of the doings of his bygone life, of the roles he played, of what he was for different people. It takes all those lids to cover—what? No one. *Niemand, outis.*

III

The purpose of these examples was to illustrate, by contrast, one aspect of the difference between the poetry of ancient Greece and modern European poetry. I would now like to try to draw some more general conclusions. This will lead me to formulate some hypotheses and to express some opinions, both extremely hazardous given the extremely slippery nature of the subject and my own limited means, as I am relatively well versed in only five languages (modern and ancient Greek, French, English, and German) and moderately ignorant of only three others (Latin, Italian, and Spanish). That is to say, my familiarity is confined to a very small part of the Indo-European domain. What gives me the courage to attempt this undertaking, in spite of it all and at my own risk, is what I perceive as the quasi general neglect, since the end of "classical" philology and the death of the great Roman Jakobson, of an extremely important research topic: the comparative exploration of the expressive resources of languages, an all-important subject for the elucidation of the ways and means of social-historical creation.

I think this neglect has to do with an aberrant contemporary phenomenon: the fear of seeming to favor a particular language or culture, thus exposing oneself to the accusation of cultural imperialism or, the worst of all crimes, of Euro- or logo-phallo-onto-etc.-centrism. This produces a rabid, wholesale leveling off, a refusal to discuss differences, and more importantly, to discuss all the sorts of alterity that constitute the unfathomable wealth of human history, under the fallacious pretext that all peoples have equal rights. As if one had to have asserted the equivalence of Greco-European and Tasmanian "philosophies" to have the right to condemn England's extermination of the latter. The imbeciles who follow that line of reasoning don't even see that they are actually giving in to the "reasoning" used to justify colonialism: if one culture is "superior" to another, then its representatives have the right to dominate (and to exterminate, in the last analysis) members of the latter. Whence, to condemn that domination or extermination one would have to condemn any comparative study of cultures, which might result in "value judgments" about them. The absurdity of this pseudo-reasoning obviously has nothing to do with the immense difficulties intrinsic to any such study, nor with the question, which is on another level completely, of the political choices we are necessarily led to make between the types of institutions created by different cultures. It is not because I proclaim my attachment to the seeds of democracy created within the Greco-European tradition that I am obliged to assert that the architecture produced by a caste society such as Hindu society is inferior to Western architecture. No more than I am forced to endorse women's excision or infibulation, practiced in many parts of Africa, because I support the rights of Africans. The internal cohesion—both self-evident and mysterious—of the various domains of cultural creativeness is a theoretical question of the utmost importance. However, it has no direct political relevancy, as shown by today's cross-fertilization (and contamination or corruption) between different cultures around the world. We can therefore launch an investigation of the different paths taken by poetic expression in ancient Greece and modern Europe without fearing that were it, most improbably, to lead us to the conclusion that the former paths were "superior" to the latter, we would be forced to fight for the reinstatement of slavery. There does remain the risk of giving in to one's "subjective" tastes and preferences in conducting such a study. That risk can never be eliminated when "esthetics" are involved, but it is rather minimal here, since we have no intention to make a comparative "evaluation" of ancient and modern poetry, but rather to describe and analyze the means used by each.

My starting point will be a remark made by Aristotle in his *Poetics*. The poet who writes tragedies, he says, must be much more *muthopoios* than *metropoios,* much more a creator of myths and stories than a creator of meters, a versifier. I think that is true not only for tragic poetry, but for all poetry. Even in lyric poetry, there is always some *muthos*—I have tried to show that in those four lines from Sappho—that is, a story, a referent (created by the poem itself of course), an object that is presented and that "unfolds" even if that unfolding is very brief, and even if the referent does not take the form of acts, but has to do with the poet's feelings and psychic states, as is the case in epic or tragic poetry. Lyric poetry is not purely exclamatory; it is not simply oh!s and ah!s. It has an object: psychic states—representations, affects, and desires—and even if that object is captured in a snapshot, it is never shown in absolute instantaneity. It is within time, caught up in time, and it makes time exist, with a before and an afterward. This may be found even in such poetry as haikus or some very short Chinese poems composed of a few terms—perhaps a mountain, a lake, a bird, sadness. This apparently static presentation contains the slightest of movements, and that is its *muthos.* What Aristotle means by *muthos* is definitely a narrative development, but between that full narration and the simple *metron* there is the space occupied by the lyric object, which is unquestionably within time.

But the poet is not simply *metropoios* and *muthopoios;* he is also *noēmatopoios,* creator of sense and meaning, as well as *eikonopoios,* creator of images, and *mēlopoios,* creator of music. The latter assertion requires clarification. Music is not intended here simply as material musicality, the rhythmic musicality of the meter and the melodious choice of words (and everything that goes with it, including alliterations, rhymes, or simply beautiful "intrinsic" sonorities), but as the music of meaning, evidencing itself not only in the *muthos* but in the verse, the way words follow each other, and even in the individual word. Significations are presented and articulated. There is signification in the *muthos,* the story told, the object presented as a whole, but there is also an articulation, literally, as in a body subdivided into members that are not separate but are linked together in an ongoing synergy. And subdivision does not mean that the overall signification is cut up in the different parts of the poetic work, in its verses, lines, and words. Minimal poetic meaning is presented in the word itself, and certainly even more in the way words are connected, linked together, as increasingly vivified elements of an overriding meaning. That minimal meaning of the word is not presented in a logical or purely descriptive manner: any metaphor betrays us here, for metaphors betray the specificity of the poetic work. Still and all, we must resort to them, to say that this minimal meaning is presented both pictorially and musically. Speaking of poetry, we are obliged to use metaphors coming from music and painting, just as we must use metaphors derived from poetry, painting, and music when speaking of music or painting. Such is the circle of artistic creation. Metaphors from geometry or physics cannot be used to discuss poetry, music, or painting. I say all this here because we need to understand the stuff of which the musicality of meaning—there is no other name for it—consists. If I am led to prefer the musical metaphor in the forthcoming development, it is because pictorial metaphors are only appropriate when the poetry refers to an "outside" object. But above all, it is because painting, unlike music, does not unfold over time, as the poem does.

There are always two dimensions at the level of the myth, as well as at the metrical level—that is, in lines of verse. The myth can be projected onto the historical dimension of what can be told, the "narration." This is what the scholiasts do, for instance, when they furnish the *hypotheses,* the point and the anecdote of the play, a résumé in terse press-dispatch style, at the beginning of the manuscripts of the ancient tragedies: "Polyneices, having taken up arms against Thebes, his fatherland, is killed in a duel with his brother who was defending Thebes. Creon, the tyrant of Thebes, forbids the burial of his corpse, but Antigone, Polyneices's sister, disobeys the order. . . . " The myth may also be projected on the dimension of signification. This is what we bring out when we analyze the content, the meaning of the story that is told. A myth that could be totally projected on the narrative axis (to take an extreme case) would be devoid of signification; it would be a tale told by an idiot, signifying nothing, or else a trivial event. A myth susceptible of being projected totally on the axis of signification would be a sort of philosophical system—Spinoza's system perhaps—certainly not a poem. Poems, like tragedies, necessarily develop on both of these dimensions.

What we are talking about here is not the *muthos,* but rather the *metron,* the "line," or lines, the subunits without which no poetic signification can be achieved. Here too we have two dimensions. As I have already said, there is a "material," phonetic, and rhythmic musicality. What is important here is semantic musicality: there is both a melody and a harmony to meaning.

The melody of meaning is the interweaving of rise and fall in the register of signification and in the level of intensity. The meaning of each word modulates the meaning of the line as it unfolds. The changes in acuity or intensity of expression create a form, a pattern. Take the mounting intensity in:

> Plonger au fond du gouffre, Enfer ou Ciel, qu'importe?
> Au fond de l'inconnu pour trouver du nouveau!

> [To dive into the gulf's depths and—
> what matters if it is heaven or hell?—into the depths
> of the Unknown in quest of something *new*][8]

or the continuous rise in:

> Demain c'est le cheval qui s'abat blanc d'écume,
> Demain . . .

> [Tomorrow is the horse collapsing, white with froth,
> Tomorrow . . .

ending brutally with the bottomless descent of:

Demain, c'est le tombeau.

[Tomorrow is the grave.][9]

The melody of meaning is the way the meanings and intensities of specific words relate horizontally as they follow each other in a succession that already contains a harmonic component of its own. For, just as when we hear the end of a melody its musical substance includes what preceded it, in the same way the unfolding of meaning in a poetic phrase, itself a temporal form, reaches an end that cannot be what it is without everything that went before it.

Strictly speaking, the harmony of meaning seems to be an illogical expression, since harmony is the consonance of several voices, whereas poems—and linguistic expression in general—are apparently monodic. But there is a harmony because there are harmonics to the signification of words. When you touch a key on a piano or pluck a violin string, a C or a G, what you hear is not only that note but its overtones, the octave, the fifth above it, and so forth. This is what gives the sound of each instrument its richness and color. The harmonics of a word may be taken as all the resonances of that particular word. What makes a word what it is, meaning-wise, is its overtones, its resonances and consonances, what is traditionally called its connotations, everything it conveys and everything to which it refers.[10] This is, unquestionably, inseparable from the listener, the concrete audience, but it is also and above all "impersonally" deposited in the language. A word cannot function within a language without those countless indefinite referrals, each of which sets off other referrals. The harmonic richness of a line of verse is the outcome of the richness of the referrals of the words composing it.

All this is true for poetry in general, irrespective of the language in which it is written.[11] What I wish to discuss here is a specific difference between ancient Greek poetry and modern European poetry, relative to the "choice" of the mode of expressiveness of musical semantics. This difference seems to be tied to one property of ancient Greek, which it probably shares with all those tongues that may be termed primary, as opposed to those we may call secondary.[12] In ancient Greek, words have an originary polysemy, a multiplicity of significations[13] that is not simply the outcome of connotations or harmonics, but corresponds to semantic spectrums in the physical-mathematical acceptance of the term *spectrum*.

In ancient Greek, different meanings cohabit within the same word in a qualitatively different proportion from what may be found in those European languages of which I am at all acquainted. Sometimes they are derived from each other, at others simply interrelated. The latter distinction should in fact be relativized, if only because there is often no way of knowing whether or not the related meanings are the result of a centuries-long derivation process of which no indications have survived. Emile Benveniste's *Indo-European Language and Society* yields an abundant harvest of these, covering, precisely, most "primary"[14] Indo-European languages, in point of fact. Greek words such as *einai, logos, phainesthai,*[15] and so many others definitely seem to have embodied, from the outset of the language and with no indication of what they stem from, whole sheaves of significations within which it seems quite impossible to establish any internal genetic order.

There is, moreover, another equally important fact. Even in the case of derivation, the internal connections between lexical terms are immediately visible; you can almost literally put your finger on them, whereas that is hardly ever true in secondary languages, and when it is true, the cases are often uninteresting, as it were. We have seen some examples of this above, with Sappho's *selanna* and *ōra,* Aeschylus' *gelasma,* and Herodotus' *ergon.* By contrast, let us consider the words *moon* in English and *lune* in French. Neither carries any lexical kinship; their connotations are either real or literary. They do not refer back to any shared matrix of meaning from which a spectrum of signifiers and signifieds would burst forth. *Lune,* in French, is inorganic, so to speak, in this respect. The word fell into the French because Latin said *luna,* just as *moon* fell into English from the Germanic root that yields *Mond.* Interestingly, the latter term is just as "inorganic" in German today.

This primordial indivisible polysemy is certainly not the exclusive privilege of the Greek language. If we are only to judge by the examples given by Benveniste in his above-mentioned book, phenomena of the same type exist in Sanskrit and ancient Iranian as they do in Proto-Germanic. It is up to students of those languages to determine the extent to which they were actively utilized in poetry.

Finally, in ancient Greek (as well as in modern Greek), there is an immense, free lexical production. It is possible to create words, and people actually do so, from Homer on, up to the fourth century and beyond, using the immanent potential of the tongue and the rules governing word formation that go with it, on an incomparably greater scale than in contemporary European languages. The use of prefixes and suffixes, the creation of verbs based on nouns or adjectives, and vice versa, and their composition, did not take place once and for all, but through an ongoing process. This does not exclude discussion and critical postures. Aristophanes, in *Frogs,* criticizes Aeschylus—who treats language like a marble worker extracting blocks of marble from a quarry—putting the words in the mouth of Euripides, who accuses him of making words that are like mountains, and of having too big a mouth, whereas he, Euripides, claims to speak the language of ordinary people.

These derivation processes, in the broadest sense of the term, seem to be ossified in modern European languages, or far more rare. The rigidity of academic French is almost grotesque in this respect. Luxuriant Rabelaisian language has been killed by Malherbe, Boileau, and the *Académie Française.* The compounding process, still numerically important in German, seems to be confined to administrative, practical, and scientific terms: I don't see many composite words in Hölderlin, George, or Rilke. Nouns are still turned into verbs and vice versa in English, but essentially in journalistic-administrative and technical jargons.

Modern European poets are obviously in no way unarmed or inferior owing to this situation, but they have been led to create other kinds of resources. Any minimally adequate description of these would require the writing of a treatise on European (that is to say, Western) poetry, which would take innumerable volumes. In my discussion above of Macbeth's monologue, I attempted to point to one of these, which I have called the developed metaphor. Of course, what is involved here is not the "elementary" metaphor, always present everywhere as soon as there is language, for every linguistic utterance is necessarily metaphoric/metonymic and, more generally, tropic. Nor is it the "poetic image"—comparison, assimilation, allegory, and so on—possibly extending over a number of lines, so often used by Homer. The three "images" given by Shakespeare in the passage discussed above communicate from within; they move from one to the other in ascending figuration/presentation, referring both to their own referent and to each other, and gaining in richness until the final acme.

If there is something that should fill us with wonder, it is the multiplicity of paths that the creative power of poets has been able to elicit in different languages to achieve the most forcefully expressive semantic musicality in poetry. We marvel, first of all, at the resources, the potential contained in each of those languages, each created by another society, another anonymous collective.

May 1984–July 1996

Koinōnia

§ 3   The "Rationality" of Capitalism

For Vassili Gondicas,
discernment personified

It may seem strange to still be discussing the "economic rationality" of contemporary capitalism now, at a time when unemployment officially affects three and a half million people in France and over 10 percent of the workforce of the EEC countries, and when the governments of European countries are responding to this situation by reinforcing deflationary measures such as the reduction of budgetary deficits. It becomes less strange—or rather, the point of the strangeness shifts—when we look at the incredible ideological regression that has been affecting Western societies for close to twenty years now. Things that people rightly viewed as established knowledge, such as the devastating criticism of academic political economy by the Cambridge school between 1930 and 1965 (with Sraffa, Robinson, Kahn, Keynes, Kalecki, Shackle, Kaldor, Pasinetti, and so on), are not being debated or refuted; they are simply ignored or forgotten, whereas some naive, far-fetched inventions such as "supply-side economics" and "monetarism" hold sway, the praises of neoliberalism are sung by people who present their aberrations as self-evident common sense, the absolute freedom to transfer capital is ruining whole sectors of production almost everywhere in the world, and the global economy is being turned into a planetary casino.

This regression is not confined to economics. It prevails in political theory as well ("representative democracy" is now unquestioned and beyond question, precisely now, when it is increasingly being discredited in all those countries that have ever tried it), and more generally in the social sciences and the humanities, as shown by the scientistic, positivistic attack on psychoanalysis that has been raging in the United States over the last fifteen years.

The social-historical background of this regression is clearly visible. It attends the social and political reaction under way since the late 1970s, of which the "socialists" have been the main artisans in France, and for the time being there is no indication that it will come to an end, except in some vague, distant future, through the self-destructiveness of this new capitalist course. But even that prospect cannot offer any consolation, because what is at stake is much more than the suicide of capitalism, as shown, among other things, by the destruction of the environment on the planetary scale. This makes it all the more imperative to develop critical analysis of the present trend. That is not the main purpose of the present text, however.

Capitalism is the first social regime to have produced an ideology asserting its own alleged "rationality." Every other type of society legitimated its institution by myth, religion, or tradition. In the present case, we have the claim that legitimacy is "rational." That very criterion—being rational (as opposed to consecrated by experience or tradition, or handed down by a hero or the gods, or other)—is of course literally instituted by capitalism, and it is as if that fact of having been very recently instituted made it unquestionable instead of relativizing it. No thinking person can avoid asking what that rationality is, what rationality are we talking about? Capitalism might assert a Hegelian position: according to Marx's old mentor, reason means acting in conformity with a goal. So the criterion for rationality would be the conformity of an operation with its goal. This would prevent us from asking: what about the rationality of the goal itself? This rationality confined to means—what Max Weber, curiously, called *Zweckrationalität,* that is, rationality relative to a goal presumably accepted, instrumental rationality—clearly has no intrinsic value. The very "rationality" by which the choice is made of the best way to poison one's spouse, or of the most efficient H-bomb to exterminate millions of people, increases our horror not only of the goal pursued but of the means used to achieve it with the utmost efficacy. Nonetheless, in its most philanthropic moments, capitalist ideology claims that the goal of "rationality" is "well-being." But its specificity resides in its identification of that well-being with an economic maximum (or optimum), or in the claim that it will certainly or quite probably be the outcome of the achievement of that maximum or optimum. Directly or indirectly, then, rationality is reduced to "economic" rationality, the latter receiving a purely quantitative definition as maximization/minimization: maximization of "output" and minimization of "costs." It goes without saying that the regime itself decides what is an output (and how it will be evaluated), just as it decides what counts as "costs" and sets the figures.[1]

Now, the relativity of the ultimate criterion for any culture is a known fact, at least since Max Weber (if we don't want to go all the way back to Herodotus). Every society institutes both its institution and the "legitimacy" of that institution. This legitimation, an improper, Western expression already referring to some "rationalization," is almost always implicit. Better yet, it is "tautological." The precepts of the Old Testament and the Koran find their "justification" in their very assertions—that "there is only one God, who is God," whose word and will they represent. Other societies—archaic societies—derive their justification from the dispositions given by the ancestors, who are to be revered and honored according to the injunctions of the institution. The "legitimation" of capitalism by its rationality is just as tautological. Who in this society, except perhaps a poet or a mystic, would dare to challenge that "rationality"?

Naturally, this circle of institution is just one example of the circle of creation. An institution cannot exist without ensuring its existence, and brute force is generally incapable of meeting that need for more than short periods of time.[2] Parenthetically, one may wonder how this will be dealt with in an autonomous society—that is, one capable of explicitly, lucidly challenging its own institutions. In one sense, it will obviously never be able to break out of that circle. It will assert that collective, social autonomy is "valid." It will certainly be able to justify its existence retrospectively by its accomplishments, including the anthropological type of the autonomous individual it will create. But the positive evaluation of those accomplishments will still rely on criteria, more broadly on imaginary social significations, instituted by itself. I say this as a reminder that, in the last analysis, no society of any sort can take its justification from an external source. There is no way out of this circle, so that cannot form the basis for a critique of capitalism.

It must be noted that lately, the regime's ideological factotums have finally dropped the pretension of justifying or legitimating it. They simply refer to the failure of "really existing socialism"—as if Stavisky's doings could be justified by those of Landru[3]—and to figures for "growth," in places where it still occurs. They used to be more courageous, when they wrote treatises on welfare economics. It is true, too, that the ex-professional critics of capitalism (Marxists and so-called Marxists) are in such a pitiful state that those ideologues can afford to set aside any pretense of seriousness, in complete keeping with the spirit of the times.

Be that as it may, my criticism will be essentially immanent. It will attempt to show that the constructions of academic political economy are theoretically incoherent or meaningless or valid only for a fictitious world, and that, empirically, the actual functioning of the capitalist economy hardly has anything to do with what the "theory" says. In other words, capitalism will be criticized using its own criteria. The discussion is divided into four parts: (1) the specificity and social-historical relativity of the capitalist institution; (2) the theoretical ideology of the capitalist economy; (3) the effective reality of the capitalist economy; and (4) the factors contributing to the productive efficiency of capitalist society and to its social-historical "resiliency."

Specificity and Social-Historical Relativity of the Capitalist Institution

From a bird's-eye viewpoint of history, what distinguishes capitalism from all other forms of social-historical life is clearly the position of the economy—of production and consumption, but also, more saliently, of economic "criteria"—as the focal point and supreme value in social life. One corollary of this is the constitution of the social "product" specific to capitalism. In short, all human activities and all of their effects come to be more or less viewed as economic activities and products, or at the least, their economic dimension is viewed as their essential, most valuable feature. Needless to say, this valuation is formulated in purely monetary terms.

This aspect was clearly acknowledged by the end of the eighteenth century, if not earlier. The justifications advanced for modern indifference to public affairs and politics refer to the primarily economic interests of modern man.[4] Both Saint-Simon and Auguste Comte extolled the "industrial" or "positive" age. In the *Manuscripts of 1844,* Marx wrote some strong, beautiful pages on the transformation of all values into monetary values. What makes them strikingly different from the opinions of the time is not their content (look at Balzac) but the virulence of the criticism. But characteristically, the acute awareness of the historicity of the phenomenon during that period was soon eclipsed by apologists of the new regime, recruited mostly among economists. This occultation was to take the form of glorification of capitalism, depicted as a "rational" economic regime, the development of which represents the triumph of reason in history and relegates earlier regimes to the obscurity of "gothic" (in Sieyès's earlier term) or primitive times. Under their pens, the historical emergence of capitalism became the epiphany of reason, assured, therefore, of an unending future. As Marx put it, for them, "there has been history, but there is no longer any."

Strangely—or not, if we consider the ideological advantages of that position—the denial of the historicity of capitalism has prevailed among economists, from Ricardo to the present. Political economy and its object have been glorified as the investigation of "the pure logic of choice" or the study of "the allocation of limited means for the achievement of unlimited objectives" (Robbins[5]), as if that choice, with its criteria and objects, could be totally independent of the social-historical form in which it operates, and as if nothing other than economics was involved (or as if every other human activity entailing a choice of any kind, from strategy to surgery, could be subordinated to economics). This aberration has enjoyed a tremendous vogue recently, with the proliferation of all kinds of "economics" and so-called economic calculations applied to just about everything (from education to the control and punishment of crime). From this perspective, it is clear that the "reasoning" of scientific economics (I write the word without quotation marks from here on, for readability) should apply by right and even in fact to any society, past or future.

These ideas have surfaced again in another form in the writings of F. von Hayek. Capitalist society, it is said, has proved its excellence—its superiority—by a Darwinian selection process, having turned out to be the only one capable of surviving in the struggle against other forms of society. Aside from the absurdity of applying Darwin's conception to the history of social forms, and the repetition of the classical fallacy (the survival of the fittest is the survival of those fittest to survive; the fact that capitalism prevails simply shows that it is the strongest, at the limit in the coarsest, most brutal sense of the term, not that it is the best or most "rational"—Hayek, the "anti-metaphysician," turns out to be the most vulgar kind of Hegelian here), we know that that is not how it happened. What took place in the sixteenth, seventeenth, and eighteenth centuries was not a competition between an indefinite number of regimes, with capitalism as winner, but the enigmatic synergy between a multitude of factors all tending toward the same outcome.[6] There is nothing mysterious about the fact that a society based on a highly sophisticated technology was then able to demonstrate its superiority by exterminating American Indian nations and tribes as well as Aboriginal Tasmanians and Australians, and subjugating many others.

There is no need, here, to enumerate the examples and studies showing that almost all of human history has taken place in regimes for which economic "efficiency," the maximization of outputs, and so on were absolutely not central to social activities. It is not that those societies were positively "irrational" in the way they organized work or in their productive relations. But almost always, at any given technological level, social life revolves around concerns that have nothing to do with improving the "productivity" of labor through technical inventions or the rearrangement of work methods and productive relations. Those sectors of social activity were subordinated to and integrated in others viewed, in each case, as embodying the main goals of human life, and above all, they were not separated as "production" or "the economy." Such separation began at a late date and for the most part was instituted at the same time as capitalism, by and for it. I would simply remind readers of the writings of Ruth Benedict on North American Indians, Margaret Mead on the Pacific Island societies, Gregory Bateson on Bali, and so on, as well as the work of Pierre Clastres on the Tupi Guarani and Jacques Lizot on the Yanomami. In the most recent period, the most satisfactory overview of these questions was provided by Marshall Sahlins in his *Stone Age Economics*. But this does not apply exclusively to "primitive" cultures, in fact. The economic anthropology of ancient Greece points to similar conclusions, as does the analysis of medieval societies.[7]

Studies on the rise of capitalism in Western Europe, irrespective of their intrinsic validity, all forcefully point to the historical "contingency" of this process. This is true of Max Weber, Werner Sombart, Richard Tawney, and so forth. Even for someone as convinced of "historical necessity" in general and of the historical necessity of capitalism in particular as Karl Marx, the development of capitalism is inconceivable without what he rightly calls primitive accumulation, which, as he demonstrates at great length in chapters 26 to 32 of the first volume of *Capital*, is conditioned by factors (especially exactions, fraud, and private and state-led violence[8]) that are in no way "economic" and owe nothing to the "market." Karl Polanyi did similar, masterful work on a more recent period in *The Great Transformation*.

Before going any further, we must address the question of how the capitalist regime may be adequately characterized. We know, at least since Marx, that the feature specific to capitalism is not the mere accumulation of riches. Wealth is amassed in many historical societies, and we also know that latifundist landowners used slave labor in their attempts at large-scale farming (in particular, not so distantly, in the Roman Empire). But simple maximization (of wealth or of production) per se does not suffice to describe capitalism. Marx perceived the crux of the matter when he posited as the crucial factors for capitalism: the accumulation of productive forces combined with the systematic transformation of production and labor processes, and what he called "the rational application of science in the production process."[9] The decisive element is not accumulation as such, but the ongoing transformation of the process of production in order to increase output while reducing costs. Here we have the fundamental feature of what Max Weber would later call "rationalization" and about which he noted, correctly, that under capitalism it tends to take over every sphere of social life, especially by expanding the realm of calculability. Georg Lukács completed the views of Marx and Weber by adding some major analyses on the reification of all of social life by capitalism.

Why "rationalization"? Like every historical creation, the fact that the trend toward such "rationalization" has prevailed is basically "arbitrary"; it can neither be deduced nor produced from anything else. We can, however, characterize it more accurately by linking it to something better known, more familiar, and expressed in different forms in other types of social organization: that is, the tendency toward mastery. This has the advantage, in particular, of enabling us to establish a connection with one of the most deep-seated traits of the individual psyche: the desire to be omnipotent. This drive, this thrust toward mastery is not exclusively specific to capitalism either; it may, for instance, be found in conquest-oriented social organizations as well. But we may come closer to the specificity of capitalism by looking at two of its main features. The first is that this thrust toward mastery is not simply oriented toward "foreign" conquest, but is aimed just as much, or more, at society as a whole. It must be achieved not only in production, but in consumption as well, and not only in the economy, but also in education, law, politics, and so on.

It would be erroneous—the Marxist error—to view these extensions as "second-order" or instrumental with respect to the control of production and of the economy, which would be the main thing. The same imaginary social signification takes over one social sphere after another. It is certainly no accident that it "began" with production: it is in production that technological changes first made domineering rationality possible. But the process does not stop at production. Between 1594 and 1607, Maurice de Nassau, Prince of Orange and *stathouder* of Holland and Zeland, with the help of his cousins William-Louis and Johann, set rules for standard musket drill. They included a series of about forty precise steps to be performed by musketeers in the proper order and by the entire company at a same set pace. Those rules were formulated by Jacob de Gheyn in *Weapon Handling: Drill Book of Musket Drill*, published in Amsterdam in 1607, which immediately circulated throughout Europe and was translated into Russian, on order of the czar, in a practically illiterate Russia.[10] The second feature is of course the fact that the thrust toward mastery adopts new means for its accomplishment, and those means are of a special, "rational"—that is to say, "economic"—nature. The means are no longer magic or winning battles, but precisely, rationalization, with its peculiar, very specific content: maximization/minimization, that is, extremization (if I may forge that term, borrowing it from mathematics, in which the maximum and the minimum are two cases of the *extremum*). It is in consideration of this series of facts that we may describe the core social imaginary signification of capitalism as the thrust toward the unlimited extension of "rational mastery." I shall explain the quotation marks further on.

This unlimited extension of rational mastery goes hand in hand with, and is embodied in, several other social-historical trends. I am not talking about the consequences of capitalism (such as urbanization and the changing nature of cities) but about those factors that were essential requisites for its rise and development:

- The enormous acceleration of technological change, a historically new phenomenon (this is a well-known fact, but must be emphasized). This acceleration was brought about by the outburst of scientific activity that had begun before the Renaissance but increased enormously during it. In recent times, this has turned into an independent trend: technoscience. One particular feature of this evolution must be stressed: technology is predominantly aimed here at reducing, then eliminating, human intervention in production. This is understandable, because human beings are the most difficult element to control, but at the same time, it leads to irrationalities of another sort (breakdowns in technical systems may have catastrophic consequences, for example).

- The birth and consolidation of the modern State. Capitalist development in Western Europe went hand in hand with the creation of an absolutist State, which in turn fed and facilitated it in several respects. Simultaneously, that centralized State became increasingly bureaucratic. An "orderly" bureaucratic hierarchy replaced the more or less chaotic feudal entanglement. The newly developing capitalist business enterprise was modeled after this bureaucratization of the State and the army.

- In the major countries (England, France, the Netherlands, and so on), the creation of a modern State paralleled the formation of modern nations. This established a national sphere, both economic (with protected national and colonial markets and government spending) and juridical (with unified rules and jurisdictions), essential for the first phase of capitalist development.

- A considerable anthropological transformation occurred. Economic motivations tended to supplant every other incentive, by hook or by crook. Humankind became *Homo oeconomicus,* that is to say, *Homo computans.* Duration was reduced to measurable time, imposed on everyone. Shumpeter's entrepreneurial type, and later the speculator type, became central. A calculating, gain-seeking mentality spread, unevenly, to the different occupational groups. At the same time a working-class psychosociology, marked by solidarity and its opposition to and challenging of the prevailing order, saw the light and developed. For close to two centuries, it was pitted against the dominant mentality and conditioned social conflict.

- Precisely, and above all, capitalism was born and developed in a society in which conflict, and more specifically the questioning of the established order, was present from the outset. This first took the form of a movement in which the protobourgeoisie strove to gain freedom for the boroughs, a form of questioning that was actually a resumption, under the conditions prevailing in Western Europe, of the ancient movement for autonomy later to expand in the form of the democratic and working-class movement. The evolution of capitalism beyond its first stage

is incomprehensible without that internal challenge, which has been a
decisive requisite for its very development, as will be recalled below.

The Theoretical Ideology
of the Capitalist Economy

What now passes for the "science of economics" has received such
scathing criticism and entertains such tenuous relations with reality that
to pay attention to it may seem as anachronistic and fruitless as whip-
ping dead horses. However, as noted above, the ideological regression is
so great nowadays, and above all, the debris of those "theories" is still
floating around in so many confused minds (and not only those of journalists), that a cursory recapitulation is needed.

There was a classical theory of political economy, which actually came
to an end with Marx. However, as Marx himself already observed, whereas
his classical predecessors had made an effort to analyze the newly emerg-
ing social reality seriously, the epigones of Smith and Ricardo soon turned
it into a defense and glorification of the new regime. Following a phase
of vulgar apologetics, political economy was attired in mathematical garb,
so that it could allege its "scientific" character. But the ideological nature
of the new science was given away by its persistent efforts to depict the
regime as both inevitable and optimal. It is easy to see that either one of
those virtues would suffice: the fact that the inevitable is simultaneously
optimal can only make us prick up our ears. I will simply attempt to
point out some of the basic postulates of this ideology and to show that
they are either vacuous or unreal.

The one overriding idea is that of *separability,* leading to the notion
of separate imputation. Now in fact, the economic subspace, like every
social subspace, is neither discrete nor continuous, with the understanding that these terms are used metaphorically here. Individuals and firms
are of course identifiable in their economic doings, susceptible of being
designated as distinct entities, but every aspect of their activity is constantly entangled with that of innumerable other individuals or firms in
countless ways that are not strictly separable. A firm makes decisions on
the basis of an "overall climate in public opinion," and if it is at all large,
its decisions will affect that overall climate. Unknown to it and unwit-
tingly, its action will make the existence and activity of other firms easier
(by enabling them to make external economies) or more difficult (they

may make external diseconomies), and in return it will undergo the positive or negative effects of the action of other firms and other factors of social life. The imputation of an economic result to any one firm is purely conventional and arbitrary: it follows boundaries set by law (private property), conventions, and habits. It is no less arbitrary to ascribe a productive result to any one factor of production, be it "capital" or "labor." Capital (in the sense of the means of production produced) and labor contribute to the productive result without any possibility of sorting out their respective contributions, except in the most trivial cases, and even then. . . . The same is true within a factory, between the different departments and shops, or again for the "result" of each individual's work. No one person could do what she does without the synergy of the surrounding society and without the cumulative effects, in her motions and mind, of what went before. Classical political economy tacitly treats these effects as "history's free gifts," but they have extremely tangible results, visible for instance when the industrial productivity of a European population is compared with that of people in precapitalist countries.[11] The social product is the outcome of cooperation within a collectivity whose boundaries are fuzzy. The idea of an individual product is inherited from the juridical convention/institution initiated by the establishment of "private ownership" on land. These notions—separability in general and the possibility of separate imputation in particular—are the tacit assumptions underlying the postulates of economic theory.

The first postulate, explicit or implicit even in its attenuated forms, is the existence of a *Homo oeconomicus,* which applies not only to individuals but to organizations (to business enterprises and the State, although curiously, the postulate of rationality supposedly characterizing every other sector of economic life does not seem to apply to the latter, no doubt because it is disturbed by political factors). The fact that these collective bodies develop specific courses of action, "rationalities," and above all irrationalities is of no great concern to these theoreticians. That economic creature is totally, absolutely a calculator who acts computer-like, constantly maximizing/minimizing the results of his action. I could easily give a laughable description of the consequences of the strict application of this fiction. For example, I would invite the reader to imagine himself waking up and, before getting out of bed, unknowingly reviewing the billions of possibilities open to him for maximizing the pleasurable aspects and minimizing the negative aspects of the new day, weighing the different combinations, then rising, always ready to revise the outcome of his calculations in the light of any new piece of information. Just as the apologists of the capitalist system seem to ignore history, anthropology, and sociology in their portrayals, this postulate turns its back on psychology and psychoanalysis as well as on the sociology of groups and organizations. No one functions by constantly attempting to maximize/minimize "utilities" and "disutilities," benefits and costs, and no one could. No consumer is cognizant of all the goods on the market, with their qualities and defects, and no one could be. Nor is anyone exclusively guided by considerations of "utility" or personal economic satisfaction ("ophelimity"). Choices must be made within whatever environment is available. They are influenced by advertising, and "tastes" reflect all sorts of social influences, more or less arbitrary from an "economic" standpoint. This applies to decisions made by organizations as well. Not only is the managerial bureaucracy that runs firms imperfectly informed, but also it generally applies erroneous criteria, and furthermore, it does not come to its decisions at the end of any "rational" procedure. It reaches them at the outcome of a struggle between cliques and clans spurred by all sorts of motivations, only one of which, and not always the prevailing one, is the maximization of the company's profits.

The postulate of mathematicization is obviously consubstantial with "rationalization," construed as exclusively quantitative. Political economy textbooks and writings are filled with equations and graphs, almost always meaningless except as elementary exercises in differential calculus and linear algebra. There are several reasons for this lack of meaning:

- This mathematicization is essentially quantitative (algebraic/differential). Now, the paradox of the actual economy is that although it is full of quantities, these cannot be treated mathematically, except in the elementary sense. There definitely are physical quantities, but as we know, they are heterogeneous. They can be neither added up nor subtracted, except when they refer to the exact same object. (I am not talking about engineering calculations here.) Nonetheless, on the marketplace, or in national accounting, they are added together by means of their prices. But the resulting magnitudes are only significant within a very narrow framework. They are not comparable over time, for example, or internationally. Only valuations in current prices can be added up, and these only provide a "snapshot," and one of limited signification. Strictly speaking, there is hardly any sense in comparing the national product over successive, somewhat distant periods of time, for example, because its composition changes in the meanwhile, and the methods invented to circumvent the famous index number problem are extremely imprecise artifices. That does not make statements such as "production was lower this year than last year," or "working-class consumption has increased over the last century" untrue, but it does make the calculations and predictions to the third or fourth decimal so commonly found in national accounting simply ridiculous.

- Political economy is constantly alluding to "capital" as a factor of production, meaning by that the whole set of means of production produced. Now, in reality, this whole is not measurable for a number of reasons: its composition is heterogeneous; valuations of the goods composing it, based on market prices, may change from day to day with the state of demand and the expectations of profit; the endless tide of technical inventions constantly modifies the "value" of the elements composing it (new machines may become worthless if more efficient ones are put on the market); changes in "tastes"—that is, more or less lasting modifications in the structure of demand—also modify the "value" of these elements. None of this prevents political economy textbooks, and even Nobel prizewinners, from going on about "production functions" and quarreling over their most appropriate mathematical formulation.

- Furthermore, differential calculus deals with continuous magnitudes, whereas economic quantities are discrete (regardless of whether we take their "physical" existence or their valuation in current prices). The derivatives and differentials that pervade economic writings are mathematically ludicrous. All those "marginal" curves—of costs, "utility," and so on—are radically meaningless. True, the same theoretical issue arises in quantum physics, which uses differential calculus although the underlying structure of the phenomena studied is probably discrete. But observable reality is nonetheless sufficiently "pseudo-continuous" to justify this treatment, as is actually demonstrated by the scientific efficiency of the methods used in physics. (The same holds for the equations used in statistical thermodynamics.) The points of a hypothesized curve may be "interpolated" from extremely close observable figures, making it possible to calculate a quasi-derivative. But a graph for which only very few points may be determined cannot be treated mathematically. This is true of every sphere of economics, but more particularly of capital and production. To take one striking but by no means exceptional example, an airline company that wishes to increase its transportation capacity can only do so by purchasing units costing tens of millions of dollars apiece.

- What all this means is that the notion of function has no validity in economics. A function is a law linking one or several values of the independent variable to one, and only one, value of the dependent variable in an absolutely rigid manner. But even supposing that those variables can be measured, there are simply no such rigid connections in economics. There certainly are a great many approximate regularities, without which real-life economics would be impossible. But the correct assessment of those regularities and their adequate utilization by participants in the economy are more of an art than a "science." We may be sure, roughly speaking, that if the demand for some commodity increases while the supply remains more or less the same, the price of that commodity will go up. But it is absurd to attempt to determine the extent of the price rise mathematically. Likewise, an increase in demand generally leads to an increase in production. But the way in which the purchasing power corresponding to this additional demand is distributed between a higher price and increased supply (production) depends on all sorts of nonmeasurable and actually not necessarily assignable factors, such as the degree of oligopoly in that particular branch, whether the firm thinks the increased demand will be temporary or lasting, and so on. The very possibility of increasing supply (that is, production) in this case cannot really be determined a priori. Only in some exceptional branches such as steel factories is the productive capacity of the fixed capital strictly determined. In most manufacturing industries that capacity may vary from a factor of one to almost three depending on the feasibility, or not, of working two or three shifts instead of one. The degree of utilization of fixed capital is unclear, and the same is true to a lesser extent to the intensity of use of labor power. More generally, to speak of economic "laws" is an outrageous abuse of the term, aside, I repeat, from a few trivial cases that cannot receive quantitatively rigorous treatment either. Even in the short term, in "static" economics, the state and evolution of the system depend above all on the actions and reactions of individuals, groups, and classes, which are not subjected to any set determinism. This holds even more for the medium- and long-term evolution. The latter is partially determined by the pace and contents of technological change, unforeseeable by definition. "If future innovation were foreseen in full detail it would begin to be made at once . . . ," as Joan Robinson already remarked in 1952.[12] It is also determined by the attitude of business firms, which in turn is motivated by their expectations, among other "irrational factors," and there is no guarantee that these are correct. It is determined, finally, by the behavior of the working class, which is equally hard to predict (for example, their tendency to make demands, and the possibility of doing so successfully, depends on psychological, political, and other factors).

• Last of all, most of the thinking of academic economics revolves around the study of "equilibrium" situations and the conditions under which they are achieved. The obsession with balance has two roots, both ideological. Positions of equilibrium are chosen because they are the only ones in which precise, univocal solutions are possible: systems of simultaneous equations provide a disguise of scientific exactness. Second, equilibriums are almost always presented as equivalent to situations of "optimization" ("cleared" markets, fully employed factors, consumers achieving maximum satisfaction, and so forth). The outcome, until the 1930s, was that persistent imbalances and catastrophic or nonoptimizing "equilibriums" (including "balanced" monopolistic or oligopolistic markets involving additional overexploitation of consumers, or the "equilibriums" of underemployment) tended to be glossed over or relegated to footnotes. One writer (A. Pigou) even managed the feat of depicting situations of mass unemployment as more or less satisfactory equilibriums, explaining that unemployed workers had actually "withdrawn from the labor market" because they refused to take the slightest cut in their wages to find a job. (This sort of idiocy is still very much alive today, when people contend that unemployment would disappear in Europe if only the "labor supply" would become more "flexible"— in other words, if workers accepted cutbacks in their wages and other benefits.) Actually, the capitalist economy is an endless succession of changing imbalances, making anticipation hazardous and the structure of both "capital" and demand at any point in time full of "fossils" (according to Joan Robinson).

The Effective Reality of the
Capitalist Economy

> "The question is," said Alice, "whether you *can* make words mean so many different things."
> "The question is," said Humpty Dumpty, "which is to be master—that's all." —Lewis Carroll, *Through the Looking-Glass*

For a long time, the new "science of economics" only concerned itself with those factors determining the price of specific commodities under conditions of static "equilibrium." Economists believed, or pretended to believe, that the same factors that determine the price of an "ideal" commodity under "ideal" conditions (perfect competition and so on) would do so for just about any price (including the "price of labor" and the "price of capital"), which in turn supposedly determined every important economic phenomenon: the overall equilibrium of the economy, the distribution of the national income, the allocation of resources produced among the various categories of users and types of utilization, and—but this remained very hazy—long-term trends. This was all supposed to be derived, with very few corrections, from the curves of costs and marginal utilities, which could easily be "proved" to intersect at optimal points of "equilibrium." They apparently did not lose any sleep over the fact that capitalism is essentially characterized by violent, spasmodic social and economic upheavals—that is, by the constant reproduction of discontinuities.

Modern-day academic economists are still singing the same tune, sotto voce, but no one seems to take it seriously any more. The reason, no doubt, is that the fiction of perfect competition, pure and perfect or perfectly perfect, has gone up in smoke (more about this later), and that it is impossible, even on paper, to go from the reality of oligopolistic markets to general "equilibriums" optimizing anything other than the profits of the oligopolies or, more accurately, of the clans that run them. Even more, the effective globalization of capitalist production with the resulting colossal differences in conditions of production between the old industrialized countries and the "emergent" countries makes it simply ludicrous to postulate even approximate homogeneity of markets for "factors of production" throughout the world.

For the "classical" phase of capitalism—that is, until around 1975—three groups of problems were encountered by any economic analysts who cared about retaining some relevance to reality and to those aspects of the economy that count for the present and future state of society. The first, clearly defined by Ricardo and taken up again by Marx, is the question of the distribution of the social product (the "national income"). It greatly affects resource allocation between categories ("sectors") of production. The second is the relationship between available productive resources ("capital" and "labor") and effective social demand, which relationship conditions the full or underemployment of those resources. It is closely tied to the third question: the evolution of the economy—that is, the actual or desirable increase in production. These three groups are closely interrelated, since, for instance, income distribution is the main factor regulating the distribution of resources, which in turn plays a key role in the quantity as well as in the content of investment, and therefore in future economic trends.

If we set aside the details, qualifying remarks, and special cases, and if, in a first phase, we exclude foreign trade (for instance, considering a worldwide economy posited to be approximately homogeneous), the answer to these questions is surprisingly simple. The evolution of the distribution of income between social classes and between social groups within each of these classes is essentially a function of the power relations between them. This distribution regulates the allocation of resources to consumption or investment, roughly estimated. Broadly speaking, workers consume what they earn, while the propertied classes earn what they spend.[13] The latter consume an insignificant portion of their income, and invest most of it—and if they do not invest, it disappears and underemployment ensues. This also determines the distribution of investment between industries producing consumer goods and those producing means of production. The "overall equilibrium"—the approximate equality of the supply capacity, that is, the use of available capital and labor, and the effective (which is to say, solvent) demand—depends primarily on the amount of investment. If we consider the total sum of wages plus the income of the propertied classes earmarked for consumption as a given, an equilibrium can only be achieved if companies invest just about enough to absorb the productive capacity of those industries producing means of production. There is no law against their doing so. But again, there is no guarantee that they will. That depends on a number of factors, the main one being their expectations as to future demand for their wares.[14] There are not many sensible things to say a priori and in general about these expectations. Whence the recurrent fluctuations in levels of activity and the "accidents," sometimes to the point of major depressions and highly inflationary phases. Roughly speaking, if we take the pace of technical innovation (and therefore also the rising productivity of labor) to be relatively constant, those same expectations and the level of investment commanded by them will determine the rate of growth of the economy on the longer term. In this case, they will be greatly affected, in terms of trend, by the accumulated experience of the capitalist economy, which tends toward expansion on the whole. In the long term, then, there will be a positive bias toward growth, but also a considerable margin of uncertainty at any particular time for each specific firm. This, combined with the rebound effects of previous fluctuations affecting the existing fixed assets, precludes the existence of balanced, "steady" (at a practically constant rate) long-term growth. This overall picture may, and of course should, be filled in by looking at other factors (an upward or downward change in the pace of technical innovation, variations in demographic trends, new parts of the world to exploit, and so forth).

Nothing in the foregoing allows us to speak of a guaranteed equilibrium or an optimal rate of growth or level of production, any more than of maximization of social utility, remuneration of labor on the basis of its "marginal output," a natural rate of profit or of interest, or any of the other cupids and nymphs that people the economics textbooks. More specifically, the profits made by firms are not determined by the "marginal cost" of their product (which normally only sets the lower limit for selling prices), but by the price they can obtain (impose, extort) for it, given the demand. This in itself excludes any talk about the "rationality" of resource allocation in the economy.

Here are some concrete illustrations of what economic "rationality" means under capitalism:

- Each firm invests primarily in its own line of production and not where it would make "marginally higher" (and therefore "socially preferable") profits. If it ventures to invest in other sectors, it is because it foresees that the rate of profit will be considerably higher.

- Almost all firms (including neighborhood shops) are in oligopolistic rather than competitive situations, when they are not actually monopolies or in producer combines of one sort or another.

- Owing to this, the notions of "commodities" as homogeneous products and of a "sector" as the sum of firms producing "the same product" are fuzzy.

- Decisions by a firm to invest or not, or to increase or decrease production, are always based on spotty, biased information. In large companies, these decisions are the outcome of infighting among "specialists" and bureaucratic clans (rather than of any "rational decision-making process," as Herbert Simon and others would have it). They are strongly biased toward retaining the current managerial team, as shown by Robin Marris's studies as early as the 1960s.

- The company's internal situation is more or less opaque for its own managers, owing to the bureaucratization of the firm and to worker resistance.[15]

- The "capital market" (and the credit market) is totally "imperfect" for a combination of reasons: because the funds available, as mentioned above, are preferably put back into the places where they were acquired, because the situation of the borrowers is opaque, and because of the very strong ties between the banks and industry.

- In close connection with the previous point, "capital," as the ability to dispose of productive resources and above all of other people's labor, is partly disconnected from ownership—that is, the possession of different kinds of values. What counts is primarily the potential access to such resources, possibly procured by other means (such as bank loans).

- The "valuation" of companies on the marketplace is fuzzy because it depends on expectations as to their future profits *and* on forecasts as to the "average rate" of profit.

- Production (and the labor market, to some extent) is full of rents due to position.

- Private ownership of land creates an absolute ground rent (according to Marx) totally unjustified and economically unjustifiable.

- Labor power is not a commodity. Its production and reproduction are not and cannot be regulated by a "market."[16]

- The effective output of labor (or the effective ratio of pay to physical output)[17] is mostly indeterminate.

In the present phase of capitalism—that is, for about the last twenty-five years—all of this remains true, but some new factors have upset the overall perspective. The effective globalization of production, made possible by new technological developments (in short, the fact that the importance of skilled labor in material production has been reduced practically to naught, quantitatively speaking, putting billions of starving people around the world at the disposal of global capitalism) and political developments (the fact that governments no longer have the arm of economic policy, and especially the total liberation of international capital flows) has had the apparently paradoxical effect of destroying the homogeneity of economic conditions of production around the world at the very time when a truly global marketplace was coming into existence. Any discussion of price setting or of anything else—including capitalist profits—in terms of "rational" factors is ridiculous in this context. I shall return to this in the last part of this essay.

Relative Efficiency, Flexibility, and Resiliency of Capitalism

The best justification of capitalism was given by Schumpeter at the end of his life, in *Capitalism, Socialism, Democracy,* as summarized by Joan Robinson: "The system is cruel, unjust and turbulent, but it does deliver the goods, and damn it all, it's the goods you want."[18]

Here again, the justification is circular. In "affluent" countries, people "want" the goods because they are reared from earliest infancy to want them (a visit to one of today's nursery schools is enlightening), and because the regime prevents them in a thousand and one ways from wanting anything else. This is true everywhere, because if capitalism has not invented *ab ovo* what we call the demonstration effect, it has taken it to previously unknown heights. For the time being, it is still capable of delivering the goods, more or less. This necessarily puts an end to the discussion: the situation will not change as long as people want all that accumulation of junk, which growing numbers of people today are increasingly less sure of getting, and with which they may or may not be fed up some day.

A few questions subsist, however. Despite all its limits, how far does that "efficiency" of capitalism go, and what supports it? How is it that the regime has been able to survive a long series of crises and historical vicissitudes and come out strengthened, at least up to a certain point in time? What changes can this new phase generate, in this respect?

The answer to the first question is not that difficult. Capitalism is the regime that aims at increasing production—a particular type of production, we mustn't forget—by all means, and at cutting its "costs"—as de-fined very restrictively, we must remember as well—by all means. The costs counted here do not include the destruction of the environment, the stunting of human lives, or the ugliness of cities, any more than the across-the-board victory of irresponsibility and cynicism and the re-placement of tragedy and popular festivities by TV sitcoms, nor could the latter be taken into consideration by any reckoning of that sort. To achieve that goal it has known how to and been able to rely on histori-cally unprecedented technological developments, which it encouraged in countless ways. True, that technology was strictly channeled, but it was appropriate to the ends pursued, which were power for those in dominant positions and mass consumer goods for the majority of the dominated, the destruction of meaningful work, and the elimination of any human element in people's role in production. But most formidably, it destroyed all previous social significations and instilled in practically every mind the urge to acquire what is or seems to be within reach, in each person's sphere, and to accept practically anything in order to do so. This tremen-dous anthropological transformation may be elucidated and understood, but not "explained."

Some time ago, but not at all from the start, another transformation occurred as well. An institutional mechanism dating back to the most ancient times, the marketplace, was stripped of every shackle and gradu-ally extended to cover every sphere of social life. That marketplace is not, has never been, and never will be for as long as capitalism persists, "per-fect" or even truly competitive, as political economics textbooks piously claim. It has always been characterized by state interventions, capitalist coalitions, information withheld, consumers manipulated, and open or disguised violence inflicted on workers. It is little else than a moderately wild jungle, and as in any jungle, the fittest have survived and continue to survive, except that the ability to survive does not coincide with any social optimum or even with any maximum production since the latter is ob-structed by the concentration of capital, oligopolies, and monopolies, not to speak of the irrational allocation of resources, unemployed capacities, and constant warring over production in workplaces. But with its ups and downs, booms and crashes, it has somehow been more or less operational within its limits and with respect to its goals.

The answer to the second question, if indeed there is one, is more diffi-cult and complex. It is essentially paradoxical. Left to follow its own logic, the minimization of costs requires that wages be as low as possible for the highest possible productivity. During the first half of the nineteenth century, capitalism spontaneously took that course, and that was the logic Marx extrapolated with his theory of pauperization and surplus production. It was working-class struggle that countered that trend, imposing wage increments and shorter working hours, creating enormous domestic consumer markets, and preventing capitalism from drowning in its own wares. Also, it turned out—it is a known, demonstrable fact, proved by Keynes—that the system, left to its own devices, does not evolve spontaneously toward a state of "equilibrium," however approximate, but rather toward alternating phases of expansion and contraction—economic crises—the most violent of which may cause, and have caused in the past, considerable destruction of accumulated wealth and breathtakingly high rates of unemployment (30 percent of the workforce in the United States in 1933). Now here too, it was social and political reactions that forced governments, starting with the United States government in 1933, to introduce interventionist economic policies.

In both cases—the distribution of the social product and the role of governments—the capitalist, banking, and academic Establishment fought those foolhardy innovations tooth and nail, believing they would bring the world to an end. For a long time, bosses did not confine themselves to requesting (and obtaining) the use of the army against striking workers. They claimed that they were absolutely unable to grant higher wages or shorter working days without ruining both their company and society at large, and they could always find professors of political economics to say they were right. Jacques Rueff, the hero of French economic policy, organized the "Laval deflation" in 1932, while on the other side of the Channel the Treasury and the Bank of England were writing one memorandum after another to prove that any use of public works policy to boost demand would bring about an economic catastrophe.

It was not until after World War II that more or less regular pay increases and state regulation of overall demand came to be widely accepted by employers and academic economists. The outcome was the longest period of practically uninterrupted capitalist expansion (the postwar boom). As Kalecki had already foreseen in 1943, this led to growing pressure on wages and prices, which was clearly felt in the 1960s. There is no proof that this pressure could not have been moderated by appropriate policies, but a specifically political factor came into play here. That moderately inflationist situation served as a signal, and a pretext, for a reactionary counteroffensive by Thatcher and Reagan—a sort of conservative counterrevolution—that spread to the rest of the world over the ensuing fifteen years. Politically speaking, that counteroffensive took advantage of the failure of the traditional "left-wing" parties, the trade unions' tremendous loss of influence, the monstrosity of "really existing socialism" regimes (already manifest before they collapsed), the apathy and privatization of whole populations, and their increasing irritation with oversized, absurd state bureaucracies. All of those factors, aside from the last one, directly or indirectly bespeak the crisis in the social-historical project of individual and collective autonomy. The outcome was a great imbalance in power relations between social forces, making possible the return to blind, brutal "free-market economics," the main beneficiaries of which are definitely the great industrial and financial firms and the groups that run them, but which exceeds their political role by far. In France, Spain, and several Northern European countries, it was the so-called socialist parties that took upon themselves to introduce and impose (or to maintain, in Great Britain) neoliberal policies. Here we witness the unmitigated triumph of the grossest forms of the capitalist imaginary.

This imaginary was primarily materialized by the dismantling of government intervention in the economy. The international circulation of capital has been freed of all controls, the fetishism of the balanced budget prevents any regulation of demand through deliberate policies, and monetary policy is now entirely in the hands of central banks whose sole concern is combating henceforth nonexistent inflation. Consequently, a high level of unemployment has been maintained for the last fifteen years. In countries such as the United States and Great Britain where the jobless rate has dropped, the price paid has been the multiplication of part-time or poorly paid work and the stagnation or reduction of real wages, along with a constant rise in corporate profits and the income of the wealthy classes. The head-on attack on workers' previously won wages and benefits, made possible by the high unemployment rate and job instability, takes the form of blackmail: the cost of labor must be cut down so as to be competitive with foreign companies or to avoid plant relocations. The idea may be to make people think that a pay cut of a few percent in France or Germany would be enough to win the battle against products from countries where wages are a tenth or a twentieth of ours (US$2.50 a day for women penned up in Nike's Indonesian *ergastula,* and even less in Vietnam). No amount of "labor flexibility" in the old industrialized countries could withstand competition from the poverty-stricken workforce in countries with a bottomless reservoir of labor power. There are hundreds of millions of potential workers, both men and women, rapidly "usable" with practically no need for training, in China, just as many in India, and almost as many in the rest of Asia, not to mention Latin America, Africa, and Eastern Europe. It is ridiculous to contend that a harmonious international division of labor can be achieved between countries initially in such vastly contrasting situations without some clashes. We are going through a brutal, savage transitional phase, on a much larger scale and over a much shorter lapse of time than any other transitional phase in the history of capitalism, and the justification given is the absurd pretext that the present course is inevitable and that no political action can counter the juggernaut of economic progression.

Given this state of affairs, it is vain to discuss any sort of "rationality" of capitalism. The regime itself has done away with those few means of control that one hundred fifty years of political, social, and ideological battling had succeeded in imposing on it. The anomic domination of predatory "barons" of industry and finance in the late-nineteenth-century United States pales in comparison. Transnational corporations, financial speculation, and even mafias, in the literal sense of the term, are now looting the planet, guided only by the shortsighted prospect of immediate profits. The repeated failure of any attempt to protect the environment from the effects of industrialization, be it civilized or savage, is simply the most spectacular sign of their shortsightedness. The foreseeable, terrifying effects of the "modernization" of the other four-fifths of the world have no effect on present policies.[19]

The prospect resulting from all this is not a general "economic crisis" for capitalism in the traditional sense. Theoretically, capitalism (global corporations) could do better and better until the sky falls on our head. However, that would suppose, among other things, that the old industrialized countries, especially the European countries, could go to ruin and billions of people in the currently nonindustrialized nations could see the end of their centuries-old lifestyle and enter a universe based on technology, wage labor, and urban development, without any major political or social upheavals. That is a possibility. I am not sure it is the most probable prospect.

Analysis can be taken to the point of raising these questions. The rest depends on the reactions and the action of the people in the countries involved.

September 1996–August 1997

§ 4 Imaginary and Imagination at the Crossroads

My subject is the imaginary and the imagination, looked at from the standpoint of their present crisis in Western societies: the crisis in the instituting social imaginary, the crisis in the imagination of singular human beings. That is why I have entitled my lecture "Imaginary and Imagination at the Crossroads."

First of all, why the imaginary? A brief discussion of the notion is no doubt called for here. I talk about the imaginary because the history of humanity is the history of the human imaginary and its works (*oeuvres*). And I talk about the history and works of the radical imaginary, which appears as soon as there is any human collectivity. It is the instituting social imaginary that creates institution in general (the institution as form) as well as the particular institutions of each specific society, and the radical imagination of the singular human being.

Just a few words about the fate of this notion in the history of philosophy. Throughout that history, the notion of the imaginary has been either ignored or mistreated. As for imagination, it was first recognized by Aristotle, who discovered it, so to speak, and perceived some essential aspects, such as the fact that the soul never thinks without any phantasm—that is, without an imaginary representation. He only arrives at the question of the imagination toward the end of his treatise *On the Soul*, however, and then drops it to pursue his line of reasoning. Some Neoplatonist thinkers occasionally returned to the question during the first centuries of our era, but after that, imagination was dealt with more or less as a "psychological faculty," on the basis of the most facile, most banal aspects of Aristotle's discussion, until the eighteenth century. In the latter half of that century,

the term is often found in the writings of English and Scottish Enlightenment thinkers, and later in Germany, in connection with current interest in questions pertaining to taste and art. Kant, in the first edition of
his *Critique of Pure Reason,* discovered what he called the transcendental
imagination: the imagination required for knowledge to be ascertained
rather than empirical. But in the second edition of that same *Critique,*
he reduced its role and importance considerably. The concept was forcefully revived by Fichte, after which the question returned to oblivion,
philosophically speaking, until 1928, when Heidegger, in his *Kant and the
Problem of Metaphysics,* rediscovered the notion of the imagination as a
philosophical notion. He rediscovered the discovery of the imagination by
Kant, noted that Kant himself had retreated on the question and occulted
it between the first and the second edition of the *Critique,* and attempted
to return imagination to a central position in the way human beings relate
to the world. Then the same story repeated itself for the third time: after
that 1928 book, Heidegger never again discussed the imagination.

But finally, it may be said that this discussion of imagination did exist
in the history of philosophy, after a fashion, with those successive periods
of covering over. But what one would seek in vain is what I call the instituting social imaginary, which is to say the acknowledgment of the basic
fact that one cannot "explain" either the birth of society or the course of
history by natural factors, be they biological or other, any more than by
the "rational" activity of a "rational" being (man). From the start of history, one sees the emergence of radical novelty, and if we do not wish to
resort to transcendental factors to account for this, we definitely must
postulate a power of creation, a *vis formandi,* immanent to human collectivities as well as to individual human beings. Consequently, it is quite
natural that we call this faculty of radical innovation, this ability to create
and to form, the *imaginary* and *imagination.* Language, customs, norms,
and technique cannot "be explained" by factors extrinsic to human collectivities. No natural, biological, or logical factor can account for them. At
most, such factors may constitute necessary conditions (generally external
and trivial), never sufficient ones.

We must therefore recognize that there is, in human collectivities, a
power of creation, a *vis formandi,* which I call the instituting social imaginary. Why has philosophy been blind to this necessity, and why does it
now continue to recoil, horrified and irritated, before that idea? People
always ask me: what is that instituting imaginary? Whose imagination

is it? Show us the individuals who . . . or the factors that . . . and so on. But what it is, precisely, is a constitutive faculty of human collectivities, and more generally of the social-historical sphere. What horrifies and irritates representatives of traditional philosophy, as well as members of the scientific establishment, is the necessity of acknowledging the existence of a collective imaginary, and for that matter, of a radical imagination in singular human beings, as a creative force. Creation here means creation ex nihilo, bringing into being a form that was not there before, the creation of new forms of being. It is ontological creation: of forms such as language, institution qua institution, music, and painting; or of some specific form, some work of art, be it musical, pictorial, poetic, or other. Why is philosophy, in the forms we have inherited, unable to acknowledge the fact of creation? Because that philosophy is either theological, and therefore reserves creation for God—creation took place once and for all, or it is continuous divine creation—or it is rationalist or determinist, and therefore obliged either to infer everything that is from first principles (and from what, then, do we infer the first principles?) or else to produce it out of causes (and from what does one produce the first causes?). But creation belongs to being in general—I will not go into this here, because I am not holding a philosophy seminar today—and creation belongs, densely and massively, to social-historical being. This is attested by the creation of society as such, of many different societies, and by the constant historical alteration, slow or sudden, of those societies.

How can we describe the work of this instituting social imaginary in detail? One aspect of it is institutions. But a look at these institutions shows that they are quickened by—and bearers of—significations, which significations refer neither to reality nor to logic, which is why I call them social imaginary significations. God, for instance, the God of the monotheistic religions, is a social imaginary signification, upheld by a myriad of institutions such as the Church. But the same is true of the gods of polytheistic religions and of founding heroes, of totems, taboos, fetishes, and so forth. When we talk about the State, we are talking about an institution animated by imaginary significations. The same is true of capital, commodities (Marx's "social hieroglyph"), interest, etc.

Once created, both imaginary social significations and institutions crystallize, or solidify, and that is what I call the *instituted social imaginary*. It provides continuity within society, the reproduction and repetition of the same forms, which henceforth regulate people's lives and persist as long as no gradual historical change or massive new creation occurs, modifying them or radically replacing them by others.

Let us consider the imagination of singular human beings. It is the essential determining element (the essence) of the human psyche. This psyche is radical imagination, first of all inasmuch as it is an unceasing flux or stream of representations, desires, and affects. That stream is continuous emergence. Never mind if you close your eyes and plug up your ears; there will always be something. That thing goes on "inside." Images, memories, hopes, fears, "psychic states" surge forth, in ways we may sometimes understand or even "explain," at other times absolutely not. There is no "logical" thought process here, with few exceptions, and discontinuously. The elements are not tied together in a rational or even a reasonable way; there is a surging, an inextricable mixture. Above all, there are representations that have no functionality. Animals, higher animals at any rate, conceivably have a degree of representation of their world, but that representation—and its components—is regulated functionally; it contains primarily what is necessary for the life of the animal and the continuation of its species. But in human beings, imagination is defunctionalized. Human beings can give up their lives to win glory. What is the "functionality" of glory? At most, it will mean a name engraved on a monument, itself eminently perishable. Glory is the subjective corollary of a value of the social imaginary that constitutes one pole in human activities, or at least in the activities of some, bringing into existence a desire directed toward it. Or again, what are the different human affects, the least commonplace of them in particular, such as the affect of nostalgia? It is a creation of the radical imagination of the psyche.

If human beings were prey to that radical imagination and nothing else, they would not be able to survive; they would not have survived. That stream is not necessarily tied either to any logic or to reality; it is completely foreign to both, at first, and the desires that spring up in it are not conducive to life in any community. One of the most powerful affects to be encountered, one that may or may not surface in broad daylight, is the affect of hate, for instance, sometimes to the point of a desire to murder. I often say, jokingly, that any person who doesn't experience a wish for someone else's death at least once a year is seriously ill and should see a psychoanalyst as soon as possible. The "natural" reaction when someone is in our way is to want him to disappear, and as we know, this can be put into effect. The radical imagination of human beings has to be tamed, then, channeled, regulated, and brought into line with life in society, and also with what we call "reality." This is achieved by socialization, through which individuals absorb the institution of society and its significations, internalize them, learn language, the categorization of things and what is right and wrong, what is acceptable behavior and what is not, what must be adulated and what hated. When that socialization occurs, the radical imagination is stifled, to a point, in its most important manifestations: it expresses itself more conventionally and repetitiously. Under these conditions, society at large is heteronomous. But so are individuals heteronomous, for they only apparently use their own judgment, whereas in fact they apply social criteria when judging. Actually, we ourselves shouldn't boast too much. Even in our societies, enormous numbers of people are in fact heteronomous; they only judge on the basis of "conventions" and "public opinion."

Societies in which the possibility and the ability to call established institutions and significations into question are exceptional, a minute number in the history of humanity. We actually only have two examples. The first is ancient Greece, with the birth of democracy and philosophy; the second is Western Europe, after the Middle Ages, that long period of heteronomy.

An extremely important phenomenon, one that is central to today's discussion, is that the history of societies is marked by pulsating processes. Phases of dense, intense creation alternate with lulls, sluggishness, or regression. There are many instances of this. They are all taken from historical cultures of course, since we can say very little about the others. There is a real possibility that "Homeric" (that is, Minoan and Mycenaean) civilization did not disappear solely or even primarily because of invasions or earthquakes, but through some "internal" disintegration processes. We know nothing about that, at least for the time being.

One example of a society that experienced a period of decadence following an age of rich, intense creativity is ancient Greece, and the Athenian *polis* in particular. The truly creative times, with the emergence of philosophy, democracy, and tragedy, not to speak of the other arts and sciences, unfolded until the end of the fifth century BCE, up to the end of the Peloponnesian war. Then, starting from the fourth century, nothing much went on any more. Propelled by its own impetus, society did of course continue to create. There is the paradox, in particular, that two of the most important philosophers of all times, Plato and Aristotle, belong to that fourth century, yet they came after that grand creative period. Theirs is probably a unique case, a flagrant one at any rate, one that illustrates Hegel's famous phrase, his claim that philosophy only appears when the works of the day are over, just as Minerva's bird only takes flight at nightfall. (The phrase is in fact literally false: philosophy took off in Greece just about simultaneously with the beginning of Greek political creation, and the same is true for modern times. The claim only expresses Hegel's wish that the history of humanity, in the strongest sense of the term, would come to a close with his own system.) Be this as it may, after the victory of Macedonia, of Philip and Alexander, we have the Hellenistic, or Alexandrian, civilization, quite comparable, if I may jump ahead, to our own situation. There was no great creation, but eclecticism, endless commentaries—very valuable ones, in fact. Philology and the art of the grammarians flourished, techniques and knowledge continued to "progress," but (with the noteworthy exception of mathematics) there was no powerful expression of any truly innovative radical imagination.

A similar case is found in the Roman Empire after the first century CE. Its fall, conclusively conditioned by the internal evolution of imperial Roman society and by the breakdown of the social imaginary significations underlying the institutions, was simply facilitated by the Germanic invasions. The barbarians had been beating at the gates of the Roman dominion since the first century BCE, and were successfully held back until the end of the second century CE. The decadence within the Empire was too flagrant at that point to be questioned by anyone but quibblers.

Similar major facts are visible in every society whose evolution is documented: in Egypt, the Middle East, India, China, and even in Mesoamerica.

What is important here, from the standpoint of the elucidation of history, is the failure of "explanations." There is nothing surprising about that. No more than we can "explain" the creative phases of history, why they occur at a particular time or the content of that creation, we are symmetrically unable to "explain" the occurrence of phases of decadence, the period in which they take place, or the stuff of which they are made. We may collect all sorts of partial facts that seem to make these alternating phases more comprehensible, but never does this yield a true "explanation." There are no "laws" commanding the radical imagination, when it flourishes and when it fades away, and Spengler's biological and botanical images obviously don't provide any "explanation."

I have already pointed out that during the Hellenistic period, as well as during the late Roman Empire, technical development continued to some extent (this is strangely reminiscent of the present-day situation). This leads us to make a distinction that is also necessary for other reasons: the distinction between culture, in the strict sense of the term, and the purely functional dimension of social life. Culture is the domain of the imaginary, in the literal sense, the domain of the poietic, of that element of society that goes beyond the merely instrumental. No society is devoid of culture, of course. No society is reduced to functionality or instrumentality; no known human society lives like the "societies" of bees or ants. There are always songs and dances, decorations, things that are "useless." Those primitive peoples, whose lives were so difficult, managed to find time for that kind of "foolishness." As you know, what are probably among the oldest, if not the oldest, known prehistoric paintings have been discovered in Portugal, on the walls of Paleolithic caves.[1] Those people spent their time in poorly lit caves to do cave-wall paintings. They felt that was more important than to develop the productive forces or to maximize the yield of their capital.

Clearly, the distinction between what I call the poietic and the functional does not reside in things themselves: it is in the relationship between the way things are done and their finality. A vase can be simply functional—serving a purpose, as a plastic vase might—but it may also be an admirable work of art, like so many old Chinese and African ones. In the latter case, an essential dimension of what makes the vase exist escapes or exceeds any finality; the beauty of a vase is "useless." These two sorts of creation, the poietic and the functional, do not move at the same pace or in the same direction. Poietic creation may dwindle without this affecting creation in the functional sphere: new inventions may be made; technical and even scientific development may continue. That is what happened, as I have mentioned, during the Hellenistic period, as well as after the culturally creative phase of Roman history. In other cases, after the collapse of "Homeric" civilization, for instance, or during the true European Middle Ages (from the fifth to the eleventh centuries CE), the poietic and the functional spheres regressed simultaneously. There is also a possibility that there have been periods of intense poietic creation while the functional component remained just about stable. This is suggested, at any rate, by the fact that many archaic societies have profoundly different cultures whereas their functional instrumentation seems to be roughly identical.

This differentiation, completely masked by Hegelo-Marxism, adds a further dimension to the immense question of the unity of a society. How can we conceive the fact that two parts of a same body may proceed at different paces? How can two—or several—sectors of life in a same society exist in such different time frames? All I can do here is raise these questions, without attempting to elucidate them.

After the Greek experience, the project of autonomy emerged once again with the birth of the bourgeoisie in Western Europe, starting in the eleventh and twelfth centuries. This is the onset of the "modern" period in the broadest sense of the term. From then on, cultural creation is seen to expand and accelerate, so richly and with such changes of tempo that it is incompressible and almost beyond scrutiny. It is practically impossible to write a history of European culture. It happened everywhere: in Italy, Spain, Portugal, France, England, in what was to become Germany, in Scandinavia, and in the Slavic central and Eastern European societies. Different activities developed at different times and in different countries, with cross-fertilization and mutually beneficial proliferation. This extraordinary profusion reached a sort of acme during the two centuries extending from 1750 to 1950. This is a very specific period, owing to the tremendous density of cultural creation, but also to its enormous subversiveness.

I see this explosion as tied to the fact that the social-historical project of autonomy pervaded society and acted as a ferment on its every aspect. It took the form of the movement for democracy, of the revolutions of the seventeenth, eighteenth, and twentieth centuries, the working class movement, and more recently the woman's movement and the youth movement. But the important point for us here is what went on in the specifically cultural field. We witness the creation of new forms and new contents, with the perfectly explicit intention of fomenting change, and this happened at a pace previously practically unknown in history, with the possible exception of ancient Greece during the period around the fifth century BCE.

As we know, there was, simultaneously, an enormous acceleration in technical inventions, out of proportion with anything experienced in other phases and other regions of the history of humankind. What I am saying here is independent of the many destructive effects ascribable to that technical development. But it was not this technical progress that could have "caused" the cultural upheavals with which we are concerned here. That progress itself depended on some all-important changes in the scientific imaginary. It was at that time that chemistry and electricity, as forms, the theory of heat and thermodynamics, field theory (Faraday and Maxwell's theories), and quantum theory and general relativity were "created" for the most part. Likewise, advances in medicine and applied biology were linked to the emergence of a new science of biology. And the creation of new disciplines such as sociology and psychoanalysis in the social sciences was definitely tied to this overall trend in society, rather than to any technical development. This is even more true of the great philosophical movements of the Enlightenment, followed by German Idealism. The general move to liberate society, and the calling into question and overthrowing of the old political forms, did not stop at the doors of specific activities and disciplines, be it in art, philosophy, or science.

Some people may be surprised to hear me include science as well as philosophy when speaking of the unfurling of poietic activity. Don't both of them express a movement of "pure" Reason? I include them because, contrary to generally accepted ideas, creative imagination plays a fundamental role in science just as in philosophy. Every great philosophical work is an imaginary creation, a creation of the particular type of significations that are philosophical significations. These are not "rational" productions. The idea *idea,* for example, is not the outcome of any empirical induction or logical deduction; rather, it is a prerequisite for both of these. The same is true of ideas such as *potentiality* and *actuality, cogito, monad,* or *transcendental.* They are all great inventions, thanks to which light is shed on a set of facts pertaining to being, the world, nature, human thought and its relationship to the other, and so forth. But the same is true in science. The great scientific advances are outgrowths of the creation of new imaginary schemes, formed under the constraint of available experience but not "following from" that experience. By definition, a logical deduction cannot bring a new hypothesis into being. (An inductive inference is only a deduction lacking stringency, one based on an incomplete set of facts combined with already existing rules, conclusions, etc. A "new" fact may—but does not necessarily—invalidate the previously accepted hypotheses. It does not provide a single milligram of a new postulate. It is in this sense that Popper's conception of "falsifiability" is basically flawed. Falsification by another observation may simply "refute" an existing conception, and even so, that is not always the case: some "falsified" theories persist for a long time, sometimes wrongly, often rightly. The situation will only change when a new hypothesis is invented.) A physician cannot formulate just any old postulates; the new theories have to account for known facts (that is the constraint) and, if possible, predict other, hitherto unknown categories of facts. That is what happened with the positing of such great new imaginary schemes as Newton's vision of the universe, Faraday and Maxwell's idea of the field, Einstein's successive conceptions, and so on.

There is a profound kinship between art on the one hand, and philosophy and science on the other. Not only does one see the creative imagination at work in all of them, but also, art and philosophy and science are attempts to give form to chaos—to the chaos underlying the *cosmos,* the world, the chaos that is below those successive layers of appearances. In the depths of being there is that indetermination, the corollary of its power of creation, the successive determinations of which are embodied by the infinite leaves of the cosmos.

The institution of society also aims at covering over that chaos, at creating a world *for* society, and it does so, but there is no way of avoiding the existence of tremendous holes in that creation, great conduits through which chaos is clearly evidenced. One of those ducts, for human beings, and no doubt the most difficult to block off, is death, which every known institution of society has attempted to make meaningful. One dies for one's homeland, to become one of the ancestors who will return reincarnated in a newborn babe, or to enter the Heavenly Kingdom, and so the essential senselessness of death is masked.

Art on the one hand, philosophy and science on the other, attempt to give shape to chaos, a shape that human beings are able to grasp. Art does it in its own way, philosophy and science in theirs. In both cases we have the creation of forms, with the difference that art, by giving and in order to give shape to chaos, creates a world, it creates some new worlds, and it does so relatively freely. It does not work under the constraint of experience. The constraints with which it must deal are of another order; they are internal. Philosophy and science, on the other hand, aim at elucidating the world as such, as it is given to us, and this imposes a very strict constraint: the constraint of available experience. Science certainly does this in its own way and in a restricted field, that of our physical experience, and it is concerned with those elements of experience that are essentially regular and are susceptible of explanation. In the case of philosophy, the point is not to explain, or even, actually, to understand (where the humanities and social sciences are concerned), but to elucidate. However, a philosophy does not hold water if it does not attempt to account for the totality of human experience. I must say, although I cannot go into this any further, that there does exist one marvelously mixed field, and that is mathematics, which in the most important instances creates new worlds, but in doing so contributes to the elucidation of the world in its given state.

~

I now come to my subject, strictly speaking: that is, the contemporary period, starting from 1950—a date that obviously has no pretension of being precise. What I see, bluntly, is that the great movement of creation is now in the process of running dry. Its exhaustion exceeds the domain of art. It affects philosophy as well, and, I think, even true theoretical creation in the scientific field, whereas the development of technique and of technoscience is accelerating and becoming increasingly independent. This evolution, this regression of creativity, is attended by the triumph, during the same period, of the capitalist imaginary, and an increasingly marked regression of the democratic movement—of the movement toward social and political autonomy.

Let me begin with philosophy. Heidegger seems to have succeeded in having his (erroneous) diagnosis of the "end of philosophy" become a sort of self-fulfilling prophecy. With very few exceptions, there are no longer any philosophers. There are extremely erudite commentators and very knowledgeable historians of philosophy, but hardly any new creation. The only experience with which philosophy tries to deal, henceforth, is the philosophy of its own history. It is condemned to feed on itself, to devour its own flesh.

In this case, at least, we may perhaps perceive an internal factor that has contributed to this evolution, although it is certainly insufficient as an "explanation." It is the influence of those two great German idealist philosophers, Kant and Hegel. Their influence most probably operated for contradictory reasons, but converged toward the same outcome. The radical break that Kant wished to establish between philosophy and science, under cover of his criticism of metaphysics—with philosophy reduced, in the domain of knowledge, to "criticism of theoretical reason"—led to the idea that the domains of science and philosophy were separated by a gulf that one could not attempt to cross without risking a fall into the abyss of metaphysical speculation. From a symmetrical but opposite standpoint, Hegel elaborated a "system" that claimed to encompass all knowledge, including scientific knowledge. The proclamation that this knowledge (scientific as well as philosophical) had just reached its completion in that system seemed to demonstrate, by the failure of that very same system, that from then on theoretical philosophy should confine itself to the domain of the theory of knowledge, barring which it would be a pathetic repetition of Hegel's vain effort. Close scrutiny discovers both of these effects in Heidegger's proclamation of "the end of philosophy in technicized science." But that watertight separation between philosophy and science, powerfully abetted by the growing specialization and increasingly technical nature of contemporary science, necessarily had catastrophic effects for philosophy. It was then condemned to set aside a huge portion of human experience (everything touching on inanimate or living nature) and either to become a distinct, limited field of no special interest—as is the case in the English-speaking world where logical positivism and "linguistic philosophy" prevails—or to consider itself to be pure "thinking on Being," empty and sterile since nothing can be said about Being outside of beings.

This factor can only have played a secondary role, however, for a similar evolution is observable in every domain. Take the case of science itself. Some major scientific advances are still being made, of course, but the two great theoretical forms on which science rests were both created over three-fourths of a century ago: that is, relativity between 1905 and 1916, and quantum theory between 1900 and the 1930s. These two theories contradict each other, however, and each contains, not puzzles, as Thomas Kuhn put it, but actual aporias that should have challenged the theoretical paradigms themselves. It is a fact that new schemes have been suggested (the theory of cords and supercords, the inflationary universe . . .), but none of them has held up against the constraints of experience so far.

The last great fundamental discovery in biology, the discovery of DNA, dates back to 1953, and it actually follows from Delbrück's work in molecular biology in 1943. Perhaps we should mention, as a possible exception, the theories on self-organization, except that they are based on the theory of automats created by Turing and von Neumann between 1935 and 1955.

It is worth our while to dwell for a moment on the situation created by advances in mathematics and physics since 1900 as they relate to philosophy. These advances have called into question some categories hitherto (and still) fundamental for our understanding of the physical world, including causality, locality, separation, and so on. In mathematics, as of 1930, some astonishing findings—the theorems of Gödel, Turing, and Church—pulverized previous prevailing conceptions of the foundations and possibilities of mathematics. This situation desperately demands philosophical elucidation. But it elicited almost nothing of the sort, as if philosophy had relinquished its role of elucidating our experience.

So we have this exhaustion of the imagination and the imaginary in the fields of philosophy and science, and there is also, obviously, an exhaustion of the political imagination and imaginary. There is no getting around the observation that the worker's movement, and more generally the movement for democracy, has degenerated. Present-day political discourse on both the "right" and the "left" is absolutely sterile and repetitious; we don't even know what distinguishes the "right" from the "left." To confine ourselves to the French scene (but the same may be said of the United States, England, Spain, and so on), there is no noteworthy difference between the various cabinets named by (Socialist) President Mitterand over his two seven-year terms and those that preceded or followed them. Some details do differ, and importantly so (pertaining to policies on the immigration question for instance), but the broad lines are the same. Mr. Juppé [the Gaullist prime minister at the time] is doing exactly what Mr. Balladur [another brand of Gaullist] did previously, which was the same as Mr. Bérégovoy [a Socialist] before him.

But it is the exhaustion of creativity in the artistic field that is most important for our discussion. When I began to write about this subject—my first observations date back to 1960, in an essay entitled "Modern Capitalism and Revolution"[2] in which I stated that the novel had come to a dead end, and I discussed it again in a 1978 paper, "Social Transformation and Cultural Creation"[3]—people said, "you're exaggerating," or "you're getting on in life; they aren't doing the same things as when you were young, so you hate the contemporary period and look back nostalgically to the good old days." Nearly twenty years have gone by since then, and I have the sad pleasure of seeing that even those "official" critics, who have been keen "vanguard" worshippers for so long, are now saying the same thing—except, possibly, with respect to the novel.

What has happened in art during the last forty years? At first there was a fake "vanguard" and a simulacrum of subversion. What is a vanguard? During the previous two centuries, starting with Romanticism but more definitely with Baudelaire and Manet, an important new phenomenon occurred: a break between creative artists and established, "bourgeois" society. Initially, and for a long time, official public opinion rejected the innovations in form and content created by art in every field. Contrary to what some people contend, this was a historically new phenomenon. Young creators may have had problems gaining recognition at other times, but that remained a matter of clans and jealousies. But from the mid-nineteenth century on, a definite break occurred in almost every domain. I mentioned Baudelaire: we may add Rimbaud, Mallarmé, and Lautréamont in France, and similar cases in other countries. In painting, the break came with Manet, the Impressionists, and all those who followed them. In music, it began already with Wagner; then there was Stravinsky and the Vienna school.

Now, that vanguard really and truly seems to have worn itself out after World War II. And what we see, then, at first, is the development of a false vanguard, a series of artificial efforts to produce novelty for novelty's sake, to subvert for the sake of subverting, by people who have nothing new to say. This is particularly flagrant in painting and music. Then, during a second phase, no one even goes through the motions of subversion. Starting even before postmodernism, but mostly when it began, we enter the era of conformism, which is to say the unabashed application of eclecticism and of collage. People imitate earlier creations, combine them, put together the most disparate assortment of plagiaries. In philosophy as well, we have witnessed a glorification of "weak thought"—that is to say, abdication of what is philosophy's job. This is the triumph of sterility.

Postmodernism is the ideology that aims at theorizing and glorifying these practices, and more generally, at depicting the stagnation and regression of the contemporary period as the expression of maturity, as the end of our illusions. It deliberately proclaims its refusal of innovation and originality, as well as of cogency of form. In 1986, in New York, I had an opportunity to hear one of the most famous postmodern architects make this memorable statement during a lecture: "Postmodernism has freed us of the tyranny of style." In the minds of these people, style is a tyranny, whereas it is actually coherence of form, without which there can be no work of art, and at the same time it is the expression of the creator's individuality.

Let's try to go into some detail here. Let's see what has happened in music, for instance. After the atonal and dodecaphonic schools, there were various experiments, which did not come to much. The music produced (that is exactly the right word) today amounts to some imitations and compilations of nineteenth- and twentieth-century pieces. Luciano Berio, for example, has integrated long quotations from Beethoven's symphonies in his own music.

The first half of the twentieth century had witnessed the outstanding creation of two art forms, both new and popular: jazz and the cinema. Now in my eyes, or to my ears if you like, the creative period of jazz came to an end when Miles Davis and Thelonious Monk died. After that, rock, rap, dance, and techno music are definitely major societal phenomena, but that has nothing to do with musical creation, for they are rhythmically totally monotonous, and the poverty of their stereotyped harmonics and melodies is dismally pathetic.

Cinema, the other great creation of the twentieth century, is on the way to being lost in industrialization, facile effects, and vulgarity. One may easily list dozens of great filmmakers for the earlier period, but practically none for the recent period.

In painting, it seems that the main way of innovating nowadays is to do a quasi-photographic representation of Campbell soup cans or ketchup bottles, to revert to various variations on realism, or to do feeble imitations of Marcel Duchamp's provocative exhibit of a bidet in 1920 (that is, over three-fourths of a century ago). Paris was recently treated to Beuys's piano wrapped in felt and exhibited as a work of art at the Centre Georges-Pompidou Museum.

The case of the novel is more debatable. There are, no doubt, still a good many excellent novelists. But do their writings really contribute something new and important, in comparison with the great novels of the past? Can we set those writers on the same pinnacle as Balzac, Stendhal, Flaubert, Tolstoy, Dostoyevsky, Henry James, Proust, Kafka, Joyce, Faulkner . . . ? Can it be that the novel as a form has now run dry? I will simply mention the case of Milan Kundera, who, having written a number of more or less "classical" novels, now feels the need, in his last two or three books, to experiment with new forms. But I'll leave the question of the novel open.

This reversion to conformism is an overall relapse into heteronomy. I have defined heteronomy as thinking and acting in ways imposed (overtly or subterraneously) by the institution or the social environment. Now presently, just as there is a *pensée unique,* a one-track, conformist way of thinking about economics, where no one dares to challenge the neoliberal inanities that are driving European economies to their ruin, no one seems to be capable of challenging the "end of philosophy," or of saying that what goes as painting is worthless for the most part; not just mediocre or barely decent, but worthless. Anyone who does will be told he is a boor and a know-nothing where art is concerned, or an old man who refuses to admit that times have changed.

This overall picture, supposing one accepts it and even roughly agrees with my interpretation of it, expresses a crisis in the overall societal institution and in social imaginary significations. As I have already pointed out, this crisis isn't incompatible with continued "progress" in technology and production, scholarship, and even science. I for one, for reasons it would be too time-consuming to explain here, have doubts as to the possibility for even that sort of "progress" to continue for very long, once deprived of the roots that formerly nourished it.

I think we are at a crossroads in history, in History with a capital H. One path is now clearly marked, at least as for its general direction. That path leads to the loss of meaning, the repetition of empty forms, conformism, apathy, irresponsibility, and cynicism, along with the growing takeover of the capitalist imaginary of unlimited expansion of "rational mastery"—pseudo-rational pseudo-mastery—of the unlimited expansion of consumption for consumption's sake, which is to say for nothing, and of technoscience racing ahead on its own, and obviously a party to domination by that capitalist imaginary.

The other path would have to be opened up; it has not been marked out at all. Only a social and political awakening, a renaissance, a fresh upsurge of the project of individual and collective autonomy—that is, of the will to be free—can cut that path. This would require an awakening of imagination and of the creative imaginary. For the reasons I have tried to formulate here, any such arousal is impossible to predict, by definition. It is synonymous with social and political revival. The two necessarily go hand in hand. All we can do is prepare it in whatever way we can, from our own particular place.

Thank you.

Answers to Questions from the Audience

Mr. Heleno's question was: in the distinction between the poietic and the functional dimensions, couldn't we say the functional is "badly" poietic? No. It is important to discuss the criteria differentiating the poietic from the functional dimension, but the functional dimension per se cannot be "bad." No human society can exist without a functional component, which is the domain of ensemblistic-identitary (ensidic) logic, the *legein* and *teuchein*. No society can not have arithmetic; there can be none in which tools have no set effects on the materials people work, where institutions are not functional to some extent, and coherent from an ensemblistic-identitarian standpoint. What is "bad," and must be fought, is what is occurring in contemporary capitalist society: the autonomization of the functional dimension, the irrational attitude consisting of conceiving everything in terms of "rational mastery," which obviously has truly preposterous results. As for the distinction between the poietic and the functional dimensions, it isn't hard to see. The functional sphere includes everything that complies with the vital or physical necessities and with logical constraints. Production as such is usually functional. But the ultimate objectives of production are never "functional," since no human society produces exclusively for its own preservation. The Christians built churches. Primitive peoples often paint their bodies or faces. Those churches, paintings, or drawings are of no utility; they belong to the poietic realm. Of course they are of much greater "utility" than "being somewhat useful." The purpose they serve is much more important than all the rest; it is the possibility for human beings to give meaning to their world and to their lives. That, then, is the "role" of the poietic dimension.

"Descending" in logical order, I think it is time to address Mr. Cometti's query. He raised a serious question, to which our answers probably differ. I think you are quite right in saying, to be brief, that philosophy, especially when there began to be great thinkers who constructed systems, did as much to obstruct as to open up. I would not say it was mainly obstructive, however. Take Plato, for instance. He is unquestionably the philosopher who has most dominated Western thought (and not only thought) for the last twenty-five centuries, and in fact still does. We continue to think in more or less Platonic terms, and even when we rebel against Plato, he is the one we rebel against, which is another form of domination. At the same time, he is the philosopher who played that very "negative" role, first of all through his hatred of democracy, which led him to give an extremely inaccurate picture of ancient Greece. He successfully staged that fantastic strategic operation consisting of imposing on posterity a despicable image of Athenian democracy, describing participants in its political life as demagogues and its thinkers as "sophists" (in a completely fabricated acceptation of the term, and one that has prevailed ever since), claiming that its poets told ludicrous fables and were merely corrupting influences, etc. Simultaneously, he nourished a whole "idealistic" school, in the negative sense of the word, in Western philosophy—through misunderstandings, but still and all, it was his writings that were at the root of those misunderstandings. All this has to be smashed; it must be demolished. But was that Plato's only contribution? There have been tens of thousands of young people who became alive to philosophy by reading Plato, and many of them became great scientists (Heisenberg, for example).

But there is another aspect to this question. Thought in general, including great thought, tends to a degree of closure. It has a tendency to shut itself off. This is perhaps because of some internal quasi-necessities. The obsession with unity, which turns into obsession with system, is one manifestation of the ongoing hold of the ensemblistic-identitary dimension in philosophical thinking. The infinite goal of philosophy, according to which everything must be elucidated, turns into *everything must be structured*. The need to account for and give reasons for every statement one advances, becomes: everything must be "grounded" and based on a "single" foundation. Here we have some almost insurmountable tendencies in philosophy, but they must be fought inasmuch as possible through internal criticism. One may have an open philosophy without lapsing into eclecticism, not to speak of what is now called weak thought, that ecstatic way of thinking that turns left, or right, and is unable to explain why it went left rather than right, or vice versa. Philosophy can only be upheld by that effort at elucidation, which cannot be achieved without a degree of coherence, but must not sink into the illusion that it can operate a closure, and close itself up as a system. Under this proviso, philosophy—which, after all, is simply one of the main embodiments of our freedom—continues to have an essential role to play. And that is not the role taken by some contemporary trends, which indulge in an eclecticism that turns into a form of irresponsibility.

Someone asked me whether interdisciplinarity has its place in this sort of modern breakdown. It is a fact that the fragmenting of disciplines contributes to decadence and even to heteronomy, because it is tantamount to breaking down the world of research and thought into noninterrelating fields, each tending to develop its own dogmatism and to blind itself to the rest. This may be tied to Mr. Pereira's interrogation on psychoanalysis. If there is one striking fact in the social sciences today, it is what I have called the psychoanalytic deafness of sociologists and the sociological deafness of psychoanalysts. Each group goes on speaking, oblivious of the fact that human beings have two inseparable dimensions, the psychic and the social dimensions. Each takes one half and talks about it as if the other half were nonexistent. And since there are no separable "halves," the "half" about which each group believes it is speaking becomes a caricature. The effects of this attitude are particularly devastating in sociology. Political theory, economic theory, and sociology—all dominated, what is more, by an unspeakably naive methodological individualism—continue to hold forth as if Freud had never existed, as if the motivations of human beings were trivially simple and "rational." But if, to take one example, people's "rational" motivations determined all of economic life, that economic life should be foreseeable, which is obviously not the case. The same thing is true of "political theories." The contribution of psychoanalysis to the comprehension of the human world is absolutely fundamental and clearly shows that human motivations are not dominated by considerations of economic "interest" any more than by any "rational" factors that would enable us to understand human behavior. Conversely, psychoanalysis deliberately continues to ignore the crucial role of the social institution in the socialization of human beings, and to claim that all institutions and social significations are derived from the underlying tendencies of the psyche. This is nonsensical on many counts.

However, psychoanalysis can and must provide an essential contribution to the politics of autonomy. This is so because each person's self-understanding is a necessary requisite for autonomy. There can be no autonomous society that does not look inward, wondering about its motives, its reasons for acting, its profound inclinations. But taken concretely, society does not exist separately from those individuals of which it is composed. The self-reflexive activity of an autonomous society is essentially dependent on the self-reflexive activity of its members. The politics of autonomy, if it is not to be naive, cannot exist without taking the psychic dimension of human beings into account. It therefore presupposes a considerable degree of comprehension of those human beings, even if psychoanalysis has not yet sufficiently developed its contribution to that understanding. There can be no democratic individuals if they are not lucid, and first of all lucid about themselves, which does not mean that everyone will have to be psychoanalyzed. But education should most certainly be radically reformed, among other things so as to give much more consideration to the autonomy of pupils and students, including its psychoanalytic dimensions, than is the case nowadays.

As for the question of the relations between democracy and the State, I must point out, first of all, that it confuses the State and power, which confusion is deliberately fed by reactionary writers. There can be no society without power: it will always be necessary to settle conflicts, or to decide that a particular act has transgressed the law of society, just as there will always be a need to make decisions, affecting every member of society, as to what may or may not be done—in other words, to establish laws and to govern. The anarchist and Marxist utopia (Marx's conception of the "higher phase of communism") is an incoherent utopia. Given what we know about the human psyche and about the issues raised by the maturation process of that psyche, there will always be a need for laws, for collectively determined limitations on human action, which may no doubt be internalized by individuals during the socialization process but never to the point of becoming totally untransgressable, since we would no longer have a society of autonomous subjects then, but a society of automats. So there will always be a power. But power does not mean a State. The State is a power-wielding authority separate from society, composed of a hierarchical, bureaucratic apparatus that stands face to face with society and dominates it (even if it cannot remain impermeable to its influence). That State is incompatible with a democratic society. The few indispensable functions presently fulfilled by a state can and must be restituted to the political community.

Paris, November 1996–Tinos, August 1997

§ 5 Primal Institution of Society and Second-Order Institutions

The object of today's meeting is, "is there a theory of the institution?" I, for one, say: definitely not. There is not, and there cannot be, a theory of the institution, because the word *theory* comes from the Greek *theōria,* meaning the gaze that looks across from, faces, something and inspects it. We cannot set ourselves across from the institution and inspect it, since the means for doing so are part and parcel of that institution. How could I conceivably talk about the institution using a language claiming to be rigorous and formalized or indefinitely formalizable, etc., whereas that language itself is an institution, perhaps the first and most important of institutions?

We are speaking French here, and I am speaking to you in French because I learned French. The fact is that my mother tongue is Greek, but there is nothing natural about either my French or my Greek. Since this gathering seems to appreciate joking, let's say that had I been born in China—I am not even saying had I been Chinese, but simply had I been born in China—I would be doomed, for my whole lifetime, not to know the difference between an "election" and an "erection," because "l" and "r" are not distinct phonemes in Chinese phonology.

But it is not simply a matter of phonetics. All of Greco-Western philosophy and thought, and the theory or theories we construct, are largely beholden to some features of the grammar of Indo-European languages, and particularly to that famous verb *einai,* "to be." Many very beautiful languages, totally appropriate to their society, do not possess the verb "to be." And if the people who speak those languages were to undertake the elaboration of a fundamental philosophy, they would not call it "ontology." I can elucidate my own relationship to language, but I cannot remove myself from it and "look at it," or "construct" it from outside.

I cannot construe a "theory" of the institution because I am inside it. In fact, I would go a great deal further. Except at an ultimate point—a point I try to approach with patients on the couch, or with myself, taking advantage of a dream, perhaps—with the exception of that ultimate point which is at an almost infinite distance, I am, as we all are, a walking fragment of the institution of society. We are mutually complementary walking fragments. We are two-legged speakers: two-legged, which reminds us of our biological nature, or rather our biological underpinning (*étayage*); and speaking, which is definitely also a reminder of that biological bedrock, for in order to speak we need our vocal cords and so on, as well as a central nervous system organized in a particular way, but we also need language as a social institution. This is neither the time nor the place to go into the endless discussion that began in fifth century BCE Greece on the "natural" (*phusei*) or conventional/instituted (*nomōi*) character of language, and has resumed a few decades ago, first with structural linguistics and then with Chomsky's conceptions and the search for universals and invariants cutting across the different languages. One thing is clear: in *Homo sapiens,* an enormous portion of language—the most important part, having to do with the significations it carries, its semantics—does not correspond univocally with the central nervous system, for if it did, languages would all be strictly isomorphic and we would be able to shift from one to another without losing or gaining anything, thanks to a series of well-adjusted transformations. Now we know that there is no such thing, strictly speaking, as an accurate or "perfect" translation of a text into a language other than the one in which it was formulated (aside from the trivial case in which that text is a concatenation of mathematical symbols). As Jakobson said, "true" translation is always poetic re-creation.

What I think and say, then, is profoundly dependent on language, and this is only one example of the prevalence of—actually, much more than that, of the thoroughness with which we are all penetrated by—the instituted elements of our native society.

Can we say, then, as someone did earlier today, that theory is the calling into question of the institution? First of all, I repeat, we have to eliminate the usual acceptation of the term "theory" in this discussion. Next, we have to note that such "calling into question" by thinking about the institution or by an attempt to elucidate the institution is an exceptional occurrence in the history of humanity, and is only encountered in one single social tradition, the European or Greco-Western tradition. I am not expressing any ethnocentric bias here, and still less the idea that this gives us some privilege, political or other. I simply take note of the fact that calling the institution into question implies a tremendous historical break, and that as far as we know no such break has taken place in the Nambikwara or Bamileke culture. A rupture of this sort is only encountered twice in the history of mankind: the first time in ancient Greece, and later in Western Europe starting at the end of the High Middle Ages. What this break means is that those same individuals who were fashioned by their society, who are walking fragments of that society, were able to operate essential changes in themselves. They were able to create for themselves the means by which to challenge and call into question their inherited institutions, the institutions of the very society that had formed them themselves, and this was obviously accompanied by a fundamental change in the entire instituted social sphere. This took the form of both the birth of a public political space and the creation of free investigation, of unlimited interrogation. The possibility of thinking about and elucidating the instituting process and institutions[1] only began to exist when the institution was called into question, in words and in deeds. Here we have the birth of democracy and of philosophy, which go hand in hand.

People stand up and say, "The tribe's representations are wrong," and they try to think about the world and about humankind in the world differently. And some people stand up and say, "The powers that be are unjust, the instituted laws are unfair, we must set up new ones." The two positions are bound together, profoundly so. What does that mean, that the powers that be are unjust? What gives you the right to say that? Do you merely want to replace them by some other, equally unjust power, or do you claim to found a power that is just? But what is a just power—what is justice? On the other hand, you are destroying the tribe's representations; you want to replace them by something else. You therefore contend that this other thing is true. You know what is true, then; but what is truth?

It is already evident here that although the institution is a basic fact of human history, and actually is one of the two factors in the hominization of man—the other being the radical imagination—one cannot discuss all institutions throughout history in one and the same way. Because in a predemocratic, prephilosophical society, there simply is no possibility of challenging the institution and calling it into question: its members do not know that the gods of the tribe are institutions. They do not and cannot know that. To be brief, I will take one of the most clear-cut and best known cases: the Law, for the Hebrews, is not a tribal law, it was formulated and handed down by the Lord in person. How could you question that Law? How could you claim that God's Law is unjust, when Justice is defined as the will of God? How can you conceivably claim that God does not exist when God defines himself as *egō eimi ho ōn,* I am (he who) is, I am being (I won't go into the quarrel over the interpretation of the original text in Hebrew). How can you possibly say "God is not," when that would mean, translated into the language of the tribe, "being is not"?

In the overwhelming majority of societies, the ones I call heteronomous societies, first of all, the institution claims itself not to be a human creation; second, its individual members are raised, trained, fashioned in such a manner as to be completely absorbed by the social institution. No one can assert ideas, a will, a desire that goes against the instituted order, and the reason is not that this would be sanctioned, but because the person has been anthropologically fashioned in that way; he has assimilated the institution of his society to the point that he does not dispose of the psychic and mental means of contesting that institution. What changes, with ancient Greece first, and then with postmedieval Europe, is that the institution of society makes it possible for there to be individuals who no longer view it as something untouchable, who succeed in calling it into question, either in words or in deeds, or both at once. Here we encounter the first historical attempt at what I call the project of social and individual autonomy.

But what does autonomy mean? *Autos,* "oneself"; *nomos,* "the law." An autonomous person is someone who gives herself her own laws (not someone who does whatever she feels like, but who gives herself laws). Now this is immensely difficult. For an individual, to give oneself one's own law (in those areas where this is feasible) demands the ability to dare stand up to the entire range of conventions, beliefs, and fashions, as well as to scholars who continue to support absurd conceptions, the mass media, a public that keeps silent, and so forth. For a society, to give itself its own law implies total acceptance of the idea that it creates its own institution, and that it does so without the possibility of alluding to any nonsocial basis, to any norm for its norm, to any measure of its measure. In other words, it must decide for itself what is just and unjust, and this is the issue with which true politics must contend (not, of course, the kind of politics we see in today's politicians).

Society cannot exist without institution, without law—and it must set down that law for itself without the possibility of resorting (except by deluding itself) to some nonsocial source or foundation. Both of these two aspects are present in the ancient Greek term *nomos*. *Nomos* is what is peculiar to each society or to each ethnic group, its institution/convention, the opposite of *phusis*, a "natural" (and unalterable) order of things. At the same time, *nomos* is the law; it is that without which human beings cannot exist as such, since there is no city, no *polis*, without laws, and there are no human beings outside of the *polis*, the city, or political collectivity/community. When Aristotle says that outside of the *polis* man can only be a wild beast or a god, he knows, and states, that human beings are only humanized in and by the *polis*, and this idea is in fact constantly expressed by the ancient Greek poets, historians, and philosophers.

So there are those two sides to *nomos*, to the law. It is, in each instance, the institution/convention of a particular society, and at the same time it is the transhistorical requisite for the existence of society. In other words, independently of the content of its particular *nomos*, no society can exist without a *nomos*. Without this dual comprehension—that we cannot exist without *nomos*, but also that this *nomos* is our institution, our doing—there can be no democracy. For democracy does not mean only human rights or the habeas corpus, of course; that is only a *derivative* aspect of democracy, which is not to say a minor or secondary one. Democracy means the power of the people; in other words, it means that the people makes its laws—and to make them it must indeed be convinced that laws are the work of men. But at the same time, this implies that there is no extrasocial benchmark for laws. Here we have the tragic dimension of democracy, for it is also the dimension of radical freedom: democracy is the regime of *self-limitation*.

Let us return to the very idea of institution. The term is indeed polysemous, and this polysemy causes a malaise, because as I have said, "everything is institution." We definitely should define the levels to which we refer when talking about institution. To begin with, we are obviously not talking about social security or a mental health clinic. We are speaking, first and foremost, about language, religion, and power, and about what the individual is in a given society. We are even talking about man and woman, who are visibly institutions. The noninstituted part of man and woman is their biological underpinnings, the fact of their leaning on a sexed anatomical and physiological constitution (their *Anlehnung,* to use Freud's term). But the definition of being-a-man and being-a-woman is different in our society from what it was in ancient Greece, and also from what it is in some African or American Indian tribe. The same is true for being-a-child. The state of childhood obviously has a biological dimension, and being-a-child is an institution of a transhistorical type in that every society must assign an instituted status of some sort to children. But at the same time, that institution is profoundly *historical,* for what being-a-child means concretely in each particular society changes with the totality of the institution of that society. The child under the ancien régime is one thing, and another thing is the child of today, with her electronic games, her television, and everything these facts assume and entail. Let me say in passing that this signification now seems to be on its way to dissolving; no one seems to know what a child is supposed to do or not do. Likewise, it seems increasingly unclear in what sense and in what form men are men and women are women. The radical and totally warranted challenging of women's traditional status has left the social (and psychical) signification of being-a-woman completely up in the air, and by the same token and ipso facto, has called into question the social and psychical status of being-a-man, since these are simply two inseparable poles of significations. What, today, is the behavior, what are the signs, the emblems denoting manliness and womanliness? Is to be a woman to have had fourteen fruitful pregnancies, as in my grandmother's time, or is it to measure twenty-four inches around the hips?

A parenthesis must be opened here, about a question raised earlier today: how do institutions die? Someone said, the birth of institutions is an easy question, what is hard to understand is why they disappear. Hearing that, I smiled to myself, for really, it is rather surprising to hear that the question of the birth of language, or of philosophy and so on, is an easy one. What is interesting, however, is that the speaker was at odds with the traditional philosophical position. In that stance, just as in popular beliefs, what goes without saying and hardly needs any explanation, is that things come to an end, they decay, die, pass on. What is scandalous is creation; therefore, creation doesn't exist, except as a divine act once and for all, at the beginning of time. The idea that the history of humankind is one of ongoing creation—as is obviously the case—is strictly inconceivable to the traditional way of thinking. Conversely, people apparently believe that only easily solved questions are raised by the fact that institutions and regimes may disappear. The truth is, however, that these two questions, these two enigmas, are perfectly symmetrical. The death of forms raises just as formidable a problem as their coming into being. How is it that "at a certain point," as we say, the idea of the *polis,* what I call the *social imaginary signification polis,* the city as community/collectivity of citizens taking responsibility for their laws, their acts, and their fate, and everything that goes along with that signification, emerged in ancient Greece? "Explanations," be they functionalist, economic, "historical materialist," and even psychoanalytic, are all powerless (and in fact absurd) in the face of this emergence. But they are equally powerless when faced with the fact that "at another point" the stuff that holds that *polis* together begins to crumble and decay, and disappears. Why is it that at the end of the High Middle Ages, in the interstices of the feudal universe, communities that aspired to be self-governed collectivities began to be constituted once again? These are the new towns or free boroughs, in which the protobourgeoisie (long before capitalism was even an idea, not to speak of a reality!) created the first seeds of modern movements for emancipation and democracy. And why is it that nowadays most of the imaginary significations that held that society together seem to be vanishing, without being replaced by anything else? Both questions are unavoidable, and no "theory" provides an "answer" to them.

The institution of the overwhelming majority of known societies has been heteronomous in the sense specified above. In two historical societies, including ours, the *seeds* of autonomy have been created and are still alive, represented by some aspects of formal institutions, but above all embodied in the individuals fashioned by these societies—you, me, the others—inasmuch as these individuals continue to be capable (at least we hope they are) of rising up to proclaim, "That law is unjust," or "The institution of society must be changed." If any politics, in the true sense, exists today, it resides in efforts to preserve and develop those seeds of autonomy. And if psychoanalytic practice is politically relevant, it is only inasmuch as it attempts to make individuals autonomous to whatever extent is possible; that means lucid as to their desire and as to reality, and responsible for their acts, meaning that they hold themselves accountable for their acts.

As I said earlier, it is the institution, for one thing, that marks the hominization of man. Why is there institution? The question is enormous,

but at the same time absurd: why is there something rather than nothing? But it must be asked, to show the absurdity of some stupid, obsolete
discourse now being heard again. The reasoning is stupid even if it is
professed by Nobel prizewinners in economics: it posits society as formed
by a collection or combination of "individuals." But where on earth are
those "individuals" to be found? Do they grow wild? The individual is a
social fabrication; and what I know, as a psychoanalyst, is that not only
would the nonsocial part of the "individual" be incapable of forming a
society, but it is radically, violently asocial. That nonsocial part of the "individual," down in the ultimate depths of the human psyche, is definitely
not what has been called "desire" for many years now. When speaking of
"desire," one always refers to something that may at least be articulated in
one way or another, if not expressed in words, and this therefore presupposes that a series of *separations* are already effective. But the core of the
psyche is a *monad,* it is a monadic psyche characterized by pure or radical imagination, initially in a state of complete nondifferentiation. The
emergence of humankind as a living species was marked by the coming
into being of that congenital tumor—that cancer of the psyche, if you
like—which takes the form of an immeasurably developed imagination,
an imagination gone mad, having broken with any subservience to the
"functional." This leads to that unique human feature, unknown to any
other living species: the replacement of organ pleasure by representational
pleasure. (Even for socialized, developed human beings, the prevalence of
representational pleasure over organ pleasure is obvious and tremendous;
otherwise, no one would get killed in war, phantasizing would not be an
essential prerequisite for sexual pleasure, and so on.)

So there is defunctionalization of representation and defunctionalization of pleasure. For human beings, pleasure is not simply a sign indicating what should be sought and what should be avoided, as it is for
animals. It has become an end unto itself, even when it goes against the
preservation of the individual and/or the species. Man is therefore not
just a sick animal, as Hegel had it; man is a mad animal, an animal radically unfit for living. Man only survives by creating society, social imaginary significations, and the institutions that convey and embody them.
Society—the institution—is not there merely to "contain the violence"
of individual human beings, as Hobbes thought, or the Sophists before
him, five centuries before the Christian era, nor is it even there to "repress
drives," as Freud thought. Society is there to hominize that wailing little

newborn monster and to make it fit for life. To do so it must inflict a rupture on that monadic psyche, force on it what the psyche refuses, deep down, from the beginning to the very end, which is: the acknowledgment that the "omnipotence of thought" only exists in one's phantasms, and that outside of oneself there are other human beings, there is a particular organization of the world (the works, in each instance, of the institution of society), that "real" pleasure can only be obtained through a series of mediations which, in turn, are both "real" and generally rather unpleasant, and so forth. So the societal institution has to integrate each monadic psyche in collective, "real" life by means of a radical violence inflicted on that egocentric, self-centered being, capable of living almost indefinitely in the pure pleasure of representation. In doing so, the institution destroys what was meaningful for the psyche, what gave meaning originally (closure within the self, the pure pleasure of "solipsistic" representation), and by way of compensation, so to speak, it provides the psyche with another source of meaning: social imaginary signification. As the psyche is socialized—as it becomes a social individual—it internalizes these significations and "learns" that the true "meaning of life" is elsewhere: in gaining the esteem of the clan, or in the hopes of being able to rest with Abraham, one day, in the bosom of God; or in being *kalos kagathos* and caring for one's *kleos* and *kudos,* or being a saint, or accumulating wealth, or developing productive forces, or "building socialism," and so forth. Here again we see how the human race is capable of substituting representational pleasure for organ pleasure. Representation here is the subjective side of the social imaginary significations conveyed by the institution.

Henceforth, then, the institution provides "meaning" for socialized individuals, but it also supplies them with the resources for bringing this meaning into existence for themselves. It does so by restoring, at the social level, an instrumental or functional logic that most probably existed, differently, in animals but was shattered in man by the unbridled development of the imagination. Through its implementation within and by means of that logic, the radical imagination of a singular human being can now become a source of creation at the collective, "real" level. A phantasm remains a phantasm for a singular psyche, but artists, poets, musicians, and painters don't produce phantasms; they create works, *oeuvres.* What their imagination sires acquires a "real"—that is, social-historical—existence, and it does so by using an infinitude of means and elements—language, to begin with—that the artist could never have created "all by herself."[2]

These are the elements that define what I call the primal institution of society: the *primal institution* of society is the fact that society creates itself as society and creates itself afresh in each instance, by giving itself institutions quickened and sustained by social imaginary significations specific to that particular society: specific to the Egyptian society of pharaonic times, to Hebrew society, to Greek society, to contemporary French or American society, and so on. And this primal institution articulates and implements itself through *second-order institutions* (which by no means makes them secondary) that we may divide into two categories. Some are *transhistorical* in their form, abstractly speaking. Language, for example, is in that category: each language is different, but there is no society without language, and so is the individual: the type of individual is different, concretely, in each society, but there is no society that does not institute some *type* of individual. The same is true of the family: the organization and specific "content" of the family change, but no society can forego the reproduction and socialization of the next generation, and the institution in charge of that is the family, irrespective of the form it takes (the baby factories in Huxley's *Brave New World* are families in this sense). Then there are second-order institutions, *specific* to particular societies and playing an absolutely central role in them, in that these specific institutions are the essential embodiments of what is of vital importance to that societal institution, its social imaginary significations.

Let us take two clear examples: the Greek *polis* is a specific second-order institution, without which the ancient Greek world is impossible and inconceivable. The capitalist *business enterprise* is also that sort of specific second-order institution. There can be no capitalism without that enterprise—and what goes under that name for us does not really exist in precapitalist societies. That institution conveys a signification, that set of arrangements and rules brings together large numbers of people, forces them to use specific tools and machines, controls their work and organizes it hierarchically, and its goal is its own unlimited self-aggrandizement. That institution and that signification are created by capitalism, and capitalism can only exist within and through this creation. In each instance these second-order institutions, the transhistorical and the specific ones, woven together, produce the concrete texture of a particular society.

I will make two closing remarks on practice since you all work on social reality, as I do, with some definite goals, and I suppose that you, like me, feel that things are not all what they should be or what we would like them to be, even if the opinion polls maintain that 80 percent of French people are "happy," or think they are. The first has to do with the fundamental solidarity, the tremendous interdependence of the various institutions of all orders in a given society. There has been a tendency to forget this in recent years, or to avoid mentioning it, under the pretext that we should not consider society as a whole, or look at the totality of society, because otherwise there is a risk of sliding toward totalitarianism. That is obviously absurd. Society *is* an extremely complex whole, and its different "parts" cohere in countless ways. For instance, there is no saying whether, with the dislocation of the traditional significations and roles of man and woman in contemporary Western society, the rest of the system will be able to simply go on functioning as if nothing had happened. This in itself shows that any politics with serious and simply "reformist" intentions is incoherent, for that sort of politics amounts to wanting to change a few pieces of a system without caring about, or even being aware of, the effects of those modifications on the rest.

The second remark has to do with an opposite, symmetrical pitfall, which would be to say that precisely, given the previous remark, nothing can be done—or else that we can only work with the immediate goal of a radical transformation of society. But precisely, a radical transformation of society, if it is possible—and I am profoundly convinced that it is—can only be the work of individuals who want their autonomy, on the scale of society as a whole as well as on the individual level. Consequently, working at preserving and extending the possibilities of autonomy and of autonomous action, and likewise, working both to help shape individuals so that they aspire to autonomy and to increase the number of such individuals, is in itself a creative political work, one whose effects are more important and more lasting than some kinds of superficial, sterile agitation.

Polis

§ 6   Heritage and Revolution

I

My title for this essay may sound bizarre. The term *heritage* connotes something conservative, if not something downright reactionary—perhaps some organization in the United States.[1] Or else it brings to mind legal papers, deeds, and notaries. *Revolution,* on the other hand, is a term that has been prostituted by the contemporary publicity industry: every now and then, there is a revolution in vacuum cleaners or toilet paper. But in common parlance, between 1789, when La Rochefoucauld-Liancourt used it for the first time in its modern sense, and somewhere around 1950, it meant a radical change, a subversion of the existing, instituted order of things (not to be confused with gun firing and bloodletting). So my title needs some explanation.

I do not think the game is over. And I do not want the game to be over. I mean the political game, in the grand sense of the term *political;* I am not talking about Mr. Reagan or Mr. Mitterrand. Nor do I have in mind the management of the current affairs of government. By *politics* I mean a collective activity endowed with self-reflection and lucidity, aiming at the global institution of society.

The historical singularity of Western Europe, and before it eighth- to fifth-century Greece, is that they are the only societies to have *created politics* in the sense of an activity explicitly attempting to change society and succeeding to a substantial extent. In all other societies we have court intrigues, group rivalries, machinations, open competitions, complicated games to obtain power—but these are always within the existing instituted framework. In ancient Greece and Western Europe (including, of course, the United States), we have *politics.*

Considered this way, politics is a moment and an expression of the project of autonomy; it does not passively and blindly accept what is already there, what has been instituted, but calls it into question. Now, what is called into question may be the constitution or a body of law. It can also be the prevailing collective representations about world, society, truth, or values. In the latter case, the calling into question is, of course, philosophy in the pristine sense. The creation of politics and the creation of philosophy, as expressions of the project of autonomy, go together, and together indeed they have gone in actual history.

These expressions of the project of autonomy also take on, almost immediately, the content of autonomy. The Greek *politai,* or the European bourgeois, did not set out to change institutions simply to manifest their capacity to do so. Rather, they tried to bring about the realization of social and individual autonomy. This is the *democratic* component of their political activity and of the resulting institutions. (The same can be said, mutatis mutandis, about philosophy as realization of intellectual and psychical freedom, but this is not our present object.)

What this means is that *our* heritage, *our* tradition, is the democratic heritage and the revolutionary tradition in their strictest senses. So much for the coexistence of these two words in my title.

Such things can of course be seen differently, even from an opposing view. It could be argued that our heritage is just what is there—that there is nothing more to be done except to manage its legacy, to take care of this fortune, large or small. We should be clear about the consequences of this position. The central part of our heritage lies in making our institutions; we can change them, and we ought to change them if we think fit. Now the assertion that we have nothing to change, at least nothing important, that there is nothing to do beyond the day-to-day legislation and management of the congress or parliament, is tantamount to the statement that things are perfectly satisfactory as they are, that we have reached the highest state of society—or at any rate, the least imperfect one. It is saying, in other words, that our society is such that any attempt to change its institutions will inevitably bring about something worse. As is well known, this position has been argued explicitly for more than a decade now.

One has only to open one's eyes to dismiss this view. Regardless of whether one is "satisfied" or "dissatisfied," the existing state of affairs is untenable in the long run because it is self-destructive, and by this I mean self-destructive politically. It produces a glacier of privatization and apathy; it dislocates the social imaginary significations that hold institutions together. An apathetic and cynical society cannot maintain for long even the few liberal institutions existing today. And a society of liberal institutions based on the relentless pursuit of individual self-interest is sheer nonsense.

Another suggestion has surfaced in the last few years: that we come to live under a new form of "democratic politics" made up of the juxtaposition of various "social movements"—or rather, nonmovements—none of which would be concerned with envisaging society as a whole, but whose additive synergy would work to produce a "democratic" state of affairs. It is not difficult to see that these "movements," stripped of general concerns, inevitably take the form of lobbies, the mutually opposed pressures of which currently contribute to stalemates of society on substantive issues. Recent developments have amply illustrated this point.

A final preliminary remark. Formulations that suggest, for example, that the ideas of the Enlightenment have not yet been fully implemented are defective in more ways than one. Our heritage goes far beyond the *Aufklärung* and has not been, to say the least, exhaustively "recapitulated" by it. The Enlightenment itself, important as it is, forms only one phrase in the symphonic creation of the project of autonomy. Many important things have happened since the *Aufklärung* that are not limited to the implementation of its ideas. Above all, if and when a new period of political activity oriented toward autonomy begins, it will carry us not only far beyond the *Aufklärung* but also beyond anything else we are now able to imagine.

II

To minimize misunderstandings, I should now make clear some of my further presuppositions. Human history is creation. It is, first and foremost, wholesale self-creation, the separation of humanity from sheer animality, which is at once never complete but abysmal. This self-creation manifests itself as unprecedented new forms of being, "models" or "causes" in the presocial world. Some such forms of being are language, tools, instituted rules, meanings, and anthropological types. Others are the particular global forms society takes on in different times and places:

Tupi-Guarani or Hebrew, Greek or medieval European, Assyrian or capitalistic bureaucratic.

These elemental facts—the self-creation of humanity, the self-institution of societies—are, almost always, almost everywhere, veiled; they are concealed from society by its very institution. And almost always, almost everywhere, this institution contains the instituted representation of its own extrasocial origin. The heteronomous character of the institution of society consists in the fact that its social law is not posited as created by society but is seen rather as having a source beyond the reach of living human beings. This is the root of the religious character of the institution of almost all known societies—and likewise of the unbreakable link between religion and heteronomy. The institution of society has found both the guarantee of its validity and its protection against internal contestation and external relativization through the instituted representation of an extrasocial origin for itself.[2] "God has given us our laws. How could you dare change them?"

Every institution of society aims at its perpetuation. And it generally succeeds in creating appropriate means for this, since human beings can exist only insofar as they are socialized, i.e., humanized, by such an institution, and insofar, too, as the modes posited by that institution conform to it and tend to reproduce it indefinitely. To put it in another way, newborn bipeds become social individuals only through internalizing the existing social institutions.

This should have entailed that a social order, once created and barring external factors, would last forever. We know that this is not so. More precisely, we know that although this was almost the case for a very long time, it then ceased to be so. We know that there have been many extraordinarily different societies, and that they are all to some degree historical in the proper sense, that is, self-altering. I shall now briefly describe two important types of this self-alteration or historicity.

As far as we know, some degree of self-alteration, however small or slow, seeps through in all societies. Language offers perhaps the most striking example of this. Every day, several anonymous and untraceable changes are introduced into the English language as it is spoken, say, in the United States, in the guise of new slang words, semantic shifts, etc. A similar process has been going on with a slower tempo for thousands of years in "primitive" or "savage" societies as well as in "traditional" peasant societies such as those under "Asiatic despotism" or those in Eastern Europe.

This minute but continual self-alteration will persist as long as there are human beings and societies, for it has to do with the nature of human beings as well as that of social institutions. If institutions were made of iron, they would still be subject to alteration, but not self-alteration; rather, like iron, they would rust. If they were made of rational ideas, they would last forever. But institutions are actually made of sanctioned social meanings and the corollary procedures for giving meaning. These meanings are at heart imaginary—not "rational," not "functional," not "reflections of reality." They are *social imaginary significations.* They can be effective, and effectively alive, only as long as they are invested ("cathected") and lived by human beings. The same is true of the procedures for the sanction of these meanings.

Human beings are essentially defined not by being "reasonable" but by being possessed with a radical imagination. It is this imagination that has to be tamed and brought under control through social fabrication, but such taming never fully succeeds, as witnessed by the existence of transgression in all known societies. Thus the activities of innumerable human beings always introduce infinitesimal alterations in the ways of doing things, as well as in the manner of effectively living, or "interpreting," the instituted social imaginary significations. As a result, a slow—and, of course, unconscious—self-alteration is always in process in actual social life. This self-alteration is usually the object of an occultation on the part of the existing institutions of society in the same way and for the same "reasons" that the creative dimension of self-institution is such an object. The occultations of self-institution (of the self-creation of society) and of self-alteration (of the historicity of society) are two faces of society's heteronomy.

The second type of self-alteration, leaving aside the extremely important class of "intermediate" cases consisting in relatively swift but fully blind social change, concerns the periods of rapid and important societal self-alteration in which an intense collective activity, endowed with a minimal degree of lucidity, is successfully aimed at changing institutions. Such periods manifest another mode of being of the social-historical, the explicit calling into question of its laws of existence and the corresponding work toward their lucid transformation. These periods I would call revolutionary. In this sense I speak of a revolutionary period in the Greek world from the eighth to the fifth centuries BCE, and in Western Europe from, say, the thirteenth century onward. During these two periods, the project of social and individual autonomy was created, thanks to which creation we today think and speak as we do.

III

I come now to the idea of revolution as an explicit political project—or, rather, as a dense period of time within which a radical political project takes hold on social reality.

What does *radical* mean in this context? Of course, the idea of a total revolution, of the creation of a social tabula rasa, is absurd. In the most radical revolution imaginable, the elements of social life that would remain unaltered—language, building, tools, ways of behaving—are immensely more numerous than are those that might be changed; they are also the most important, heaviest parts of the sociopsychical structure of human beings. This can be seen as a great fact that, made explicit, sounds like a truism. But it can and must also be seen as a crucial problem for political action.

This problem, as far as we know, was raised explicitly for the first time by Plato. Given what humans are—which means, for Plato, given that human beings are utterly and hopelessly corrupt—how is it possible to make changes, and who is going to bring them about? Plato's answer in the *Republic* is well known: philosophers ought to become kings, or kings philosophers. Plato himself considers both eventualities unlikely.

Plato's position is unacceptable to us, or at least to me. Certainly, to call Plato a totalitarian is to misuse and abuse terms; it is even silly. It is also wrong to call him a conservative: what he intended was not at all the conservation of an existing state of affairs or the return to some previous one. Any decent Athenian conservative would recoil with horror at Plato's proposals regarding property and women and children. Rather, Plato aimed to arrest the movement of history (this can be more clearly seen in the *Laws*), and the hidden, certainly not fully conscious, presupposition behind his political attitude and his bitter hatred of democracy was the understanding that history is the work of the human collectivity. Once you give free rein to the will of the many and to its expression, then *genesis*—change and becoming, the negation of true Being—and the concomitant decay, set in.

Nevertheless, the diagnosis of the problem was correct, and its formulation remained, by and large, the same during the subsequent millennia.

How can you change society if both the actors and the instruments of change are living individuals, that is, the embodiment of that which is to be changed? Accordingly, Rousseau could write in the second half of the eighteenth century, "Celui qui ose entreprendre d'instituer un peuple doit se sentir en état de changer, pour ainsi dire, la nature humaine" (The one who dares to endeavor to institute a people must feel himself capable of changing, so to speak, human nature).[3] It is true that in this passage Rousseau deals explicitly with the question of "first" institution; but the whole of his political writing shows that he is in the grip of Plato's problem. To give institutions to a people, one has to change, first of all, the mores, the *Sitten,* the ways of being of the people. Without such a change, the new institutions are useless and cannot even function. But it is precisely in order to bring about change in these ways of being that new institutions are required.[4] Rousseau, like Plato, like Machiavelli, like Montesquieu, like all great political thinkers (and in contradistinction to recent political theorists), was lucid on this point. There cannot be a "political" institution that is not, from top to bottom, from its most superficial to its deepest level, linked to the mores, the *Sitten,* the whole anthropological, sociopsychical structure of the people living in that society.

Let us dwell a bit longer on Rousseau's formulation. "The one who dares to endeavor to institute a people, to give institutions to a people." Behind this statement one sees the image, the figure, and the story of *the* legislator, the canonical list of whom includes Machiavelli, Moses, Theseus, Lycurgus, Numa. . . . Now Rousseau is a deep thinker, and, in a sense, a democrat. Why, then, does he think only of *celui qui . . . ,* "*the one who . . . ,*" as a subject of action and of the people, *le peuple,* as a *passive object* of this action, an object that has to be *formed* (*formed* is the precise term in the first version of the *Contrat:* "celui qui se croit capable de former un peuple"), formed by the active legislator not only in terms of a narrowly conceived political constitution but also in respect of its mores, its ways of feeling, thinking, doing, and being? That Plato could speak in these terms is understandable. Regardless of any contradiction that this view might have with his ideas about the human being or the soul, he firmly believes that the people are rabble, and he says so repeatedly. But Rousseau?

One could argue that Rousseau is pessimistic, indeed gloomy, about the people of his time and about human nature in general. Contrary to widespread, popular misunderstanding, this was indeed the truth of the matter—and, as we know, events rapidly proved him wrong (the *Contrat Social* was published in 1762; Rousseau died in 1778). What is more important and deeper is the fact that the common ground on which Plato and Rousseau stand is the philosophical equivalent of the imaginary of heteronomy. Both Plato and Rousseau would recognize that people have been active in bringing about the given state of political affairs. But they would also be quick to point out that it is a bad, corrupted state of affairs—and necessarily so. Framed in these terms, the aporia has no solution. Indeed, that is what Rousseau says in the first paragraph of book 2, chapter 7 of the *Contrat:* "il faudroit des Dieux pour donner des loix aux hommes" (Gods would be required to give laws to humans), an echo of Plato's "God is the measure of all things."

People, and history, can bring forward something "new"—but only in the sense of *destruction,* of *decay,* of a *less good* state of affairs. By virtue of the Platonic conflation of Being and Good, *less good* means also *less being, hitton on.* Such a "new" thus is new by virtue of a deficit or negation and therefore not truly new.

In the view of the heteronomously instituted society, laws are not created by men. According to Plato and most other philosophers, the laws are humanly made, and that is precisely why they are so bad. They ought to be the reflection (or translation, or whatever) of a superhuman order, mediated by an "exceptional" being (for Rousseau, see the whole of book 2, chapter 7 of the *Contrat*), and protected against human attempts at their alteration by a "noble lie," the fable of their divine origin (*Republic,* 414b–c).

But the trails of Rousseau and Plato, because they are radical thinkers, lead to the heart of the matter. Let us reformulate the idea in question: "one who wants to institute a people has to change the mores of the people." Who in actuality changes the mores of people? The answer is obvious: the people themselves. Thus we have at least a formal answer to our question. If there is to be a true change in institutions, it must be accompanied by a deeply consonant change in mores. Changes in mores are brought about by the people. So the only assurance for this consonance is that the people be as active in bringing about the political (formal institutional) change as they are in changing their mores (though, of course, in a different way).

We may recall that Marx confronts this same question in the third of his *Theses on Feuerbach:* "The materialist theory of the change in circumstances and of education forgets that circumstances are changed by man and that the educator must be himself educated. . . . The coincidence of the change in circumstances and of human activity can be rationally considered and understood only as revolutionary praxis." The problem as posed by Marx is that human beings are conditioned by their own times and that such times cannot be changed except by their actions. But why should human beings want to change their times, if they are conditioned by them to function in conformity with them? Marx's apparently facile answer, "revolutionary praxis," means that people change by changing the circumstances in which they find themselves.

Things will become clearer, I hope, if we use the ideas I introduced before. It is through the same historical process that people change "anthropologically," that is, change their mores and sociopsychical organization, and also change the (formal) institution of society. It appears that all of the elements required for the solution of our problem presuppose each other, and that we find ourselves caught in a vicious circle. It is a circle, but it is not "vicious," for it is the circle of historical creation. Did the Greek *politai* create the *polis* or the *polis* the *politai?* This is a meaningless question precisely because the *polis* could only have been created by the action of human beings who were simultaneously transforming themselves into *politai.*

Why and how, one may ask, do people start changing themselves and their institutions? And why is it that they do not do so all the time?

We have, in a sense, already answered this question. Human history is creation. We can elucidate this creation in its general character, or in its concrete contents, after it has happened. But we can neither "explain" nor "predict" it, because it is not determined; it, rather, is determinant. Likewise, its tempo and its rhythm are themselves part of the creation. It is only in an external, descriptive sense that historical processes take place in measurable, homogeneous calendar time. Intrinsically, in its concrete content and texture, the time of a historical epoch is an integral part of it and congruent with its deepest imaginary significations. That Greek time, or Western European time, differs deeply from Trobriand or Pharaonic Egyptian time hardly needs stressing, but it does require thinking.

It is useful to revert for a moment to Marx, for he has been until now the most explicit thinker of revolution. I cannot enter here into the ambiguities and antinomies of Marx's thought, which I have discussed elsewhere.[5] Despite the third *Thesis on Feuerbach,* quoted above, and similar formulations, when it comes to the socialist revolution, Marx is unable to maintain the irreducibility of praxis. To put it more sharply, he proves unable to see its creative character, looking instead for solid causes—that is, guarantees—of and for the revolution. The direct result is that he pays scant attention to the problems of political action and organization proper. Instead he looks for economic "laws" that would somehow engineer the collapse of capitalism. Such laws, even if true, would of course be irrelevant and useless. There is nothing to ensure that a collapse of capitalism would be followed by socialism rather than fascism, the *Iron Heel, 1984,* or even cannibalism.

More to the point are Marx's attempts to find in capitalist circumstances the conditions for the creation of a "revolutionary class," not just a class striving to overthrow the system but a class capable, after this overthrow, of establishing a new society with a fully "positive" character, capable, in Marx's terminology, of the "inferior," then the "superior," phases of communism. This class is the proletariat, or the working class. But why should this be so?

There are three kinds of answer to this question in Marx:

1. The proletariat is subject, under capitalism, to total alienation or absolute deprivation; it is a pure negation, which therefore can only produce the absolutely positive. This Hegelio-Christian position has to be immediately dismissed as factually erroneous, logically nonsensical, politically inconsistent, and philosophically arbitrary.

2. "Laws of history" demand that capitalism be fulfilled by an "end of history," or, rather, an end of "prehistory." This is communism. The proletariat will thereafter be "historically compelled, in conformity with its being," to do whatever is necessary to bring about the new society (*The Holy Family*). This arbitrary eschatology does not need to be discussed either.

3. Capitalist circumstances, especially work in the factory and life in working-class neighborhoods, positively instill into the proletariat a new mentality consisting of solidarity, practicality, soberness of mind, depth of understanding, "humanity," etc., which is intrinsically homogeneous with the new society to be established. In other words, capitalist circumstances produce not only a working class but also, in the person of this class, a new anthropological type and a new sociopsychical structure, which are the necessary conditions for the production of a new society. Capitalist

circumstances change human beings in such a way that they will in turn change circumstances in the wished-for direction.

For a series of reasons, the most compelling of which is the huge quantitative decline of the proletariat in its Marxian sense, this discussion might appear to have only historical interest. In fact, it brings us back to the center of our theoretical and political preoccupations.

Marx was correct, to a considerable degree, in diagnosing a change in the sociopsychical structure of the working class. In the main capitalist countries, the working class in the nineteenth and first half of the twentieth centuries behaved and acted in a way no other exploited and dominated class had ever behaved and acted before. This was not the "product" of "circumstances" but truly the self-creation of the working class as a class and as an active factor in capitalist society. The passage from a proletariat "in itself" to a proletariat "for itself" was not (and is not) "necessary," nor was it determined by the objective conditions of life and work under capitalism. It was the British, the French, the German, and then the American workers who struggled to free themselves from illiteracy; to acquire, shape, and spread political ideas; to organize, formulate, and finally impose demands aimed at altering their "circumstances."[6] Some, but not all, working classes in other capitalist countries showed similar performances.

Now the difference between, say, English workers of the early nineteenth century and Brazilian workers until 1964 (or, for that matter, today's English workers) is certainly not a reflection of genetic disparities. Part of the difference may just be "there," and unexplainable. But part may be accounted for by dissimilarities in historical endowment, in the total "circumstances" of the countries involved, including their political traditions, beyond the establishment of capitalism per se. The fact is that the first, most important, inaugural and instituting steps in the worker's movement took place in countries where a tradition of struggle against oppressive authority in favor of popular political regimes, or in favor of freedom of thought and inquiry, was part of the historical sediment. Once started in these countries, the movement could and did spread elsewhere—though not, emphatically not, everywhere—with these characteristics, despite "capitalist circumstances."

The worker's movement in the "European" (*sensu lato*) countries created itself, but it was able to do this on the basis of the heritage, the tradition, of the democratic movement it found in the history of these countries, the tradition that was, with reference to the social-historical project of autonomy, born within the "European" world. It is therefore also fully comprehensible that before its bureaucratic degeneracy (whether social-democratic or Bolshevik), the worker's movement created institutions of a deeply democratic character, some of which go beyond the forms of the bourgeois democratic movement and resurrect long-forgotten principles embedded in ancient Greek institutions, such as can be seen in the rotation of people in posts of responsibility within the British trade unions of the first period, the importance of sovereign general assemblies, and the permanent revocability of delegates introduced by the Paris Commune and revived or rediscovered every time workers formed autonomous organs like councils (as they did in Hungary in 1956). The radical demands of the worker's movement concerning the ownership of the means of production belong to the same sphere of signification. Democracy entails the equal sharing of power and equal possibilities of participation in the process of political decision making. This is, of course, impossible when individuals, groups, or managerial bureaucracies control centers of economic power, which, especially under modern conditions, immediately translates into political power.

IV

Our heritage, our tradition, includes many contradictory elements. Our history has created democracy—but it is also the only history to have created totalitarianism. The Athenians are accountable both for *Antigone* and for the dreadful massacre of the Melians.

But our tradition has also created another sense of freedom: the possibilities and the responsibility of choosing. Choosing is a political act at the basis even of philosophy, properly speaking. To enter philosophical activity, one has to choose for thinking and against revelation, for unlimited interrogation and against blind acceptance of what has been inherited.

Our heritage contains antinomic elements. And it contains the possibility of and the responsibility for choice. This entails freedom in a sense much deeper than the "constitutional" one. When reading Thucydides, one never sees the Athenians complaining that their plights are brought by god's wrath; they recognize in them the results of their own decisions and actions. Neither, I hope, would people within today's democratic tradition seek extrasocial causes for their collective predicaments.

In this heritage, we choose the project of individual and collective autonomy for an endless series of reasons, but ultimately because we will it, and all that goes with it. "All that goes with it," that is the best in our culture, as we know it. Will is not "voluntarism." Will is the conscious dimension of what we are as beings defined by radical imagination, that is, defined as potentially creative beings. To will autonomy entails willing some types of institution of society and opposing others. But it entails also willing a type of historical existence, a type of relation to the past and to the future. Both of them, relation to the past and relation to the future, must be progressively recreated.

Today the relation to the past is either through cheap touristic archaeology or by erudition and study of museums of various sorts. We must oppose pseudo-modernity and pseudo-subversion—the tabula rasa ideology—as well as eclecticism ("postmodernism") and servile adoration of the past. A new relation to the past means that we revive the past as our own *and* as independent of us; it entails being able to engage in discourse with it and let ourselves be questioned by it. Here again, perhaps the relation of fifth-century Athenians to their past offers itself not as a model but as a germ, as an index of actualized possibilities. Tragedy does not "repeat" the myths; it reelaborates and transforms them so that they, originating in a past immemorial, can vest themselves in the language and the forms of the most vivid present, thereby addressing human beings in all possible futures. This uncanny "dialogue" with the past, two one-way runs apparently disjointed and yet actually not so at all, is one of the most precious possibilities our history has created for us. In the same way that we ought to recognize in individuals, in groups, in ethnic or other units their true alterity, and organize our coexistence with them on the basis of this recognition, we must recognize in our own past an inexhaustible source of proximate alterity, a surface of rebound for our endeavors and a line of resistance to our always imminent folly.

And we have to establish a new relation to the future, so that we stop seeing it as an indefinite "progress" giving us ever more of the same, or as the locus of undefined explosions. Neither should we bracket our relation to the future with the disingenuous term *utopia.* Beyond the so-called possibilities of the present, fascination with which can only generate repetition, we must, without abandoning judgment, dare to will a future—not any future, not a blueprint, but this ever-unforeseeable, ever-creative unfolding, in the shaping of which we can participate, working and struggling, for and against.

§ 7 What Democracy?

It may be useful to recall that with the events of the last four or five years in Latin America, and above all, the collapse of communism in Eastern Europe in the autumn of 1989, journalists and also some serious writers have begun to talk about the triumph of democracy, the irresistible, planetary advance of democracy, and other concoctions in the same vein, full of hot air. What democracy?

Etymology doesn't solve every substantial problem, but it does sometimes stimulate thought. Democracy: *dēmos* and *kratos*, the *kratos* of the *dēmos*, the power of the people, like the aristocracy is the power of the *aristoi*, the best, the noble, the great, and autocracy is the power of *autos*, oneself, of he who is not accountable to any other or others. Where do we see the power of the people nowadays?

Two confusions, introduced by two great modern writers, must be cleared up before the subject can be taken any further. The first writer is Rousseau. In *The Social Contract*, the definition of democracy is crystal clear—and untenable, in that it is derived from a pure set of abstract concepts. Democracy as conceived in *The Social Contract* is when the sovereign and the prince, that is, the legislative body, or more radically, the instituting body and what is called the "executive" nowadays, that is, the government and its administration, are one and the same. Speaking of this regime, Rousseau says it would be excellent for a people of gods, but cannot be achieved by human beings. No such regime has ever existed, nor could it exist, even in a tribe of some fifty individuals. For the sovereign and the prince to be one and the same requires that the political body make and carry out its every decision collectively, irrespective of what is involved, down to collectively replacing a burned-out lightbulb in the room where the general assemblies are held. In such a regime, there cannot and must not be any delegating of responsibility. That is clearly not what people mean when they talk about democracy, and that definition does not apply, for example, to the Athenian regime.

I wish to take advantage of this simple allusion to Athenians to repeat something I have often stated (but there are none so deaf . . .), which is that I have never set the Athenians up as a model, nor have I ever claimed that nothing politically important has been done since their times. Modern Europe created itself as modern Europe; it took what it would and could take from the Greeks, and above all, it constantly recreated them in accordance with its own imaginary. Also, it went much further, particularly with respect to universality, as applied in all sorts of domains. To take one obvious example, the Greeks created mathematics, but European mathematics represents an extraordinary creative effort that breaks the closure of Greek mathematics. Greece is important for us in that some forms developed there give us or are susceptible of giving us food for thought, and in the political field in particular, they show us that some democratic forms of governing are possible and feasible. This applied to collectivities of some thirty thousand citizens. What can happen when we have thirty million, or three billion citizens? That's another question, and it's the real problem for present-day democracy, which none of today's thinkers about democracy seems to want to broach, and which they avoid with their allusions to national sovereignty. We will get to it.

Just a few words, now, about Tocqueville's understanding of the word "democracy." He was a stupendous thinker who was barely thirty when he arrived in the United States, spent a few months there, and perceived things that no one else saw, to the point where even in the United States, political scientists and sociologists have been turning to him for several decades now to understand their own society. Needless to say, his reflections on the ancien régime and the French Revolution are extremely important. In France, he was rediscovered a mere twenty years ago, in the 1970s, and actually as an ideological recourse when Marxism went into crisis. A strange swing occurred, actually, through which Marx was thrown overboard—certainly a necessary move in some respects, and one I myself had made since 1960—but at the same time, what was thrown out with the dirty bathwater was not just the baby but the bathtub, the bathroom itself, and ultimately the whole house. That is, under the fallacious pretext that Marx was allegedly wrong in contrasting the actual functioning of society with what is written in the lawbooks, the social-historical reality in which the political regime is immersed is purely and simply erased.

Tocqueville is being rediscovered, then, which is excellent news, and he is being turned into the thinker of contemporary "democracy," which is strange. Tocqueville visited the United States in the early 1830s, but the country he described no longer existed by that time. The social situation he depicts actually harks back to Jeffersonian times, or more accurately, it is what would correspond, ideally (slavery aside), to what Jefferson would have wanted as the foundations of democracy: namely, a society that has achieved "equality of conditions." Tocqueville was anything but a formalist. He doesn't analyze constitutional arrangements, he describes a social situation (and a cultural one—an imaginary institution, in my sense of the term) characterized by "equality of conditions," an equality that would have the *chance,* to use Max Weber's expression, the significant probability, of effectively being achieved in that society. Unfortunately, Tocqueville described that state of affairs in the United States at the very time when it was disappearing. That was the Jacksonian period, with industrialization striding forward, workers laboring seventy-two hours a week, and so on. "Equality of conditions" was in a very bad way—in fact, it had been from the outset. (Let me say, in passing, that the sycophants of the American republic generally forget that the Founding Fathers wrote the Constitution partly against the subversive social movements of the time, including the demands for the abolition of debts, and so forth.) How relevant, then, are Tocqueville's descriptions for the question of democracy today (in 1990)?

The Jeffersonian political imaginary was quite "classical" (Greco-Roman). Marx formulated the same vision admirably almost a century later, when he said that the genuine socioeconomic basis of the ancient democracies was the community of independent petty producers. The availability of land in the United States preserved a semblance of relevance for that schema throughout the nineteenth century, until the "closing of the frontier." But by 1830, the great slave-owning estates of the South, a heritage of the past, and the rapid industrialization of the North, along with the rise of powerful, corrupt political machines, were heralding the future, showing that this schema no longer corresponded (supposing it ever had) to the pivotal realities of North American society. In one way or another, powerful oligarchies had seized political power.

But Tocqueville's description was essentially "sociological" rather than political. Or more accurately, it was social-historical. Its object was not so much political power as that tremendous upheaval in the imaginary of modern societies that rejects *hereditary* differences in status, or to put it differently, that refuses any status that would be permanent, and beyond reach for the "ordinary citizen," by right, de jure. As we know, Tocqueville was an aristocrat and visibly nostalgic of some features of the ancien régime (partially "justifiably" so, actually), praising the excellence of individuals, or of what Marx would have called the organic community between the lord and the small collectivity of which he is chief, judge, and father. He was struck by the fact that all this had been eradicated in the United States, or rather, had never existed there. "Equality of conditions" is the general trend of human societies that he brilliantly intuited (like Marx inferring industrialization and global capitalism from the situation in a few factories in Manchester) and projected on modern societies in general, and which leads those societies to reject the old forms of social discrimination. You can spend July on the French Riviera, August in Biarritz, September in Deauville, October in Scotland, November in France's Sologne region, and December in Cairo without having anyone ask you whether you have the right to do so; you do—as much a right as any duke married to an American heiress. You will of course need a lot of money, but we are not talking about such vulgar matters here, you see, we are talking about the "political sphere."

But what is the "political sphere"? The "political sphere" means power, and how it is acquired and exerted. Tocqueville has very little to say about that, and his conception of "democracy" is of no political use.[1] This is further demonstrated by an absurdity: Tocqueville's idea of "democratic despotism." What he means by that is not the perfectly feasible case where a "tyranny of the majority" would be taken to the extreme, oppressing individuals or minority groups, thus violating its own laws (as the Athenian *ekklēsia* did in 406). No, he is thinking of a perfectly "democratic" society, in his sense of the term, where there is perfect "equality of conditions" but in which citizens are so politically apathetic, so lethargically conformist, that they leave every power in the hands of a "tutelary state" (or maybe in the hands of a triumphant demagogue, and why not? perhaps even of some Stalin or Hitler). But what would that "tutelary state" be, concretely speaking? Certainly not a pure concept. It would be, precisely, a state, meaning a bureaucratic pyramid filled with privileged petty despots, solidly entrenched in their position, and who would be more equal than the others, to borrow a famous saying. Although a regime of that sort would remain "democratic" in Tocqueville's sense (that is, in the legalistic sense, refusing any inequality of legal status), it would simply be what we see all around us: a liberal oligarchy, not a democracy.

The evolution of Western societies shows that they really are tending toward the "equalization of conditions" in the Tocquevillean sense. This is one dimension of the challenging of the old order, combining the trend toward achievement of the project of individual and collective autonomy with the capitalist transformation of money into the true general equivalent and by the same token the general substitute (Balzac described this at great length well before it was formulated by Marx). There is a tendency for some conditions to be equalized, and at the same time for others, constantly reproduced and ever present, to be unequalized. From the standpoint of effective social-historical reality, not of the letter of the law, we live in highly inegalitarian societies, including and above all, with respect to power of all sorts. It hardly matters, as regards this inequality, that the ruling classes may be revitalized by recruiting or co-opting the most capable, clever, and intelligent members of the dominated classes.

What should be understood by the word *democracy?* Certainly not a tendency to equalize conditions of just any kind: Judaism, Buddhism, Christianity, and Islam, each in its own way and aside from a few details, achieve complete equalization of the most important of all conditions, the metaphysical conditions governing the eternal life (or nonlife) of their followers. I have explained my own position on this repeatedly, most recently in "Power, Politics, Autonomy" and "Done and to Be Done."[2] But to set things straight, let me recall two points.

First, democracy is the power of the *dēmos,* that is, of the collectivity. Immediately, the question arises: where does that power end? What are its limits? Obviously, that power must stop somewhere; it must have limits. But it is just as obvious that when society no longer accepts any transcendental norm, or even any inherited norm, *nothing,* intrinsically, can set the limits at which that power must stop. The outcome is that democracy is essentially the reign of self-limitation. Human rights are an example of such self-limitation. In several countries they are constitutional. In France they have a somewhat bizarre status, both constitutional and "more than" constitutional. But in spite of this, I don't think any jurist would claim that it is impossible to abrogate the French declaration of human rights perfectly legally. There is always the possibility of revising the constitution, and there is nothing to prevent the modification, the repeal, or other, of the preamble referring to the *Declaration of the Rights of Man and of the Citizen* in the course of that revision. The idea of a nonmodifiable constitution is a legal and factual absurdity. But to say that a constitution is revisable is to say that only the activity of the constituent body—the people, in the case of a democracy—can set limits to this revisal, and in particular can guarantee human rights, a degree of separation of powers, rules such as *nullum crimen, nulla poena sine lege*—no crime, no punishment without a law, etc. All these provisions are worth fighting for. But they all depend on explicit action on the part of the constituent—that is, instituting—body. Democracy is the regime of self-limitation; that is, the regime of autonomy and self-institution.

Taken in the fullest sense, these three terms are actually synonymous. For the same reason, democracy is a tragic regime. Tragedy means exactly that: the question of mankind is *hubris,* there is no ultimate rule to which one can refer to escape it, no Ten Commandments, no Gospel. The Sermon on the Mount tells me nothing about what laws I should vote for (in fact, it tells me there is no need for laws; love is enough). It is up to us to discover what laws to adopt. The limits are not set in advance; *hubris* is always possible. This is the subject of Athenian tragedy, that democratic institution par excellence, constantly reminding the *dēmos* of the need for self-limitation. When Euripides staged *The Trojans* (often viewed by the moderns, stupidly, as an antiwar manifesto, which is not at all its point) following the atrocious massacre of the Melians by the Athenians, what he showed the Athenian spectators was the Athenians themselves: the Greek people after the fall of Troy, depicted as dreadful monsters carried away by their *hubris,* incapable of setting any limit to their acts. He depicted them as wreaking that era's equivalent of Auschwitz or Katyn. He showed that to the *dēmos,* saying *tua res agitur*—what is done is your responsibility—and the *dēmos,* that same *dēmos* that did those awful things, or condoned them, rewarded him with the laurel wreath.

This power does not accept any limits coming from outside (I am not talking about trivial limits such as natural ones, for instance). But it is also a self-instituting power. Democracy is a regime that explicitly, continually, institutes itself. This does not mean it changes its constitution every day, or on the first of each month, but that it has taken every necessary step, legal and concrete, so as to be able to change its institutions without a civil war, without violence or bloodshed. Of course no one can vouch that violence will be eliminated from human history once and for all if democracy is established.

Second: what does equality mean in the context of an autonomous, self-governed, and self-instituted society? What is the logical and the philosophical transition from one (autonomy) to the other (equality)? First of all, people cannot reasonably desire autonomy for themselves without desiring it for everyone. But also, because there is a collectivity and because that collectivity cannot live without laws, there can be no effectively autonomous—free—people if they are not effectively able to participate in determining those laws. Freedom and equality mutually require each other. I live within society, and therefore I cannot live outside of its laws. (Life in society is not an incidental attribute of human beings, it is to be human. And laws are not a desirable or unfortunate addendum to society. The institution is the being-society of society.) Laws cannot be defined by each individual, for herself only. That idea is just as meaningless as the idea of a private language. The only sense in which I can say that laws are *mine* is that I was able to participate in creating law, although I may have been beaten in the vote. The point is that I approve the law or the process by which it was elaborated and adopted because I was able to participate in it.

Strictly speaking, then, equality means the equal possibility—effective, not just on paper—for everyone to participate in power. That does not simply mean going into the polling booth; it means, for instance, being informed, as well informed as anyone else, about the issue at hand. We may make a distinction between the *oikos,* strictly private matters, the *agora,* the private/public sphere, the "place" where citizens meet outside the political domain, and the *ekklēsia,* the public/public sphere which, in a democracy, is the place for deliberation and decisions on matters of common concern. In the *agora* I talk with other people, buy books, or do other things. I am in a space that is public, but at the same time private, for no political decision (be it legislative, governmental, or judicial) can be made there. The collectivity, by its legislation, simply guarantees freedom within this space. In the *ekklēsia,* in the broadest sense, including the "popular assembly" as well as the "government" and the courts, I am in a public/public space. I deliberate with other people in order to *decide,* and those decisions are sanctioned by the public power of the collectivity. Democracy may also be defined as when the public/public sphere—which in other regimes is actually more or less *private*—becomes truly public. It is not only under the ancien régime that "public" politics are the monarch's *private* business, or in totalitarian states that it belongs to the party apparatus. One of the many reasons why it is laughable to call contemporary Western societies "democratic" is because the "public" sphere is in fact private—be it in France, the United States, or England. This is true, first of all, in that the real decisions are made behind closed doors, backstage, or in places where those who govern meet informally. It is well known that they are not really made in those official places where they are supposed to be made. By the time they are presented to the Council of Ministers or the House of Representatives, the game is over. Next, the motives behind them (the real ones, in any case) are secret, and in most instances legally beyond reach. In England, public archives cannot be consulted for thirty years; in France, I think it's fifty years. Be it fifty, thirty, or ten years, or even one month—that is enough to make my point. Wait fifty or thirty years and you will be able to find out why your father, brother, or son was killed at war. That's "democracy."

Naturally, for the public/public sphere to become truly public, there is the obligation for the collectivity and the administration to effectively inform citizens of everything concerning the decisions to be made, of everything they need to know in order to make a fully knowledgeable decision.[3] Before going into any discussion of the issue of "direct democracy" versus "representative democracy" then, we note that present "democracy" is anything but a democracy because the public/public sphere is in fact *private*. It is in the hands of a political oligarchy, not of the body political.

But when we say "equality means the equal, effective possibility for everyone to participate," we are obviously not referring exclusively to access to information. What is involved here is effective judgmental ability, leading directly to the question of education, as well as to the *time* needed to keep informed and to give thought to issues, which brings us just as directly to the question of production and the economy. Furthermore, given the barrage of demagogy and sophistry nowadays, it is important to keep in mind that we are talking about *political* equality, equal participation in *power*. Equality does not mean that the collectivity promises to make everyone capable of running 100 meters in 10 seconds, or of playing Chopin's *Etudes* perfectly, any more than to have children all succeed at school with the same grades, or even to have them all pass, purely and simply. That has nothing to do with political equality (although some trends in contemporary society do indicate that it may have something to do with Tocquevillean equality).

Some writers have attempted to define democracy on the basis of other considerations, viewing it as the regime of "indetermination," for example, or as the regime that abolishes unified norms for various social sectors, or unity between knowledge and power. It has also been described as the regime of openness, an expression in which I recognize some things I myself have written, vagueness aside. But we are talking about contemporary Western societies. Any political philosopher in the classical ages would have recognized them as liberal oligarchies: oligarchies because they are dominated by a specific stratum of people, liberal because that stratum consents a number of negative or defensive liberties to citizens. What, then, is the concrete content of that "openness" today, in these societies? It is generalized conformism. And what is the content of the "indetermination" of these regimes? Inasmuch as the functioning of a social-historical regime can be "determined"—which it obviously *never* is, even in a primitive tribe or a totalitarian regime, since a social-historical regime is neither a machine nor a Newtonian universe—inasmuch, then, as it may be determined, that regime of so-called indetermination is perfectly "determined" by real, informal mechanisms. These are essentially distinct from the formal (juridical) rules but are permitted and covered by them, and they ensure, as far as possible (there are surprises everywhere, even in Russia and China; history means surprises), that nothing changes. It is that very reproduction of sameness that we see in contemporary "democratic" societies, except, once again, for the unforeseeable and the indeterminate, which are the core of any social-historical regime. Be it in the economy, politics, or culture, we have reproduction of the same.

Can we say that different sectors apply different norms, that there is no single norm governing every sector today? It is amusing to note that this differentiation or separation of norms (which, incidentally, was what Marx, in his youth, viewed—wrongly, however—as the very definition of alienation) is invoked at a time when two norms, and only two, are increasingly becoming the rule. One is the hierarchical-bureaucratic norm within those huge organizations of all sorts (be they productive, administrative, educational, or cultural) in which most people spend their lives. The other is the norm of money, wherever today's pseudo-marketplace setups prevail. This mixture of the norm of money and the hierarchical-bureaucratic norm is enough for us to continue to characterize these rich, liberal societies as fragmented bureaucratic capitalist societies.

The "dissociation of knowledge and power" is a multifaceted hodgepodge that only takes on a semblance of meaning in contrast to Plato's *Republic* or to the *pretensions* of the Stalinist regime (which was actually the power of the ignorant). The kings of France did not reign because they "knew," but because it was God's will. Even Hitler didn't contend he "knew"; he claimed to embody the destiny and the mission of the German race. As for what is desirable, that dissociation does not say any more than the myth of Protagoras in the dialogue of the same name: politics, as I have written dozens of times, is not a matter of *epistēmē* but of *doxa,* and that is the only nonprocedural justification of majority rule. To say that is not enough, for all *doxai* are not equivalent, and there is a sort of knowledge, in politics, that is not a "science" but a matter of judgment, caution, and verisimilitude (which is why Plato looked down on rhetoricians whereas Aristotle wrote a *Rhetorics*). As for contemporary reality, it rather tends to achieve the opposite of that dissociation. This is visible in any hierarchical-bureaucratic structure, where the director, the tenured professor, or the board of examiners is necessarily right (power claims to imply knowledge). This may also be seen in the attitude of the population, inasmuch as it takes an interest in politics. Why is so-and-so "apt" to run something (the government, the party, and so on)? Because he "knows": (pseudo) knowledge legitimates power. The fact that, precisely, it is almost always pseudo-knowledge is quite unimportant here (but is certainly very important in other respects).

All this absolutely does not prevent us from classing Western societies as different from other known social-historical regimes. In these societies, the project of individual and collective autonomy has come into being once again, after the Greek experience and in different forms. They have been agitated by that project for close to ten centuries now. The struggles and revolutions inspired by that project—as well as the slow but colossal changes in individual behavior, for that matter—have led to the institution, implicit and explicit, of arrangements that, although they have not succeeded in effectively achieving autonomy and self-government, have nonetheless made these societies open societies, in which active contestation from within remains possible, and individuals and groups enjoy some rights and freedoms thanks to which they may, formally and to some extent effectively, think independently and challenge the establish-ment. These rights and freedoms are the outcome and the heritage of the emancipatory movement that has been a driving force in the West for centuries. It is their existence, but also their essentially negative, defensive character, that lead us to call Western political regimes liberal oligarchies, and the societies that sustain them, relatively open societies. To what ex-tent are the effective social-historical processes we are now witnessing pre-paring another closure? That is a second question, to which I will return at the end of my talk.

A good deal of present-day discussions, at least in France, take place as if there were a political sphere totally independent of the rest of social life, or else one that determined the rest (that is, historical materialism in reverse). Furthermore, that political sphere is not discussed on the basis of any real processes, arrangements, or effective mechanisms, or even accord-ing to the true spirit of the laws, but according to the letter of the laws. Reality is obliterated, formalism is preferred, the implicit is replaced by the explicit, the latent by the manifest. The development of those ratio-nalizing constructions that presently stand in lieu of "political philosophy" is made possible by the disregard and the eclipsing of the actual nature of the social-historical regime in which we live.

What goes on around the question of "representation" is particularly comical in this respect. People who write about politics today do not offer any "philosophy of representation." Nowhere have I seen any grounds for or elucidation of what political "representation" might be, and I don't see what its content could be. Is it conceivable, within the Western legal con-ceptual framework, and generally speaking, for a rule to prevent me from modifying my will, or from revoking any delegation of powers supposedly in *my own interest only* (and not under contract)? "Representation" means that we give someone an *irrevocable* mandate for a period of four, five, or seven years (no matter how many), in *our interest only* (and not in the in-terest of the "representatives" as well). But an irrevocable mandate in the *sole* interest of those who gave it, even for a set period of time, is obviously nonexistent in private law, and it is absurd, juridically impossible to con-struct. A proxy, representative, or delegate only "exists" to express the will of the person represented and can only bind that person to the extent that she expresses that will. With the system of "representation," however, the collectivity gives an irrevocable, long-term mandate to "representatives" whose action may produce irreversible situations, the outcome being that they themselves determine the parameters and the themes of their "reelection."

These "elections" themselves are an impressive resurrection of the Mystery of the Eucharist and the true Presence. Every four or five years, on a Sunday (a Thursday in Great Britain, where Sundays are devoted to other mysteries), the collective will melts, turns liquid, and is collected drop by drop in sacred/profane vases called ballot boxes, and in the evening, following several other operations, that liquid, condensed one hundred thousand times, is poured into the henceforth transubstantiated minds of several hundred elected officials.

There is no philosophy of "representation," although there is an implicit metaphysics; nor is there any sociological analysis. Who represents whom, and how? Forgotten, without any discussion, is the criticism of "representative democracy," starting with Rousseau and considerably amplified since, unrestrictedly validated by the most superficial observation of contemporary political life. Obliterated, the alienated sovereignty of those who delegate to the delegates. That delegation is supposed to be limited in time. But as soon as it is established, the game is over. Rousseau was wrong in this respect: the English are not even "free once every five years." For throughout those five years, the so-called choices on which the constituents will be asked to vote will have been completely predetermined by what their deputies did in between the two elections. The effects of these five-year mandates are of course cumulative, and the voter's "choice" turns out to be reduced to such grandiose dilemmas as Mitterand or Chirac, Bush or Dukakis, Thatcher or Kinnock, etc. And as soon as any small, separate political body exists, it can only look after its own prerogatives and interests, and enter into collusion with the other de facto powers, economic ones in particular.

True, all this is vulgar empiricism—Judeo-phenomenal reality, as Marx would have said. What do we care about ridiculous anecdotes, such as the implication of practically every U.S. senator in the savings and loan scandal (for an estimated cost of US$700 billion, with estimates constantly being revised upward)? Is a billion dollars a political concept? Of course not. You are forgetting, sir, that those objects are not worthy of our thought, which only addresses the political sphere and the essence of democracy, consisting in the fact that the seat of power is empty and that no one can claim to occupy it. Sorry about that, we thought, stupidly, that decisions by which people are sent to be killed, reduced to unemployment, or confined to ghettoes must come from a seriously occupied "seat of power."

Of course there are elections for the Senate and the House of Representatives in the United States. Of course, too, once you are elected senator, you are senator for life, barring some accident. That is a well-known fact that nobody there doubts. You have to be a complete political ignoramus not to know it, just as obviously as the fact that Washington, D.C., is the capital of the United States. Why is that? Because to be elected senator, you must have money—a lot of money (a "nonpolitical" concept) to finance your campaigns (TV and so on included)—and that money is given by the political action committees (PACs), provided for by the legislation, which regulates activities and "limits" contributions, theoretically rather strictly. Who donates money to the PACs? Probably not the bashed neighborhood bum. More likely, it is people who have both money and reasons to give it to the Republican PACs instead of the Democratic PACs, or vice versa. One knows, more or less, who gave how much, just as one knows very precisely which senators voted what. The money is given by those who have it to those who vote properly. But any senator who is financed by a richer PAC than his opponent is practically sure to be reelected. Actually, incumbent senators are extremely rarely, not to say never, defeated in elections.

That takes care of the reality of representation. But the truth is, we should not discuss the reality of representation for the simple reason that we are fighting windmills. In most cases, elected representatives hardly have any power. What power does the French Parliament have? Or even the English Parliament? Practically none. The levers of power are in the hands of the extraparliamentary "political" bodies, the political parties, and always, the majority party. This real, fundamental political entity of the modern world, gloriously ignored by our political thinkers, holds all effective power. People talk about the separation of powers. What separation of powers? The majority party controls the legislature. It also controls what is hypocritically called the "executive," suggesting that it simply "executes" the legislation, which is rubbish. The "executive" does not execute anything; it decides and governs. Bailiffs and typists "execute." The "executive" power is actually the power to *govern*. It makes decisions that are not predetermined by any law. It does not "enforce" the law; it acts within the legal framework, which is quite another matter. Its decisions, on important matters, are discretionary and definitive. Can the French Conseil d'Etat, that admirable institution, cancel action taken *by* the government? Yes, in the case of trivia; no, when truly important action is involved, what it itself has very aptly called acts *of* government (see the Couitéas case, 1912), and which, according to it, cannot be attacked for excessive or abusive power. Naturally, most government action involves, precisely . . . acts *of* government. Administrative acts are of secondary interest by comparison, even if it is important to protect citizens against arbitrary decisions by subprefects.

The majority party prevails over the legislature and the government, then, and controls the administrative functions proper, through nominations to hundreds or thousands of high-ranking positions. As for the judicial power, the question must be addressed with a modicum of realism and common sense. Before the separation of powers became constitutional (and it actually existed in Western Europe several centuries before the French Revolution in the case of courts), one may doubt that the absolute monarch ever interfered in conflicts between peasants or merchants, or in trials of thieves and so on. To this day, the authorities have no reason to intervene in the functioning of the judicial apparatus in general, or any interest in doing so, in ordinary civil or criminal cases. But they have good reasons and enormous possibilities to do so in cases that matter to them, and that is what usually happens. As soon as there is a "political" aspect to a case, the government can intervene in various ways, and effectively does so. France has had the gendarmes in Nouméa, the amnesty of deputies, Urba-Technic, and so on.[4] In Great Britain, a great deal has been written about the "decline of British liberties" (poor Burke!). The situation is still quite different in the United States (where, actually, we are witnessing a hypertrophy of "judicial power," correlative to the gradual obstruction of the legislative mechanisms); but the politics of the Supreme Court (packed by the last three presidents) tend to veer toward the political options of the judges appointed by the president (and approved by the Senate).

So it is largely deceptive to speak of the "separation of powers" today, and to speak of "representation" is equally deceptive. "Representatives" are members of parliament, and the majority (and in fact the minority) does what the party head (or its leadership) says. That is what happens in truly parliamentary countries such as England, the mother of parliaments). Or else, as in France, it does what the president told the prime minister he should get parliament to do, except when the president thinks that only menial matters are involved and leaves the legislature to its own devices. This fundamental phenomenon, both in reality and for political thinking (for example, how would a genuine democracy deal with the party question?), is constantly ignored, except, may I remind you, by Robert Michels, who already said all this. That's right, and so did Max Weber and a few others since then. Let me simply add one other long-known fact: that parties are not mere opinion groups, or even interest groups. The main point about contemporary parties is that they themselves are bureaucratic apparatuses dominated by self-co-opting clans, as shown, in France, by what happened at the Socialist congress in Rennes, or in the ["neo-Gaullist"] RPR party, and so on. There is of course the possibility that tomorrow, after ten years of Thatcherism, the British Conservative party, in a reflex of self-preservation, will overthrow Ms. Thatcher to avoid losing the elections.[5] That will simply mean that the clan (or clans, having fought it out and come to a compromise) heading the Conservatives has realized that it has to sacrifice its glorious leader in order to save itself. There is nothing "democratic" about all this. The process is as old as the world, and similar cases may be found in the ancient empires as well as in contemporary dictatorships, and down to the logic behind the replacement of the likes of Dillinger or Al Capone. The logic is the same in every strictly hierarchical structure topped by a dominant group with a more or less powerful, charismatic leader, and it has nothing to do with democracy.

The reality of parties is set aside altogether, then. So is the nature of the State. The State is implicitly represented as an abstract operator of societal unification. The fact that it is structured as a hierarchical-bureaucratic apparatus, largely autonomous and separated from the people it administers, is forgotten. I won't go any further into the question of the State except to express my astonishment, once again, at a "political philosophy" that does not even mention it.

In an issue of the periodical *Le Débat,* Marcel Gauchet, in a sort of overview of the state of humanity in general and of France in particular in 1990, speaks most excellently of the "flat electroencephalogram of the party in power," that is, the Socialist Party. The expression is most accurate, but why limit it to the party in power? Are the electroencephalograms of Messrs Chirac, Pasqua, Giscard and so on—not as individuals, of course, but as (right-wing) political leaders—any less flat than those of the Socialist Party? Given what their encephala have produced, one may legitimately have some doubts. And why confine ourselves to France? In the United States, everyone has been lamenting for decades, and especially since 1980, over how hopeless the Democratic Party is, discovering that it has no ideas and nothing to say, and were it not for the customary obsequiousness toward the president and the constant bluffing of the Reagan era, they would have said—and are already saying—the same thing about the party in power. Political electroencephalograms are flat everywhere. They are just as flat in Germany, whence the divine surprise for Chancellor Kohl: the events have turned someone who everyone considered a nothing into the great chancellor who achieved the unification of Germany. The poor man didn't have anything to do with it. Don't say he could have bungled it; it's hard to see how.

As early as 1960 I was already writing about the lack of imagination on the part of contemporary "politicians."[6] Things have only gotten worse since then. But we must go further. Why, indeed, is that electroencephalogram flat? Has humankind degenerated in just a few decades? Is it by chance that the encephalogram of French parties—"the classic land of politics," in Marx's words—is flat? Doesn't it say something about that society? Can it be that the only thing a "democratic" society is able to do is to put parties with flat electroencephalograms in power? What kind of "democracy" is governed by men in that state? Just as a doctor whose patient's blood pressure is high doesn't merely take note of the fact but asks why, we have to wonder why that encephalogram is flat. This should lead us to an in-depth analysis of the entire social-historical organism involved, and of the reasons that make it produce such appalling governmental structures.

Another point that is strikingly absent from contemporary "political thought" is the weighty, massive reality of the nation. How can the universal tenets to which people refer in another context to "found" "democracy" be reconciled with the numerous "national sovereignties" (the vast majority of which, it should be said in passing, function by constantly violating those tenets)? What is "national sovereignty," philosophically speaking? A huge lump of raw facts, in the face of which philosophy resigns or makes shameful compromises with "reality." It seems that unlike one well-known late-eighteenth-century writer, our "philosophers" have never met any Frenchmen, Englishmen, Poles, Turks, Greeks, or other. They have only dealt with human beings.

Last of all, and most important, it is as though the capitalist-bureaucratic structure of society is totally irrelevant to its overall or political functioning. We are not talking about the sixty or two hundred richest families, or about men in top hats smoking huge cigars and buying governments. That is not the point. The real point is the question of the anthropological structures corresponding to the social and economic structures, which is to say, the psychosocial structures of contemporary individuals, the way they act and take part in society, and the kind of behavior the very functioning of that society constantly tends to produce and reproduce. The dominant social imaginary around which contemporary individuals are structured is purely and simply ignored. That is what happens when people talk about individualism, or like Pierre Rosanvallon, about the "advent of the individual." As if that "individual" was completely indeterminate, or as if there were individuals in and for themselves whose advent would attend this so-called democracy!

It is actually a very peculiar kind of individual whose advent occurs under modern capitalism. It is some very specific kinds of men and women, not just any men and women. Who are they? They are not Bamileke, fifteenth-century Florentines or Russians from the Times of Trouble, but men and women living under late-twentieth-century capitalism. Our job is not to look into their deepest unconscious, nor can we; suffice it to look at their social manifestations, their activities and tastes, the way they raise their children, and so forth. These are the individuals who give its concrete content to "individualism."

But the ideology in circulation today aims at building the entire political system on the idea of an ahistorical, asocial individual. It claims to grant to—or to recognize for—that individual the greatest possible autonomy, without ever raising the question of the content of that autonomy and of its utilization. (Such a carefree attitude would perhaps be defensible from a Kantian viewpoint; that is, in a philosophy with no flesh and bones.) The fact is, contemporary individuals use the liberties granted them by the regime to practice some apparently harmless activities: to go to supermarkets, drive cars, watch television, and so on. It is nonetheless legitimate for us to wonder, philosophically speaking, what would happen if those individuals put another "content" into their autonomy, or if it turned out that their activities were not all that harmless—for instance, because they are directly or indirectly polluting or destroying the environment. But above all, what those "autonomous" individuals do is naturally not at all individual, except in the physical sense.

They are purely and simply acting socially, and this is almost as true for contemporary society as for traditional society. People do what they have learned to do or are brought to do, and at this very moment, at 10:25 PM, most French households are getting ready to turn their TV set off, having almost always turned it on at 8 PM, and go to bed, every man (and woman) of them alike.

As construed by the (rare) coherent spokespeople for contemporary "individualism," law itself is not susceptible of any rational justification. To be truly consistent with its premises, "individualism" should limit the rules liable of social sanctions to those derived from a single precept: "it is prohibited to do anything that encroaches on another person's autonomy" and should otherwise retain only strictly formal and procedural regulations.[7] It is inconceivable, however, for a normative legal system to be totally divested of the slightest substantive "content" exceeding the mere preservation of "freedom" for all. First of all, there is *nothing* in this freedom and its predicates—not even bodily integrity—that goes absolutely without saying, or in other words, that is radically independent of *any* social-historical institution of the humanity of humankind. (Both Nozick and Rawls, blinded by their historical provincialism, view as axiomatic what is more or less self-evident in their own country, today.) Next, both the criminal code and the civil code necessarily contain clauses that can only be justified by substantive considerations. The battle over the right to abortion, for instance, can only be decided on the basis of substantive arguments; either the present freedom of a woman in one "sector" is preferable to the "total" but merely potential and future freedom of an embryo, or vice versa. The amount of alimony a divorced parent must pay for his children is calculated on the basis of that parent's financial "means"; in other words, it has nothing to do with the children's "freedom"; it purely and simply integrates the rule of the hereditary perpetuation of the existing distribution of economic resources. (In point of fact, inheritance law as a whole has absolutely nothing to do with the preservation of any "individual autonomy" whatsoever—except if and when it grants complete freedom to bequest, and that, I believe, is not true anywhere.) Society cannot last if its children are not socialized, that is to say, "raised" and "educated" in one way or another. Having children be born in one country rather than another is already an encroachment on their "freedom," and the same is true of raising them in one way instead of another and teaching them this or that at school. Should the State-cum-police shield children's "freedom" by tearing them away from their parents at birth (and therefore "raising" and "educating" them according to *its own* State norms), or else should parents protect them from any outside influence, including their own? If a minimal state is to be maintained so as to enforce the minimal rules of social coexistence, its running expenses must be covered. It would be interesting to see what absolutely *neutral* taxation with no social effects would look like.

The existence of collective norms, trivial or not, is logically and really impossible without taking into account something located beyond "individuals"—some sort of "commonweal." It may be "the happiness of the greatest number," the power of the state or of a tyrant, opportunities for supermen to develop without being contaminated by the moral standards of slaves, justice, "racial purity," or anything else. It is really impossible because every normative system is necessarily inspired by and unavoidably results in the fostering of substantive values, and logically impossible because the norm says "all," implying something that transcends the "individual." In the simplest cases, if the norm is to protect each person's "autonomy," it must encroach on the "autonomy" of each person—that is to say, of all. That anonymous, indefinite "all" is neither a specific individual nor a concrete collection of specific individuals, but rather, the "abstract" possibility of continuing social life as such. If that continuation is not posited as an unquestionable value, there is nothing in "individualistic" metaphysics that can go against the well-known line of reasoning that begins with Callicles and Thrasymacus, includes Sade, and goes on to Stirner and Nietzsche. If it is posited, it leads to norms and decisions, the substantive content of which goes far beyond formal, procedural rules that preserve individual freedom.

What we may call Hobbes's response to Callicles—that no man is so strong as to be able to brave a coalition against him of a multitude of the weak—is only meaningful on the radically presocial terrain to which Hobbes resorts for the sake of his construction. If human beings were absolute brutes who had not yet learned to ensnare each other with fine phrases, magic and miracles, divine revelations, divisive maneuvers, and so on, the simple brute force of the many would win out. But of course the entire history of humanity testifies against that, with all the instances of domination by sacred kings, oligarchic minorities, dictators, emperors, parties entrenched in power, etc. Hobbes's construction attempts to derive a very relative "law" from a fictitious "fact"—fictitious not because that "state of nature" cannot ever have existed (which is probably true), but because had it existed, it would not have been the state of a *human* collectivity, that is, of a collectivity of speaking, and therefore imagining and instituting beings.

Today's liberal ideology conceals the social-historical reality of the established regime. It also occults a crucial question: that of the anthropological basis and correspondent of every politics and of every regime. This question tormented those philosophers—Plato, Aristotle, Hobbes, Spinoza, Montesquieu, Rousseau, and Kant—who wrote about the political sphere. A democratic person is not just any sort of "individual," and we are now seeing that fact in action. It has also been evidenced dramatically in the opposite courses taken by the recent events in Czechoslovakia and Romania.

The anthropological content of the present-day individual is, as always, none other than the expression, or the concrete accomplishment in flesh and bone, of the central social imaginary of our times, which shapes the regime, its orientation, values, what it is worth living and dying for, the *thrust* of society, even its affects, and the individuals who will make all that exist concretely. The central imaginary of this period, as we know, is increasingly the central capitalist imaginary of unlimited expansion of so-called rational so-called mastery—in actual fact, of the economy, production, and consumption—and less and less an imaginary of autonomy and democracy.

This is the angle from which we should view the capitalist "innovation" to which Marcel Gauchet was referring. Inasmuch as it exists, that innovation is not indifferent either. Guided by the capitalist imaginary, it moves in a specific direction and excludes other directions. At present, we experience it mainly as innovation in technology, production, trade, and finance, and almost never, any longer, as political, artistic, cultural, and philosophical innovation.

∽

A long digression on the economy is required here. A little earlier I used the term *ignoramuses* in reference to the regime of representation. I reiterate the expression, and even more strongly, with respect to the economy and capitalism. We hear talk everywhere, nowadays, about the "triumph of the market economy over the plan." But there is no more a genuine market in the capitalist countries than there was a plan in the to-talitarian bureaucratic countries. In short, there is no marketplace under capitalism, because where there is capitalism, there is no marketplace, and when a marketplace exists, there can be no capitalism. There is simply an oligopolistic, more than "imperfect," irrational pseudo-market. That it functions a billion times better than the aberrant bureaucratic lunacy seen in Russia and elsewhere is unquestionable, as is the fact that it is infinitely preferable to live here than there. But this does not mean that marketplace and capitalism are synonymous, or that the capitalist pseudo-marketplace is the optimal mechanism for the allocation and distribution of resources, as is contended. The market has existed at least since the Phoenicians; it existed under the Greeks and the Romans, and it was highly devel-oped in the Mediterranean world. It regressed considerably during the true Middle Ages (from the fifth to the tenth centuries), then expanded again, paralleling the constitution and development of the bourgeoisie. It was then caught up in the development of capitalism, but it took both violence and state intervention for the marketplace to take its capitalist form, as both Marx and Karl Polanyi have amply shown. The market is infinitely more "efficient" as a setting for exchanges than any authoritar-ian allocation of resources such as bureaucratic pseudo-planning, but its actual functioning has nothing to do with that textbook mechanism ra-tionally optimizing resource allocation so idyllically served to students of political economics.

For the market to be rational, there would have to be:

1. Perfect competition between firms. It does not exist. We live in, and capitalism is *necessarily*, an economy of oligopolies, monopolies, explicit or tacit deals, and so on.

2. Perfectly informed consumers. Just try to visualize what that might mean. You will see it is absurd.

3. Perfectly informed producers. Same remark as above.

4. Perfect fluidity of production factors, which is to say not only com-plete *mobility* but complete *transformability* of concrete units of capital and labor. Strictly speaking, this implies assertions such as: buildings can be changed into airplanes instantly and at no cost, or unemployed dock-ers in Marseilles can be converted into programmers in Maubeuge (and why not into airline hostesses in Atlanta?) at no expense and at the drop of a hat. In other words, it means that in this ideal economy there are no frictions, losses, or costly, irreversible decisions, which is tantamount to

saying that time does not exist and that workers are capitalists (able to advance whatever money they need to get any training they may find advantageous, without any problem).

5. Rationality of production costs, especially of the price of labor, the "cost" and "price" of capital and the price of nonrenewable resources. This is all meaningless. Under the regime of private property, the price of nonrenewable resources (land, mines, and so on) is necessarily a monopoly price. The "price of labor" is undetermined and undeterminable by theory. In actual fact, it expresses the power relations (explicit and implicit) between employers and employees at the moment, and at the same time it reproduces the established structure of income distribution, which is to say, the unequal initial distribution of resources and conditions. In other words, labor power is not a commodity. The "cost of capital" (taken as the material set of instruments of production produced) is determined only as "historical cost," which is totally irrelevant in an economy where techniques change (the introduction of a new machine or a new product can annihilate the value of existing machines). Like any durable good, its "present value" is determined primarily by expectations as to its future value, which have nothing to do with any "production cost" whatsoever. Interest rates, in a capitalist economy, are an essentially monetary phenomenon (having nothing to do with any "return on capital" or with the "scarcity" of the latter) determined, on the one hand, by the policies of the central bank, and on the other by the expectations of the stock markets as to that very policy and as to other equally irrational phenomena, such as trends in prices.

6. Spontaneous achievement of equilibrium on the global marketplace; that is, use of productive resources to their full capacity. This is clearly not the case, and we know, at least since Keynes, why it cannot be.

If I talk, grossly, about ignoramuses, it is because most of the above has been known for a long time—actually, since the 1930s, with the work of Robinson, Chamberlin, Keynes, Kahn, Sraffa, Shackle, Kalecki, and others. It was pretty much generally acknowledged around the mid-1950s. A tremendous regression then began to take place, the same as in political philosophy. It may have been slightly less gratuitous in economics inasmuch as Keynesian regulation of overall demand raised other problems (and especially the problem of the chronic inflation generated by a sustained, long-term, high level of overall demand). This regression accompanied the Reagan-Thatcher attack on trade unions and wages. Thanks to it, those arrant liars, the Chicago boys, were able to trot out their stale ideas (actually, the quantitative theory of money), refuted long ago, the "experts" from the International Monetary Fund could put a few more nails in the coffin in which they were burying the poor countries, and Mr. Guy Sorman, in France, could become the apostle of an economic Enlightenment.

If we disregard these painful, pathetic, trivial episodes, the questions are basically far from trivial—from the purely theoretical standpoint, that is. To begin with, the economy does (also) have to do with "quantities," and economic "quantities" are not real quantities: they usually are not *measurable* because they are not mutually comparable. They become comparable conventionally (by second-degree institution, so to speak) and *after the fact*, ex post, as soon as approximately fixed rates of exchange are established, and in particular, when *money* is introduced. Money is the veil of pseudo-comparability draped over incomparable "objects." In a *static* economy, theoretical comparability might be arranged by reducing all inputs required for production to a single one, and in particular, for obvious reasons, to labor time (this, broadly speaking, is the opinion of classical writers beginning with Locke, and certainly Smith, up to Marx). But even this reduction has nothing to do with reality, for all sorts of reasons: work itself is not homogeneous; there are nonrenewable resources; and last, exchanges are mediated by prices that both reflect and achieve the distribution of surpluses (and of overall output) between workers and nonworkers as well as between various groups of workers, which distribution is only marginally determined by "economic factors" and primarily by the ceaseless, polymorphous struggle between the different parties. But second, the problem to be solved, even purely theoretically, does not apply to a static economy but to one in which techniques change (and so do "tastes," that is, the composition of the final demand). Now in this sort of economy, the technical coefficients of production—the relative amounts of goods required to produce a given object—change over time. (A change in a *single one* of them is enough to modify the entire picture.) Technically speaking, the matrix M, representing the economy (whose vectors correspond to the different productive activities and to the components of final demand) changes over time, t. A daring economics teacher with a degree in math might say: that's all right, we will say $M(t) = f(t)$. But that would be comical, of course, not only because the function f is unknown, but because the idea that one could know it is intrinsically absurd. Were we to know the function *f,* we would know what next year's technology will be and we could simply apply it immediately, and so on until time's end, in *saecula saeculorum.* But there is an even more serious flaw, if possible, in that technological change is not simply a change in the matrix of technical coefficients of production and of final demand: it involves changes in the very same linear space within which we would be attempting to formulate that matrix (which formulation, moreover, is practically impossible). To put it simply, every invention of a new product, tool, or production process means that new dimensions are added to the linear space of the economy, and that other, not necessarily "corresponding" ones, are eliminated. If our friend the daring teacher of mathematical economics then attempted to write: $S(t) = g(t)$, where S is the linear space and g another "function," he should definitely be fired because you cannot introduce a function without being able to give a minimal definition of the whole within which its values are taken, which in this case would be tantamount to claiming that one can define *all* possible technologies (at present or in a million years) *and* the law of their succession over time. To be even more straightforward, the reasons for which a real economy is not "rational" are for a large part the same as those for which there is no stringent "science of economics." If there were one, all economists, and economists only, would be infinitely rich.

That's not all. The entire construction of the so-called science of economics is necessarily predicated (including by Marx) on the idea of the feasibility of *separate imputation* of production costs (or of output, which amounts to the same thing) to production units and production factors. But any such separate imputation is theoretically completely fallacious. The overall product is the outcome of overall activity (and of all of previous history). The postulate of separability, and the corresponding imputation of "shares" of the product, is the pseudo-theoretical translation of the institution of private appropriation (Marx himself fell victim to that mystification).

It is the economic system *taken as a whole* (including its previous history) that produces goods, not any particular factory or worker. There is no economic topology, either discrete or continuous (I am obviously not talking about the physical universe underlying the economy and participating in it). It is *because* there is private appropriation that an accountancy boundary is drawn, indicating where a firm's "own" costs (and its "own earnings") stop. That boundary is fictitious from another viewpoint, if only because there are *externalities* (now being discovered, owing to environmental problems), costs borne by entities outside the firm and earnings for which the firm did nothing. To take an extreme but eloquent example, the "costs" and "profits" of a same factory, with exactly the same machines and personnel, will certainly not be the same depending on whether it is located in the Ruhr Valley or in Anatolia. And if modern factories can produce the way they do, it is *also* because there are the "external economies" made possible by all of previous history and the entire present human environment—free "gifts," not of "nature" but of the Western social-historical context, from which India, Africa, and even Russia have not benefited.

Every imputation decision is a *political* decision since it is simultaneously and ipso facto a decision as to *attribution*. The essential, never explicitly formulated, content of the political decision underlying the capitalist economy is the reproduction, broadly speaking, of the existing structure of the distribution of resources and of incomes (although not exactly of individual beneficiaries of that distribution). In a democratic society, the fundamental decisions as to imputation and attribution will have to be made explicitly and completely knowledgeably. I shall return briefly to this question below.[8]

To say that today's capitalist economy is "rational" is tantamount to saying that this applies to the micro level as well. Now, that micro level is the business enterprise, a hierarchical-bureaucratic structure brimful of contradictions and struggles, especially between order givers (*dirigeants*) and order takers (*exécutants*) (which actually do not oppose two distinct groups within the enterprise but cleave individuals themselves, most of the time). Marcel Gauchet wrote in the journal *Le Débat* that we are still awaiting a theoretician of the irrationality of bureaucracy. I hope that when that theoretician does appear, he will draw somewhat on the analysis I have been developing for the last forty years of the irrationality of both the overall political bureaucracy and workplace bureaucracies.[9] I also hope he will come in my lifetime, so I can see on what crucial points my own analyses fell short. I must say, however, in passing, how surprised I am to hear people get all excited about the bureaucratic management of the economy as a whole and seem to believe that the managerial bureaucracy of IBM, General Motors, Peugeot, Mitsubishi, or others is any different.

These contradictions and struggles within present-day enterprises result in what is diplomatically called "malfunctionings," for which the only solution found by capitalism is the increasing automation of production. But aside from the intrinsic problems raised by this automation (which cannot be discussed here, but are obvious, for example, in its most advanced sector: computer technology), it simply puts the problem off or transfers it to the not-yet-automated parts of enterprises or of the system as a whole.

Last of all, irrespective of whether it exists or not, economic "rationality" could never be anything but the "rationality" of a system of *means*, any judgment of which hangs on an assessment of the rationality of the ends achieved by these *means*. The allocation of productive resources in the capitalist system, and the organization of that system, are subordinated to an end that is neither "rational" nor simply reasonable: namely, the indefinite expansion of (pseudo-)rational (pseudo-)mastery, and concretely, the indefinite expansion of production, justified by the indefinite expansion of consumption it supposedly would allow. This brings us, finally, to the unlimited expansion of consumption as an end in itself, which is an absurdity. People who want to defend contemporary capitalist societies "philosophically" should defend its values "philosophically." Those values are absolutely unambiguous: one lives and dies to increase consumption. I would love to see a "philosopher" get up and say, we are on Earth to consume in ever-greater amounts, and to hear him try at least to defend that proposition, if not to ground it. But I don't see that anywhere. All I see is talk about "democracy" and the equalization of conditions, but not even a word about the question of which "conditions" are to be equalized.

There is of course a last line of defense, and it cannot be rejected straight off. In the last analysis, it is individual people themselves, in their vast majority, who want this regime and these orientations, or at least who do not reject them. I myself have emphasized this point repeatedly. But that is a statement of fact, not a political judgment, and it says nothing more than what we know about any regime: the regime is not separable from individuals, nor individuals from the regime. People are the products of the regime, which they constantly reproduce. Muslim societies produce Muslim individuals who reproduce Muslim societies. Soviet society produced Soviet men and women, who reproduced it—up to the point where that became impossible, and *even beyond that point* (look at present-day Russia). More generally speaking, no society can exist (lastingly) if it does not produce a modicum of support of its institutions and imaginary significations among most of its population. By this yardstick, societies are all "democratic," which is idiotic. None of them, moreover, could ever experience any *political* challenge to the established institution, nor *should* there be any since it would be "antidemocratic." This is nothing but a sophism designed to conceal the radical *conformism* of contemporary supporters of the established order.

In conclusion, a few words about the principles on which, in my opinion, any democratic organization of the economy should be based:

1. Autonomy for individuals is predicated on their sovereignty as consumers—and therefore on a true marketplace (with no monopolistic or oligopolistic situations and no manipulation of consumers).[10]

2. It also means they have collective decision-making power as producers, which implies self-management of units of production.

3. Private appropriation of unearned income of any sort is inadmissible.

4. Market prices should reflect the extent of relative demand and the "production costs" corresponding to the production level entailed by the demand for the particular product.

5. As we have seen, there is always something arbitrary in the way "production costs" are determined; such determination is necessarily based on conventions, the broad lines of which should therefore be set by explicit political decision of the collectivity.

6. The rules guiding these conventions are:

- One hour of work = one hour of work.

- The cost of utilization of a piece of equipment is equivalent to the present and foreseeable cost of its renewal divided by its expected duration plus, in some cases, a margin, the same for all kinds of equipment (see 7, below).

- Positive or negative externalities, to the extent that they are assignable, are imputed (in the form of taxes or bonuses) to the units that generate them.

7. The collectivity decides democratically how the consumable product is to be split up between overall private consumption and public consumption, as well as how the total net product is to be distributed between consumption as a whole and net investment. In other words, the collectivity decides whether or not it desires growth, and if so, the rate of that growth. This rate then becomes the margin (the "rate of profit," or "rate of interest" for Von Neumann, 1934) added to the cost of utilization

of the existing "capital." In a static economy, this "rate of profit" obviously can only be *nil*.

I do not contend that these rules are enough to solve every problem. They are simply what I view as the point of departure of any discussion of the issues involved in a democratic economy qua *economy*.

~

What are the prospects for the liberal oligarchic regime in affluent countries?

First of all, the continued existence of this regime postulates the continued presence of some natural conditions. It is true that fantastic economic expansion has taken place under capitalism, infinitely more impressive than what Marx's most lyrical praise of the progressive role of the bourgeoisie would have led us to suspect. The system is extremely efficient at producing, and its technological development is unprecedented. Nature—natural reserves of all sorts—was a necessary factor in the extension of that production. The fact is that the enormous productive and economic development of the last one hundred fifty years was made possible by the irreversible destruction (consumption) of natural or accumulated reserves, produced by the biosphere over hundreds of millions of years. This irremediable destruction is continuing. Right now, tropical forests and species of living beings are being destroyed. The measures taken or envisioned to end that destruction are ridiculously inadequate. So that, to speak of man's domination over the anthroposphere and the world created by it, as Marcel Gauchet did here, simply reproduces the old Cartesian-capitalist-Marxian illusion of man as master and possessor of nature, whereas man is more like a child who finds himself in a house with chocolate walls, and who sets out to eat them without understanding that the rest of the house is soon going to fall on his head.

Now, until further notice, this destruction is necessary for the survival of the system. The regime of liberal oligarchy, with the apathy and privatization that make it possible, presupposes that people really do spend their time in supermarkets and in front of their television sets. Those countries in which people are able to live that way represent something like 800 million people—which is to say about a seventh of the total global population of close to 5.5 billion. In the rich regions where the former live, the annual per capita GNP, measured conventionally, is somewhere around US$20,000. In the others, with their 4.7 billion people, the average GNP probably does not exceed five or six hundred dollars (there are much greater differences both between countries and between social strata here than in the former group; for a number of reasons, these figures simply indicate orders of magnitude). Now if, as I believe, there is effectively a link, not between democracy and capitalism but between the state of political debilitation thanks to which affluent societies manage to function more or less and the standard of living in the capitalist sense of the term, then the universalization of this "democracy" would require that the standard of living, thus defined, of the poor countries be brought up to par (within about 20, 30, or 50 percent) with the level in the affluent countries. In other words, the global annual production would have to be multiplied by about 200 (roughly, by 7 to account for the number of people and by 30 for the "standard of living"). By the same token, the annual rate of destruction of the natural world, the volume of pollutants and so on, would be multiplied by 200. Supposing that some magical operation could achieve that level, global production would have to continue to rise by 2 to 3 percent a year—that is, it would have to double about every thirty years. People whose goal is universal Western-style "democracy" and who look scornfully on "utopias" and "utopians" have to tell us how these challenges will be met.

But even more important, if possible, there are the anthropological requisites of the system. As capitalism developed, it irrevocably wore out a historical heritage created by earlier periods, and which it is unable to reproduce. This heritage includes, among other things, honesty, integrity, responsibility, conscientious work, respect for others, and so forth. Now, in a regime that constantly proclaims, in words and in deeds, that money is all that counts, and where the only sanction is meted out by the criminal justice system, why wouldn't judges put their decisions up for bids? There is a law against that, of course—but why should the people in charge of enforcing it be incorruptible? *Quis custodes custodeat?* Who keeps the keepers? What, in the logic of capitalism (or of modern-day "democratic individualism"), prevents an income tax inspector from taking bribes? Why should a teacher bother trying to get her pupils to learn when she can make a deal with the inspector? A first-rate mathematician, a university professor, earns somewhere around 16,000 francs in France and "produces" young mathematicians. Those of them who are aware of what goes on in the world (that is, almost all of them) won't go on in mathematics. They will go into computer science and be hired by a firm that will pay them maybe 30,000 francs as a beginning salary. Who do you think will become a mathematician in the next generation, then? According to the logic of the system, just about no one. One may say: there are always some inoffensive crackpots who prefer a beautiful mathematical demonstration to high pay. But I say that, precisely, according to the norms of the system, there should not be any such people. Their survival is a systemic anomaly, and the same is true of conscientious workers, honest judges, Weberian bureaucrats, and so forth. But how long can a system count exclusively on systemic anomalies to reproduce itself?

I will conclude with some "latest news items," that is, two surveys on American youth (in the June 29, 1990, issue of the *International Herald Tribune,* pages 1 and 5: "US Youth in 90's: The Indifferent Generation").

> John Karras, 28, was in a card shop the other day as the radio, which provides the sound track for his generation, offered a report on the dead and missing in the floods that had just flashed through southeastern Ohio. The cashier, who was a bit younger that Mr. Karras, looked up at the radio and said: "I'm sick of hearing about it." Mr. Karras, a doctoral student in education at Ohio State University, recalled the incident to illustrate what he called a "pervasive" attitude among the members of his generation toward the world. "Young people do not want to hear about it," he said, unless it's "knocking on their door."

> The findings of two national studies concur. The studies, one just released by the Times Mirror Center for the People and the Press and the other late last year, painted a portrait of a generation of young adults from 19 to 29 years old . . . that "knows less, cares less, votes less and is less critical of its leaders and institutions than young people in the past." Surveys by the Census Bureau reveal that since 1972 almost all of the decline in voting has been among those under 45, and that the sharpest drop is among voters between 18 and 25.

The article goes on to discuss the crisis in citizenship. Young people are only interested in issues that affect them personally, and those issues they care most about involve government interference with their personal freedom. When asked to define citizenship, one of the people interviewed answers: "It's the right not to be harassed by the police." (The implication behind this definition is obviously that the police can harass noncitizens—be they simple residents, illegal immigrants, or even tourists!—as much as it likes. So much for "human rights" and so forth.)

For my part, I could not dream of a better corroboration of my claim as to the negative, defensive character of freedom under the present regime. That is what freedom is, and that is how it is perceived by contemporary youth, and rightly so. The head of the *Times Mirror* survey has what I think is a perfectly accurate interpretation of these young people's attitudes. Unlike people from the previous generations, they are not so much disappointed or disillusioned as they are uninterested. For this generation, he says, the thirty-second TV commercial is the most appropriate medium. All of these young people constantly stress their "rights" and say nothing about their responsibilities. That reminds me of something a French philosopher said recently, to the effect that the fight for democracy was a combat for "more and more rights." Rights against whom?

What we have here is not the effects of a conspiracy of Corporate Capital or of the activity of the transnational firms. We have the whole system, people shaped by that system, what people become under this regime in affluent countries. And as shown by the example of former East Germany, the inhabitants of other countries all seem to long for one single thing: they want to find themselves in that same situation. We have the emergence of an anthropological type of individual (vaguely reminiscent of Roman citizens after the defeat of the Gracchi and until the end of the Empire) that has nothing to do with the anthropological type that created this regime, on the political or even the economic plane (Schumpeterian entrepreneurs have been replaced by managerial bureaucracies and financial speculators). These men and women could never have made the American or the French Revolution, or even do what the great figures of the industrial revolution did. Under these conditions, the continued self-reproduction of the system, and especially of its liberal components, is becoming increasingly problematic.

This raises some extremely serious questions about the future of the project of autonomy. It is no longer a matter of proving that the project is feasible, is not intrinsically incoherent, and does not run up against any impossibility. Because its achievement demands that human beings adopt an attitude radically opposed to the one described above, it is a matter of the desire and the capacity of those human beings to divest themselves of that condition, and to make something else emerge. The revolution required to do so is infinitely deeper and more difficult than taking the Winter Palace or winning a civil war.

The roots of the situation we are experiencing are to be found in the collapse of what replaced transcendent norms when society became de-Christianized and secular, rejecting any orientation based on those norms: the imaginary of progress, be it in its capitalist-liberal or its Marxist form, which only survives as a shell, emptied of any value-content, of any content that people might value unconditionally. This imaginary and the ideologies that turned it into common coin construed human history as a progression toward more and more freedom, more and more truth, more and more happiness. There was of course that *more and more*, both repulsive and laughable, but not of just anything: the *more* had to do with objects that everyone in society would agree to as valuable. What is left of it is the expanding consumption of just about anything and the now autonomized expansion of technoscience, which has replaced the religious beliefs of yesteryear. One wonders to what extent the superstitious attitude of contemporary mankind in the face of technoscience is sociologically different from the attitude of primitive peoples toward magic. The object is different, of course, but what about attitudes and modes of adherence? Do people know more about its assertions, the reasons behind those assertions, and why they believe them? Is there any difference in the effects of that mixture of hope and terror with which they contemplate it?

If this is the prevalent imaginary of humankind in the contemporary Western world, the rebirth of the project of autonomy requires tremendous changes, a real earthquake, not in terms of physical violence but in terms of people's beliefs and behavior. It involves a radical change in the representation of the world and of the place of human beings within the world. The representation of the world as the object of increasing mastery or as the backdrop for an anthroposphere must be destroyed. The world, with its chaotic, forever unmasterable dimension, will never be separable from the anthroposphere, and humankind will never master it. How could it, when man will always be unable to control the weft of the fabric underlying the succession of acts composing his own life? This grand, empty phantasm of mastery serves to counterbalance the grotesque accumulation of ridiculous gadgets. The two work together as distractions and entertainment, to mask the essential fact that we are mortal, to pervert our inherent inclusion in the cosmos and make us forget that we are the improbable beneficiaries of an improbable and very narrow range of material conditions making life possible on an exceptional planet that we are in the process of destroying.

The thrust and the affects corresponding to that representation must be destroyed as well: the thrust of limitless expansion of so-called mastery and the curious constellation of affects, the irresponsibility and insouciance, that goes with it. We must denounce *hubris* in ourselves and in those around us, and achieve an *ethos* of self-limitation and caution, accept our radically mortal nature so that we may at long last become as free as we can be.

What is at stake here, then, has nothing to do with tranquilly managing the prevailing consensus, extending the "spaces of freedom" millimeter by millimeter, or demanding "more and more rights." How this can be done is another matter. No great collective political movement can be created by the act of will of a few individuals. But as long as this collective hypnosis continues, there is a provisional ethical and political stance for those of us who have the weighty privilege of being able to speak up, namely: unmask, criticize, denounce the existing state of affairs. And for everyone: try to be exemplary in one's behavior and acts wherever one finds oneself. Whatever depends on us is our responsibility.

Psyché

§ 8 The Psychical and Social Roots of Hate

There may perhaps have been wars that solely mobilized "limited" aggressive drives, including for instance the minimum of aggression involved in self-defense. But what we have been witnessing for years now in Europe and Africa, as well as what happened in Europe and East Asia during the last world war, is an explosion of unlimited aggression, expressed through racism, indiscriminate murder of civilians, rape, destruction of monuments and homes, killing or torture of prisoners, etc. And what we know of human history compels us to think that twentieth-century innovations in this field mostly pertain to the quantitative dimensions and the technical instrumentations of the phenomena, or their articulations with the imaginary of the groups concerned rather than with their nature. Whatever the importance of other concomitant factors or conditions may be, it is impossible to understand the behavior of the people involved in these events unless we see in it the materialization of extremely strong affects of hate.

I will try to show here that there are two sources of hate, reinforcing each other: first, the fundamental drive of the psyche to reject (thus, to hate) that which is not itself; and second, the quasi-necessity of the *closure* of the social institution and the imaginary significations it bears.

The Psychical Root

"Hate is older than love," wrote Freud, and this is true if one takes love in the usual sense, as object love. But hate is not older than archaic, primordial love of "self," what is inadequately called "primary narcissism"—

the representational, affective, and desiring closure on itself of the original psychic nucleus, which I term the psychical *monad.*[1]

This self-closure had been glimpsed by Freud. He used Bleuler's word *autism* to characterize it and likened this primordial state of the human being, including the feeding function of the mother, to the fullness of a bird's egg.[2]

This closure becomes the matrix of meaning for the psyche. More precisely, what the psychical core will forever "understand" or "consider" as meaning is this "unitary" state, where "subject" and "object" are identical and where representation, affect, and desire are one and the same because desire is immediately representation (that is, psychical possession) of the desired and therefore affect of pleasure (which is the purest and strongest form of the omnipotence of thought). This is the meaning that the psyche will search after forever, which of course will never be fully attainable in the "real world," and for which the substitutes will be long chains of mediations—or unworldly "mystical" visions. Unless we understand this, we will never be able to understand why identification—to persons, to tasks, to collectivities, to significations, to institutions—is such a potent and omnipresent process in psychical life. Nor will we understand why society can play with the plasticity of the psyche almost without limits, on one condition only: that it supply meaning—rigorously speaking, substitutes for the original psychical meanings—to the subject in "real life."

From the moment (perhaps a theoretical or "ideal" limit) this primeval state of "psychical tranquility" (to use Freud's expression) is broken—as broken it must be if the infant is to survive—the initial "energy" of this self-love is split into three parts:

1. One part of it remains as self-cathexis of the core of the psyche, and its influence impregnates all the subsequent phases of psychical development of the subject and the corresponding strata of the mature personality.

2. Another part is transferred, in the form of *self,* to the breast: *Ich bin die Brust,* "I am the breast," is one of the last sentences Freud wrote.

3. A final part is transformed into hate of the "external world," which we have to take here as that which is external to the psychical monad, and thus *includes* the avatars of the developing psychical and somatic "reality-ego" (*Real-Ich*).

The first part (remanent self-love) accounts for the ineradicable egocentricity that, in a more or less thinly disguised way, dominates all our thoughts and deeds in the last instance. From another apparently unrelated point of view, this is the ontological egoism necessarily immanent to any being-for-itself. Everywhere and always, I am the origin of spatial and temporal coordinates, my here and now is *the* here and now, the world is my representation.

The other two parts become intermingled and entangled very quickly, whence the fundamental ambivalence of all affects, and to begin with, of the relation to the first separate love object, the mother. They become entangled because "the breast is so often missed by the child" (Freud). The absence of the breast amounts to a destruction of the closed totality of the *infans,* whence the collapse of the meaning of its world. Initially, this destruction is palliated by an imaginary creation, the hallucination of the breast. When the *infans* is no longer able to cover up the break in the closure of the original monad by means of this hallucination, it is left with a gaping hole in its world and reacts with rage and anguish. This hole, the absence of the breast, is absence of meaning, and here as always, the absence of meaning (or its destruction, actual or imminent, real or imagined) is a source of anguish. As the *infans* possesses the rudiments of an inductive intelligence—that is, as its imagination makes something out of repetition or regularity—a link is quickly established between the hole and the memory of the object that "normally" fills it: the habitual becomes normal because it corresponds to the desire. The character or value of this object is split into two contradictory attributes, the good breast (which is present) and the bad breast (which is absent). These attributes, like the affects and desires accompanying them—briefly speaking, love and hate—are subsequently transferred to the image that has been linked with the breast, the mother as an entity or person. This becomes the matrix of the ambivalence that will henceforth be inherent in all of the subject's relationships.

But there is an additional and more important point. The result of the process of maturation/socialization is the formation of the social individual, in itself an almost alien and strange "object" from the point of view of the monadic core of the psyche. (In Freudian terms, the *Real-Ich,* the reality-ego, presents all the attributes contradictory to those of the *Lust-Ich,* the pleasure-ego.) It thus becomes at the same time the support of a transfer of self-love, which will allow it to survive, and the object of hate of the "unreal" psychical agencies—hate that, as already mentioned, burdens everything that is "external" to the psychical core. The reality-ego cannot escape being the object of ambivalent affects. Usually, love of this ego prevails sufficiently over the hate of which it is the object to ensure the survival of the subject within reality. But hate of the ego goes on living in the psychical depths, almost silently.

We thus have, from the psychoanalytical point of view, two vectors of hate. The first, hate of the "real other," is simply the reverse side of the positive cathexis of self. It is sustained by a powerful and elementary sophism, which is also present in the collective forms of hatred or contempt and is perhaps more easily perceived in the latter: I am good; (the) good is me; she is not me; she is not good (or is less good than me). I am French (American, British, etc.); to be French (American, British, etc.) is to be good; she is not French (American, British, etc.); therefore, she is not good.

The second vector is self-hate, for the ego is one of the first strangers encountered by the psyche. This is also one of the meanings of Rimbaud's *Je est un autre*, "I is an other," a meaning not at all different from its apparent, prima facie meaning. The I, essentially a social construct, is no more "me" than any neighbor or passer-by. Contrary to what seems to be generally believed, this self-hatred is universal. Clearly, this form of hate (or more accurately, the subject carrying it) can only survive if it is severely tamed and/or displaced toward truly "external" objects. Through this displacement, the subject can maintain the affect while changing its object. This process is clearly visible in the phenomenon of racism, to which I will return below.

The Social Root

The link between the psychical and the social roots, in the case of hate as in all others, is the socialization process imposed on the psyche, through which the psyche is forced into society and "reality" while society takes care, more or less well, of the paramount need of the psyche: the need for meaning.

The *infans* may die, or, much more frequently, be socialized. This socialization leans on a biological need (hunger) but also, much more strongly, on the psychical need for meaning. Neither of these needs is absolutely insurmountable: anorexia and autism demonstrate, in this case also, the afunctional and asocial nature of the psyche. The psychical need for meaning, once the initial monadic closure is broken, has to be satisfied by the environment of the *infans*—an environment made up of already socialized individuals, who cannot convey anything but the meanings they themselves have already absorbed and cathected. To be socialized means first and foremost to cathect the existing institution of society and the imaginary significations this institution is carrying. Gods, spirits, myths, totems, taboos, kinship, sovereignty, law, citizen, state, justice, commodity, capital, interest, and reality constitute such imaginary significations. Reality is obviously an imaginary signification, and its specific content for each society is heavily codetermined by the imaginary institution of that society.

This meaning-giving dimension of the social institution is clearly more than multifaceted and extraordinarily complex; it is, in fact, the creation of a world, of this society's world. One of its main dimensions is of course language. Language is not an "instrument of communication," as if there existed ready-made and fully formed "individuals" eager to "communicate" and lacking only an "instrument" for that purpose. Language is the element within which "objects," "processes," "states," "qualities"—and various kinds of relations and links among them—are established.

What interests us here is the intrinsic reasons for which this institution of each society has up until now almost inevitably taken the character of *closure* of various types. There is thus always a "material" closure, in the sense of more or less well-determined territories or borders, and/or, in all cases, thoroughly restrictive definitions of the individuals belonging to that particular society. But the most important closure is the *closure of meaning*. Territories and all the rest only acquire their importance because of the specific significations attributed to them: the Promised Land, or the sacred character of territory for the Greek *poleis* and, in general, the strident character of border disputes everywhere. This, as we will see, is also true of individuals: a *stranger* [*étranger*] is so because she is a bearer of foreign, always necessarily meaning *strange*, significations [*significations étrangères et étranges*]. Yet a signification can only be nonstrange if it is positively cathected. In the previous sentence, one can simply replace the term *nonstrange* by the term *familiar* to see that it is in fact a tautology.

The metaphor of open and closed societies has been in use for some time already. But here I am sticking as closely as possible to the mathematical sense of the term *closure*.[3] A world of meanings is closed if any question capable of being formulated within it either has an answer in terms of given meanings, or is posited as meaningless. Thus the worlds of archaic or traditional societies are closed, whereas the ancient Greek world or the modern European world (European in the broad sense of the term) is more or less open.

Almost all known societies have instituted themselves by means of and within a closure. They have created for themselves a metaphysical niche of meaning, which is tantamount to saying that they have been religious, or that they have been heteronomous in the sense that they cover up the fact of their self-institution, and instead attribute their institution to an extrasocial source. I cannot develop here the reasons for which these two characterizations are more or less equivalent.[4] Suffice it to say that these traits correspond to two constitutive elements of a heteronomous society: first, the "need" or "necessity" for an extrasocial (extrainstitutional) foundation and guarantee of the institution; and second, the "need" or "necessity" to make it impossible to call the institution into question, that is to stop any discussion about ultimate foundations by contending that it rests on something beyond the ken of living humans.

During and by virtue of the very process of their socialization, individuals must cross over from an initial meaning coextensive with their own psychical, private sphere (monadic meaning) to shared, social meaning. As already implied above, monadic meaning is completely alien to what we consider meaning to be in waking life. It knows not time and contradiction, any more than distinction, separation, and articulation. Through a series of concentric circles—family, kin or clan, locality, age group, social group or class, nation, "race," and so on—the subject's world of meaning is gradually enlarged. This goes together with an extended and more or less strong identification with these larger units. (That these identifications can sometimes be antinomic has supplied tragedy with a recurrent theme.)

All this is, or ought to be, quite well known. What needs to be stressed is the consequences for the psychical organization of the individual. All the identificatory bearings of the individual are part and parcel of the instituted world of social significations, essential components of which are, of course, those referring to the various collective instituted entities of which the individual is a member or an element. Consider the expression, "I am the son of X." What a son is—beyond the simple biological fact of procreation that, moreover, is initially unknown and at any rate always uncertain—and what he has to do qua son; who and what X is and the very idea of an "I" and an "am," have no meaning whatsoever outside the socially instituted world of signification in general and the specific significations peculiar to the society being considered. A Roman son from 500 BCE and an American son of today have very little in common, for obvious reasons: the closer we are to a completely closed, archaic society, the stronger this identification is. There are well-known cases of "savages" who died just because well-meaning Europeans insisted on taking them far from their tribe and their gods. And it is also well known that most of the time this identification supersedes self-preservation. To kill and be killed in a family vendetta, in tribal conflicts, in feudal warfare, in national wars—*pro patria mori* in all its versions—is a universal fact, an obligation that societies impose on their members and that these members always and everywhere proudly and gladly accept, except in a small geographical area and during recent historical times in some modern societies.

For the psyche, meaning is identical with the indivisibleness of its initial totality. The breaking up of this totality is only possible if substitutes of self and substitutes of meaning are continuously supplied to the psyche. This is the identification process, through which quanta of psychical cathexis, taken from the initial cathexis of the self, are initially transferred to the immediate objects and subsequently to the various forms of instituted collectivities as well as to the significations that sustain them. In a manner that has perhaps become incomprehensible to some "individuals" in modern societies, the savage *is* his tribe, the fanatic *is* his church, the national *is* his nation, the member of an ethnic minority *is* this minority—and vice versa.

Evidently, this identification with collectivities also offers a substitute for the lost omnipotence of the psychical monad. The individual can feel that it partakes of the actual power of five thousand or fifty million other people. On the front, both sides share the common illusion that "we shall win because we are stronger." This identification also induces the suspension of guilt and inhibition that makes possible the unrestricted deployment of murderous destructiveness in war, but frequently also in mobs, as has long been observed. It is as if in such moments, without knowing it, individuals were recovering the certainty that the source of the institution is the anonymous collective, capable of positing new rules and lifting old prohibitions.

Outcomes

There are, as stated previously, two psychical expressions of hate: hate of the other; and self-hatred, the latter in general not appearing as such. But we must understand that both have a common root, the refusal of the psychical monad to accept what is *foreign* and *strange* for it: the socialized individual whose form it has been forced to adopt, and social individuals, whose coexistence it has been obliged to accept (an existence always less real than its own existence for itself, and therefore also much more easily *expendable*). This ontological structure of the human being imposes insurmountable constraints on any form of social organization and any political project, which cannot be discussed here. Suffice it to say that it irrevocably discredits any idea of a "transparent" society as well as any political project aiming at an immediate, universal reconciliation and claiming to short-circuit institutions.[5]

During the process of socialization, the two dimensions of hate, or at least some of their more dramatic manifestations, are significantly tamed. In part, this is achieved through a permanent diversion of the destructive tendency toward more or less "constructive" social ends: the exploitation of nature, various forms of interindividual competition (potlatch, "pacific" agonistic activities such as athletic or other games, economic and political competition and rivalry for prestige, intrabureaucratic infighting, etc.), or much more simply, ordinary intersubjective malevolence. In all known societies, all these outlets channel a part of the hate and of "available" destructive energy—but never the whole of it.

Yet up until now, this channeling seems to have been possible only if the remaining part of hate and destructiveness was kept, as it were, in a reservoir, ready to be turned into formalized and institutionalized destructive activities against other collectivities—that is, into war—at regular or irregular intervals. This is not to say that psychical hate is the "cause" of wars; it is not a question we need to discuss here. Clearly, one finds various types of war in history—from the Germanic or Mongol invasions up to the "lace wars" of the eighteenth century, not to mention civil wars—for which hate is not the primary source. Yet hate is certainly not only a necessary condition for war, but it is an essential one. I call a condition *essential* when it maintains an intrinsic relationship with that which it conditions. "Let victory in this war rest with those who fought it without loving it": André Malraux's sentence in *The Walnut Trees of*

Altenburg expresses a wish contradicted by the reality of almost all wars. Otherwise, one would not understand how it was possible for millions and millions of people throughout the entire known history of the human species to be ready, at the drop of a hat, to kill unknown people and be killed by them. And when the resources of this reservoir of hate are not actively mobilized they rampantly manifest themselves under the guise of contempt, xenophobia, and racism.

Parenthetically, let it be noted here that psychoanalysts often speak superficially about the taboo on murder. Truthfully, only intraclan murder is clearly and exclusively intended by the Freudian myth in *Totem and Taboo*. It is also the only type of murder that is socially sanctioned, whereas murder during war or in the course of a vendetta glorifies the killer.

The fatal conjunction here is that the destructive drives of individuals fit admirably with the quasi-necessity for the institution of society to close itself up, to reinforce the position of its own laws, values, rules, meanings as uniquely excellent and truthful by asserting that the laws, creeds, gods, norms, and customs of others are inferior, false, wrong, disgusting, abominable, diabolic. And this, in turn, is in complete harmony with the needs of the identificatory organization of the individual psyche. For the latter, what is outside the circle of significations it has so painfully cathected along the road to its socialization is inferior, wrong, meaningless. And for it, these significations are coextensive with the instituted collectivity (and network of collectivities) to which the individual belongs: clan, tribe, village, nation, religion. Conflicts among these various poles of reference are certainly possible, but we also know that they arise much less frequently in archaic environments than in modern ones. At any rate, what must be clearly understood, as the basis for all the rest, is that roughly speaking and in principle, any threat to the paramount instituted collectivities to which individuals belong is experienced by them as more serious than a threat against their own lives.

As said above, these characteristics can be observed with the greatest intensity and purity in fully closed societies: in archaic and traditional ones, but even more, in modern totalitarian societies. The cardinal fallacy is always: our norms are good; the good is our norms; their norms are not our norms; their norms are not good; or our God is true; truth is our God; their God is not our God; their God is not a true God. It has always seemed almost impossible for human collectivities to consider alterity as just that—otherness—as well as to consider other people's institutions as neither superior nor inferior, but simply as other institutions, and in fact, mostly incomparable to their own.

To sum up an argument I have already formulated elsewhere,[6] a society's encounter with others in general opens up three possibilities of evaluation: these others are superior, equal, or inferior to us. Were we to accept their superiority, we would have to renounce our own institutions and adopt theirs.[7] If they were equal, to be a Yankee rather than a Crow Indian, a Christian rather than a pagan, would be a matter of sheer indifference. Both entail, or seem to entail, that the individual abandon his own identificatory bearings; that he abandon, or at least call into question, his own identity so dearly acquired during the process of socialization. Therefore, only the third possibility remains: the others are inferior. To be sure, this excludes the possibility that they may be equal in the sense that their institutions and ours would be, prima facie and in toto, incomparable. It is not difficult to see why the emergence of such a view is historically improbable. It would lead to accept in others what is abominable for us—something that is in principle impossible for any religious society. Even in the case of "secularized" cultures, this may sometimes raise questions that are insoluble at the strictly theoretical level: what does one do when faced with societies that do not recognize human rights, inflict cruel penalties on their members, or practice customs that are simply horrifying to our eyes (for instance, excision and infibulation of women)? Attaining the idea of a possible incomparability of cultures is only possible for a society in which, regardless of the degree of adherence to its own institutions, a first internal dehiscence (cleavage) has already appeared, making it possible to distance oneself from that which is instituted.

That is why the movement toward the recognition of this essential alterity starts at the same time and with the same deep motivations as the movement toward a break in the closure of meaning—that is, the calling into question of the given institution of society, the end of full heteronomy, the freeing of thoughts and deeds; in sum, the birth of democracy and philosophy.

From that time onward, the idea that others are neither wicked nor inferior begins to make its way (in Homer, Herodotus, Montaigne, Swift, Montesquieu, etc.). It would be both tempting and encouraging to be able to say that the opening up of thought and the partial and relative democratization of Western political regimes have advanced in step with the decline of chauvinism, xenophobia, and racism. But even leaving aside the terrifying explosions of racist and xenophobic barbarism in the twentieth century, one could only accept such a statement with many strong qualifications. In particular, we should reflect on the extreme virulence of the resurgence of nationalism, xenophobia, and racism during the present century in "civilized" and "democratic" countries. As for the non-Western world, the appalling contemporary situation speaks for itself.

One must add that the unfathomable multiplicity and heterogeneity of the historical forms of institutions defies any simple scheme of understanding. Hostility toward strangers covers practically the whole spectrum of possibilities, from immediate murder up to the most generous hospitality. *Xenia* was common to all Greeks, but the Lacaedemonians had instituted *xenelasia,* entailing the expulsion of strangers after a minimal stay.[8] But it must be added that this instituted attitude and the goodwill it entails refer *exclusively* to foreign *individuals* and never to their institutions as such, only to foreigners "passing through" and almost never to those residing permanently. (Multiethnic empires are in a class by themselves, for obvious reasons: in this case, the central authority usually imposes tolerance of subjected minorities—which, as we well know, has not prevented pogroms against Jews and massacres of Armenians.)

My entire discussion up to this point provides an account of the exclusion of the external other. It is not sufficient to "explain" why this exclusion turns into discrimination, contempt, or confinement, and may finally explode into rampant hatred, rage, and murderous folly. Considering the varied and extreme forms such behavior can take, as well as the acute explosions of it during specific moments in history, I do not think there can be a general "explanation"; only historical investigations can make partial sense of the extraordinary diversity of historical facts. Yet this comprehension requires that we be able to recognize and correctly gauge the extraordinary quantity of hatred contained in the psychical reservoir, which the social institution has proved unable or unwilling to divert toward other objects.

Nevertheless, one particular factor can be mentioned in relation to the massive explosions of national and racial hate during the modern period. In capitalist societies, almost all significant intermediate collective bodies have been dissolved, and with them the possibilities of alternative identifications for individuals. This has certainly produced defensive identificatory stress and strain around the entities of "religion," "nation," or "race," along with immensely exacerbated misoxeny in the broadest sense of the word. The situation is not essentially different in non-Western societies, which are subjected to the frontal onslaught of modernity, and thus to the pulverization of their traditional identificatory bearings—to which they react by increased religious and/or national fanaticism.

A final remark on racism. It is astonishing that, as far as I know, the principal and defining characteristic of racism, immediately visible to the naked eye, has been overlooked by writers on the subject. That characteristic is the *essential inconvertibility* of the other. Any religious fanatic would gladly accept the conversion of infidels; any "rational" nationalist would rejoice at the annexation of foreign territories and the "assimilation" of their inhabitants. Not so the racist. German Jews would have been content—or at least most of them would have accepted and demanded—to remain citizens of the Third Reich, but the Nazis would have none of it. It is precisely because in the case of racism the object of hate must remain *inconvertible* that the racist imaginary has to invoke or to invent the existence of would-be physical (biological), that is, irreversible characteristics in the objects of its hatred: the color of the skin and facial features are the most appropriate support [*étayage*] of this hate, for they supposedly would mark the irreducible strangeness of the object and eliminate all risk of its being confused with the racist. Hence, also, the particularly strong repulsion against cross-breeding, which would blur the borders between the pure and the impure, thereby demonstrating to the racist that it would take very little for him to find himself on the other side of the barrier of hate. Finally, it would certainly be justified to link this extreme form of hate of the other to the most obscure, most somber, and most repressed aspect of hate: self-hatred.

Heteronomy and hatred of the other have one common root: the quasi-"need" or "necessity" for the closure of meaning, arising from the intrinsic tendencies of the institution and from the singular psyche's search for ultimate certainties, leading to extremely strong identifications with hermetically closed bodies of belief shared and supported by real collectivities. Autonomy—that is, full democracy—and acceptance of the other are not the natural inclination of humanity. Both face the same tremendous obstacles. We know from history that up until now the fight for democracy has been marginally more successful than the fight against chauvinism, xenophobia, and racism. But for those who are committed to the only reasonably defensible political project, the project of universal freedom, the only way open is to continue this uphill struggle.

§ 9 Psyche and Education

JACQUES ARDOINO—Our journal, *Pratiques de formation,* is publishing an issue on multireferentiality. We would like to take this opportunity to question you about the issues of education and the shaping of subjects, and to put your own theory of the imaginary and the psyche to the test on this theme.

RENÉ BARBIER—I personally have the feeling that one major point is not broached in that theory, and perhaps rightly so. It is the question of what the Oriental tradition calls meditation—that is, a state of being, a state of consciousness, which is not "consciousness of" something, achieved through personal experience. In the ultimate phases of this meditation, there is both extreme alertness and absence of representation. There is neither concept nor image. In this zone of the psyche the imaginary would be "silent," so to speak. This would contradict your conception of psychic life as the continuous, uninterrupted flow of images, shapes, figures, and so on. What are your thoughts on that?

CORNELIUS CASTORIADIS—I am somewhat familiar with Oriental philosophy, although insufficiently, but I am totally incompetent as to Oriental meditation practices. . . . I do not think anyone can discuss the subject without having some personal experience of those practices. But even then, one wonders to what extent people who have gone through this type of experience are able to talk about them correctly. Aside from what one might call a borderline state (not in the psychiatric sense of the term), and even then, I don't see how a mental state could be anything but a flow of

representational-emotional-intentional material. What do we know about
these borderline states? There are those fleeting milliseconds of orgasm,
what the ancients called "little death," *petite mort,* translated by Lacan
as a "fading" of the subject: a momentary "disappearance" of the usual
subject, an evanescent moment, beyond words. In the Western tradition,
there are mystic "experiences": perhaps everyone can go through similar
experiences (what Romain Rolland and Wilhelm Reich call the "oceanic
feeling," which, as we know, Freud claimed never to have known). As a
first approximation, we may say that these are states with no representation and no intention, although not without affect. I don't know what an
Eastern meditator familiar with our conceptions would have to say about
that. As far as I am concerned, this description seems inadequate. These
states are much more suggestive of regression toward the initial monadic
state of the psyche, toward a sort of primal, undifferentiated state, a lack
of differentiation between oneself and the other, between affects, representations, and desires, essentially characterized by a striving for perpetual, identical continuation, for the permanency of that particular "being."
As you know, that is how I see the initial, originary state of the human
psyche, inasmuch as we are able to reconstruct it—or postulate it—by going back in time, taking the basic observable features of the psyche as our
starting point. But this is only possible precisely because the psyche has
always already partially broken out of that state.

This is what I think is to be found, in an impure form, mixed with
"ideas" about the presence of an other (Christ, God, etc.) in the Western
mystical writings with which I am familiar (those of Saint Theresa, Saint
John of the Cross, and others). We should probably also compare this
with the phenomenon of the trance, on which I must admit I am incompetent as well, and for which we should consult our friend Lapassade. But
it seems probable that what is involved, once again, is the re-merging of
elements, usually distinct in mental life, and which tend to return to their
"primordial unity." The closest analogy I can find in my own experience
is what happens when I listen to music—not just any music of course.
One gets completely absorbed, so to speak, in something outside one's self
(this, actually, is the original meaning of the word emotion: *ex motus*). But
here again, it is in a flow of representations and affects that one is caught
up. Auditory representations, no doubt, which have the extraordinary
peculiarity of being both completely distinct (the more one knows the
piece in detail, the more one loses oneself in it) and constantly merging

with each other, both vertically and horizontally. But there are also affects, even though they betray their object as soon as we try to name them. For, contrary to popular beliefs, music does not "express" or "represent" any otherwise known affects; it creates them. Here we have a meaning that is not discursive (which is why verbal remarks on the "content" of music are usually inane). There is also desire, close perhaps to the desire for a state of nirvana (see Schopenhauer, Wagner, etc.): a desire for that to go on forever—but which is achieved, nonetheless, at least in Western classical music, in and by movement and a balance between change and repetition (the process is different in flamenco and gamelon music). That is probably what comes closest, for a westerner like me, to the states to which you are referring. But once again, a priori, and until proved otherwise, I cannot believe those people who claim that at the extreme peaks of meditation representation no longer exists. If this were the case I do not see how they could talk about it afterward, or even remember it.

R.B.—The people who experience that type of state of consciousness do not talk about it in terms of representations, I think, but rather, they refer to a state of consciousness that is not "consciousness of" something. In the last analysis, what we are probably dealing with here is philosophical postulates.

C.C.—They speak about it.

R.B.—Yes, they do, afterward. But they do not talk in terms of representations, except those who have had visions, and so forth. But that is something else. I am not talking about ecstatic visions. . . .

C.C.—But if they talk about it, that means that even at the most acute point in that experience they perceived, in the vaguest sense of the term, something that was there and at the same time that was themselves.

J.A.—One thing about which we are certain, if I understand you properly, is that there is, at the least, an intention or even a will, for that state of meditation can only be reached by deliberate asceticism. An effort is made to reach that state, or to return to it.

C.C.—An effort at excluding all the rest.

J.A.—There is also intentionality when a person talks about it afterward since there is a will to signify something to someone, which is to say to account for or at least to say something about that experience. So the intentional element is clear. But I wonder, then, whether there isn't something that has to do with a search that we are obliged to call regressive (the word *regressive* is not necessarily used in a pejorative sense), that is, returning to the mother, ultimately to the primal undifferentiated state. In the case of meditation, asceticism, and a spiritual quest, that regression is deliberate, yielding something else. It is out of the question to reduce it to the purely regressive aspect, in the original sense of the term, but still and all, something of that order is involved.

c.c.—Yes, except that I would not bring in the mother: the monadic state is a state prior to the mother, like there is a state before what psychoanalysis calls the part object, as a separate object.

j.a.—But can there be a memory of the monadic state?

c.c.—There is no memory, conscious or even unconscious. That is what I tried to say in chapter 6 of *The Imaginary Institution of Society,* inasmuch as it can be put in words. The monad is not repressed, it is prior to repression; but if we do not postulate a monadic state, all the rest of the history of the psyche remains incomprehensible. Where, for instance, does the magical "omnipotence of thought" come from? First of all, it is absolutely not "magical." Freud calls it magical because he is thinking about reality, but it is real. We are not talking about the reality of the subway, of course; we are talking about the only reality that interests psychoanalysis, to begin with—that is, psychic reality. The unconscious may forge, and actually does forge, the phantasm that satisfies a desire. In this respect, the psyche truly is omnipotent. What is the origin of that omnipotence? Then we say that at a certain point the infant ascribes that omnipotence to its mother. But how can an infant produce a schema of omnipotence? Where does it find it? It finds it within itself, and it operates a projection. Here we have a fundamental feature of the subject's radical imagination: the subject can only perceive the world, at the outset, as itself. We should not even say *as in its power* since that implies some differentiation, but as itself, infinitely pliable to what it "desires," although the word itself is abusive, for there is no distinction at this stage between desired and represented.

Some potent remnants of that state are to be found even in adult individuals. Why must there be that hard schooling in reality, to distinctiveness, and differentiation? Why is it so intolerable that an other is truly other and not simply another exemplar of oneself? And where do we get that mania, that rabid need for unification that we find in politics as well as in philosophy? The monad exists before the fused state that is the extension of the baby's need to see the entire world as itself. That view is already present, in fact, in Freud's phrase in his last notes, in 1939: *Ich bin die Brust,* "I am the breast." What can that mean? That I am the breast and the breast is me—that there is no difference. Only later is the breast perceived as belonging to someone else, who does what she likes with it; but because that other, too, must be a part of the world of the self, the world of the subject, the baby tries to establish a fused state with its mother. We still have powerful echoes of that in adult love. In act 2 of *Tristan and Isolde,* Tristan says "Isolde is no more," and Isolde answers, "Tristan is no more." The two lovers, and the listener as well, are absorbed in that fantastic music, a music of copulation both in the most elementary and in the most philosophical sense of the word, a merging of two parts, previously separated but belonging to each other.

The monadic state precedes any differentiation from the mother, and therefore any fusion with the mother, since fusion presupposes the existence of two separate things.

R.B.—Does that mean that you make no distinction whatsoever between the experience of a baby and the experience of someone whose psyche is as elaborate as that of Krishnamurti?

C.C.—I make a fundamental distinction. I say that Krishnamurti, by dint of asceticism, or of efforts, or of I don't know what, succeeds in reproducing a state that is obviously not the same as the baby's state, since he conceives that state as a merging with the whole of being and the abolition of distinctions, whereas this is all meaningless for the baby. Only someone who conceives of differentiation is able to conceive the abolition of every differentiation. This is obviously not the same state as the baby's, but one cannot avoid talking about it in the same terms. I am the whole, the whole is me, all differences are abolished—but Krishnamurti has a representation of all that, retrospectively.

Now, once representation ceases to be that unintelligible, unrepresentable monadic state, it always implies multiplicity and differentiation. At the least, it implies one figure. But it implies much more than that. Now if we begin to consider what that much more is, we realize that we cannot account for it in terms of ensidic (that is, ensemblistic-identitary) logic. For example, there is no saying how many elements that multiplicity contains. We are sitting here, and each of us has a perception, and more than one perception. If we try to enumerate the "elements" contained in our perception, we immediately discover that that is impossible. That eludes set theory, algebra does not apply, topology does not apply. Where are our boundaries? We are talking. I am here, you are there, I am speaking to you. My words enter your ears and you think about some things. What relation do those things have with what I am saying? They are certainly not the strict reproduction and repetition of what I say; you are thinking them and thinking something else to yourself at the same time. But the state you are in is not the same as if you were alone and didn't hear me, and the same is true for me. There is no boundary, then, no topology. Nor are there any order relations either. No logical-mathematical structure applies here, substantially. But there is some differentiation nonetheless.

Whereas in the monadic state there is no differentiation: I am everything, I am being itself, being is me, and I am pleasure, pleasure is me. Of course all this is being said in our adult language, but it is experienced as exactly the same—what is me, what is everything.

FLORENCE GIUST-DESPRAIRIE—Couldn't the fact that growing numbers of people look to spiritual experiences be seen as a protest against an increasingly atomized, fragmented, unbearable world? If so, they would be attempting to discover, to rediscover something else through those experiences of unity. . . .

C.C.—I definitely think so. What has been abusively, exaggeratedly called the revival of religion is of that order, but so is the [popular] Zénith music hall. What we have been seeing for the last thirty years or so, those huge music halls where the music can never be deafening enough, inevitably brings to mind those states of near trance, of loss of identity, a lack of differentiation from others, and a pseudounification and pseudosignification, attempting to reach beyond signification. People live in the instant, feel penetrated by the music, the sheer amount of decibels is a sort of real violation of one's physical integrity, bodies mix in a diffuse sexual encounter, joints circulate—but that is not important. These are all things on which to lean [étayages], through which to return to a situation that seems to achieve a total meaning and at the same time precedes any articulated meaning. I agree with you that attempts to do Oriental meditation are very much the same thing in individuals who despair in this depersonalized, privatized Western world.

R.B.—Your interpretation of the phenomenon is sociological. I would like to get back to the nature of the phenomenon. You say that the baby is in a monadic state. If I understand you correctly, that monadic state is, so to speak, the unconscious taking into account of the state of chaos, in the sense of what you refer to as the chaos/abyss/bottomlessness.

C.C.—It's not the same thing.

R.B.—What's the difference? What relationship do you see between that monadic state of the *infans* and chaos/abyss/bottomlessness?

C.C.—The chaos/abyss/bottomlessness is what is behind or under every concrete existent, and at the same time it is the creative force—what we would call the *vis formandi* in Latin—that causes the upsurge of forms, organized beings. The singular human being is a fragment of that chaos, and at the same time a fragment or an agency of that *vis formandi*—that force, in other words, the creativity of being as such. Both aspects are found in the subject's radical imagination: the monadic form is precisely that, what we adults would express by saying, "I am everything."

J.A.—The monadic state. "I am everything" is pantheistic, at that point, and that is funny, in fact, because it is always Leibniz who comes to mind of course, but we should also look to Spinoza.

C.C.—The monad's "I am everything" means: everything is me, nothing is outside of me. Whereas that is not the case for a true pantheist: everything is God, God is everywhere, I am a fragment of that whole/God, etc., and I may possibly gain access to that whole, through knowledge of a third kind for example. But the state I am trying to describe is really what Leibniz would have called the windowless monad, except of course that there is no preestablished harmony, no harmonious integration of all monads in an overall symphony, the monad's "perception" is a perception of the self, its conatus is directed toward itself and is in no way harmonized with that of other monads. That stays with us forever, even as adults: "You are alone in death." Even a great philosopher is always the center of the world in his own eyes: the world will end, irrevocably, for the self; one plunges into absolute darkness, even with the knowledge that "it will go on."

J.A.—But the monad also contains everything.

C.C.—No, the monad contains that thrust toward the unification of the whole, and that, ultimately, is what later enables it to hold together, in one sense, what would otherwise be a sort of absolute dispersal. Let us take a look at what happens to an infant—to a living being in general, actually. All sorts of things happen: sensory stimuli, internal bodily pain, sensations of hunger, "shadows" moving around—shadows that gradually, fitfully turn into "objects," into a "breast," then a "mother," and so on. All that has to be held together and can be held together, first, and to begin with (and in fact, at the end), only: (a) because the life of that being is subjected to the absolute necessity that it hold together (in adult language, that it be meaningful), and (b) because it has the capacity to do so—to hold it all together—in some fashion. We come back to the interrogations of philosophy from another angle. When Kant, in his "Deduction of Categories," said, "the *I think* is the principle of the transcendental unity of apperception," he saw the adult, cognitive segment of the issue. But the "principle" of any subjective life is, "I am the whole." Subjective life, to begin with, refers everything to itself. The world is my representation (and my mood, and the infinitely pliable material of my desire). This must be abandoned to enter adult life. At the start, "words" have the meaning I give them (and this is residually true to the end). We must laboriously learn that words have a socially set meaning, and that we cannot make them say anything we like. The infant who begins to take possession of words takes the same point of view as Humpty Dumpty in *Alice in Wonderland:* words mean what I want them to mean.

J.A.—So by the same token, the monad is timeless.

C.C.—In the sense that it is unaware of time. Freud says that about the unconscious, but when he says that the unconscious does not know time and does not know contradiction, his formulation is exaggerated. That may be said of the monad, but it cannot be said of the Freudian unconscious, which does not know ordinary time, social daytime, but it clearly does develop a time of its own. A dream unfolds in a dream time and it creates, it brings into being, a dream time. The dream has its own time frame, just as there is a time frame specific to the unconscious, more generally speaking. It is not the same as "our" time frame as socialized adults. Noon may come before 9 o'clock: that doesn't matter; there is a before and an after.

J.A.—But as a unifying force it is timeless, whereas representation is necessarily within a time frame.

C.C.—Definitely.

J.A.—And by the same token representation is plural.

C.C.—Definitely.

J.A.—Which brings us to multireferentiality.

C.C.—The radical imagination gives rise to its time, which is its own specific time, and its space, which is a specific space. I am always, to this day, the origin of the coordinates. The zero point of axes x, y, and z is always me, here and now. It is in the social sense that all those origins are referred and integrated in a social "origin"—the first Olympiad and the omphalus of Delphi, the birth of Christ and the Greenwich meridian, and so forth. But also, and above all, the radical imagination gives rise to a "content," a spontaneous, endless, uncontrollable representational-affective-intentional flux. You lie down to sleep, you are tired but in a good mood, then suddenly an idea or a memory occurs to you, your mood changes completely, you are unable to fall asleep. That's a trivial but striking example of the psychic flux.

R.B.—That is not true of everyone.

C.C.—What do you mean, that is not true of everyone?

R.B.—Of course, that is the most frequent case, but I believe that some individuals are able to stop that mental flow. Krishnamurti, for example, did not have that intentionality, that determination to achieve mastery: he was said to be in a sort of perpetual vacuousness. I don't think we can go any further on this subject, and we still have some other very important points to discuss. But nonetheless, I am still dissatisfied with your assimilation of the meditator to a little child. To my way of thinking, there is a dimension of another nature in the former, which is not a regressive tendency. What occurs in her is a sort of renewed bonding, but which is not of a fusion type.

c.c.—I don't want to prolong this discussion. As I have already said, I am not competent. But still and all, I wonder why on earth Krishnamurti, or anyone who meditates, would want to achieve a state of rebonding at all costs. Why does he want to reach that state rather than a state in which all things are infinitely differentiated and articulated? Where did he get that idea?

r.b.—I think he doesn't want to reach anything. I think he has no project.

c.c.—Oh, come on now . . . Krishnamurti and his likes spend their whole lives trying to reach that state. They might have tried to prove Fermat's last theorem, or gamble at Monte Carlo, or run after women. . . . Where did he get that particular desire?

r.b.—That's the question. . . .

c.c.—The answer, in my opinion, is that the monad is always lurking in the background, whispering, "I must retrieve. . . . "

r.b.—I'll answer that question. The desire comes from the fact that Krishnamurti, like everyone else, and like the world, is chaos/abyss/bottomlessness, and in this conception I include a whole destructive and creative dimension. It is from that, within oneself, that this desire originates. It is the desire to retrieve, to return to [retrouver] fullness (plenitude) in fluidity. . . .

c.c.—But you say retrieve, return to (plenitude) fullness! To retrieve: look at what you are saying, with to retrieve. . . .

r.b.—Yes, but it is to retrieve in a different way. Because there really is a difference. . . . I am in complete agreement with your conception of the imaginary institution of society, which somewhat violently removes the partitions in the infant's monadic psyche, and which gives the infant access to a process of autonomization. That really seems very clear to me, whence the importance of society, of the social-historical dimension. But at the same time, with the psyche of a "sage" like Krishnamurti, we are talking about something different from a "reunion" [*retrouvailles*]. It is something that has to do with rebonding, which I see as different from fusion. . . . But we are undoubtedly at the limit of the describable here. . . .

c.c.—We are in the realm of the totally unverifiable. Which is not true of psychoanalytic experience.

r.b.—Except for what one may experience oneself.

c.c.—Yes, but which is incommunicable by definition.

r.b.—Of course, that is why the true wise man keeps silent.

c.c.—Still and all, before going on to another subject, there is the question of the extent to which such wise men can form a collectivity.

r.b.—That's another question.

c.c.—Yes, but an important one, it seems to me.

r.b.—I agree. That is why, being a somewhat "hybrid" westerner, I defend the perspective of a paradoxical Krishnamurti-Castoriadis approach (*laughter*)! All the more reason to broach the second theme of our talk, education.

j.a.—You have dealt with the subject of education on several occasions, but you never make a distinction with pedagogy, or teaching skills. This involves going from a primitive nucleus of drives to *anthrōpos,* that is, to a being who is capable henceforth of a degree of autonomy and by the same token has forsaken omnipotence. We view education as a whole set of aims and goals, so that education is already within the realm of the political.

c.c.—I am in complete agreement with that. I explicitly wrote that in "Power, Politics, Autonomy"[1]: the object of true politics is to transform institutions, but to transform them in such a way that those institutions educate individuals, putting them on the road to autonomy. No doubt, there is no autonomous society in existence. It is so-called modern and contemporary political philosophy that has "overlooked" the question

of education, which was the main concern of all of the great philosophers, starting with Plato and Aristotle and up to Rousseau. Today, political philosophy starts with the assumption that these societies have been
given "free individuals," in some unknown way—probably supplied by
factories—and that the only problem is to arrange the relations between
them. But those relations will only be what those individuals are. Marx
was perfectly aware of that when he talked about the old problem of the
relations between educators and the students they educate, and recalled
that educators themselves must be educated. But he thought he had the
solution, because he thought he had identified the great Educator: the
socioeconomic reality of capitalism, the "objective" circumstances would
truly shape both the educators and the students. Now this is not true, or
more accurately, that reality shapes both educators and students in the
spirit of existing society. Only an autonomous collectivity can shape autonomous individuals—and vice versa, whence the paradox, for ordinary
logic. Here we have one aspect of this paradox: autonomy is the ability
to call the given institution of society into question—and that institution
itself must make you capable of calling it into question, primarily through
education.

R.B.—Don't you distinguish between pedagogues, teachers, and educators?

C.C.—I haven't given specific thought to these questions. I see education, and especially its basic orientation, as immensely important, but
some distinctions and articulations are clearly required. First of all, we
must remember that education begins at birth and ends at death. The
main part of the education provided to individuals by contemporary society is not dispensed in schools, but circulates day in and day out in the
mass media, especially television, advertising, and so on, and over and
beyond that, through everything that goes on in society, in politics, city
planning, songs, and so forth. Plato already said that even the walls of the
city educate children and citizens. It is obvious that someone living in a
city such as ancient Athens must have been, or such as Florence used to
be and still is to some small extent, receives a different education from an
inhabitant of a slum, in France or elsewhere. We absorb society through
our every pore.

Now, within education in the broad (but stringent) sense defined here, there are certainly more specific "sectors" or "times" such as pedagogy—that is, education aimed at individuals who are not yet formed as adults. A large part of pedagogy, perhaps the foremost part, begins before school: when a mother feeds her child, she is doing pedagogy, whether she knows it or not. . . . Then, there are of course teaching skills, pedagogy in the traditional, narrow sense, in specific institutions, and its relations with formal learning itself, which are not simple.

J.A.—To borrow your terms, I think an interesting distinction could be made, first, between pedagogy and education. We might reserve the word *pedagogy* for the interpersonal aspect in the transmission of knowledge to the child within the educational system, an effort that tends, fundamentally, to concentrate on the ensemblistic-identitary logic and on the subject's radical imagination. Whereas the notion of education does effectively involve the articulation between that imagination and the creative social imaginary. It is constantly formulated in terms of leaning-on, of *étayage,* which is to say on both registers, the psychic and the social.

Second point: I tend to use the term *authorization* here, perhaps more than the notion of autonomy, which has more to do with the imagination and the subject. Lacan used it in his famous saying, "authorization comes only from oneself," even if his practice was in contradiction with that, but that's another story. . . . The notion of authorization, but in the reflexive sense, of authorizing oneself, making oneself one's own author (or one's own coauthor, so as to avoid the psychotic form), is an invaluable notion that helps us to avoid some sociological utilizations of the concept of autonomy. The way sociologists dedialecticize ideology, for instance, sets up a radical break, allowing them to claim that racist conceptions function autonomously, for example. . . .

c.c.—I think we must be firm on this point and retain the term *autonomy.*

J.A.—But still, for the more social, more institutional facet. . . .

c.c.—It clearly has two facets. The interaction between the social imaginary and the singular radical imagination is present from the outset. The rupture in the monadic psyche begins with that. And the main agent of that break, of the socialization of the *infans,* is its mother. Psychoanalysts, as I have written ad nauseum, talk about the mother as if she came out of the blue and was a specifically, exclusively psychoanalytic entity. But what is a mother, really? She is the representative, for her baby, both of the existing society and of three million years of hominization. Of course she is present with her own unconscious, with its crucial effects on the child. But that unconscious itself, the mother's unconscious, has been thoroughly worked over by all the socialization to which she has been subjected. Had she not undergone that socialization she would not have been a mother, or at any rate, she could not have taught her child to speak. So that interaction between the social imaginary and the singular imagination is always present.

The difference with respect to education in the more general sense to which I referred a moment ago is that it is not aimed at any one person in particular. When the authorities—let's suppose they are democratic, the Athenian *demos* for instance, or a modern-day self-governed community—decide to organize the city in a particular way, to put the *agora* and the *ekklēsia* side by side, with the public buildings in an open space in the heart of the city and the private dwellings on the outskirts—which decisions are clearly, profoundly political—they aim at the present generations, but also the future generations, extending into an unlimited future. They are not targeting any particular, nominally designated individuals. Conversely, if I am a parent, an elementary or high school teacher, or a college professor, I am always dealing with specific individuals. I am interacting directly with their mind, and that is where the other component of pedagogy, literally speaking, begins. This is a dimension that is always overlooked, and it was visible in the high school crisis last fall [1990], in a fantastically unsettling and at the same time ludicrous way. No one talked about the teacher-student relationship, which is what holds it all together, without which there can be no pedagogy, and not even any formal education. There is no pedagogy if the pupil does not have any investment, in the strongest sense of the term, both in what she learns and in the learning process; and she can only make that investment—that is a fact, human beings are that way—provided she invests a concrete person, through a platonic Eros. Now that person is not and cannot be an ordinary wage earner, no different from other wage earners. No one says that, or dares to say it, because we have all those teachers' unions, the FEN, the SNES, the SGEN, the SNE-sup, etc., whose only concern is the wage scale and "working conditions," as in any other occupation. No one dares to raise the question of the ability of teachers to arouse the Eros of their students.

The teaching profession is not a commonplace one. Of course, teachers must be paid, much better paid than they are. Of course they should have working conditions that enable them to do their job. But it is not by taking measures on those levels—the only ones the trade unions and ministers are capable of considering—that the crisis in the school system will be solved. If teachers are incapable of inspiring love in children, love both for what they are learning and for the very fact of learning, they are not teachers. If they do not do that, high schools may possibly turn out whizzes at passing examinations, but not receptive individuals, open to the world and passionately interested in knowledge, that huge dimension of human existence. If I was able to make something of my life it is thanks to my parents, but also thanks to the tremendous good luck I had, in the course of the miserable Greek education I received during my childhood and adolescence—the luck of having at least one of each year's ten-odd teachers with whom I was in love, in a sense.

r.b.—I am struck by one thing right now. Two writers, Henri Atlan[2] and Michel Serres,[3] have just published books on education, ethics, values. . . . To my knowledge, so far, no psychoanalyst has published a book on that subject recently. Why do psychoanalysts have so little to say about education, although it is effectively central to the psychic evolution of the subject?

c.c.—As you know, it is professionally unethical to criticize one's colleagues, but I have been clear enough in my writings to be able to be critical here. Present-day psychoanalysts are deaf to everything that is not "their psychoanalysis": the couch, the psychical apparatus, their professional associations, and so forth. They are deaf to social issues, deaf to politics, deaf to pedagogy—deaf and blind. This is flagrant, with a few infinitesimal exceptions. As for me, I have tried to establish contact between the psychoanalytic dimension and the social-historical dimension, both in chapter 6 of *The Imaginary Institution of Society* and in several other texts, and again, quite recently, in my "Psychoanalysis and Politics,"[4] which takes off from Freud's famous statement about the three impossible professions: psychoanalysis, pedagogy, and politics. If psychoanalysts were not deaf and blind to the social, the political, and the educational, they could have tried to think about those objects and to say something about them—not by "psychoanalyzing" politicians or voters, which would be ridiculous, but by attempting to elucidate those objects from a psychoanalytic standpoint, thus perhaps making people act more lucidly. Freud had formulated some hopes along those lines in various papers, both before and after 1914. Psychoanalysts have rarely followed up on those exhortations, or else with some rather uninteresting deviated, vitiated developments.

But I would like to take the opportunity offered by Ardoino's reminder about transference to complete what I said in "Psychoanalysis and Politics."[5] A fundamental distinction must be made in this respect, one I did not make in that paper, and I am grateful to you for bringing it back to my mind. That is what makes discussion so valuable, and as we were saying a while ago: who is the author of a thought, and where does the originality of a thought lie? Where is the boundary? All of what we have said so far can be looked at from the perspective of transference. What is transference? It is definitely when the subject enters a regressive state. Regression does not mean he will pee on the couch. It means he relives his infantile love and hate for the adult figure he sees in the analyst's place. As a rule, these are the parental imagoes, but they may also be other figures, necessarily with the intensity of those affects and desires directed toward those figures in the past, even if they are masked, censured, and so on. The psychoanalytic catharsis occurs, if it occurs, when the subject, by means of that regression, goes through the initial incandescent flux again, melds into it, and makes himself anew in it, to use Ibsen's images in *Peer Gynt*. That is psychoanalytic transference in its full-fledged form. But in pedagogy there can only be sublimated forms of transference, if I may use such a bizarre expression. I mean that in this case, transference has to be supported by and directed to that which is sublimated, which is to say on those activities that are social objects—knowledge is a social object par excellence—and are sources of a pleasure that is neither organ pleasure nor mere representational pleasure (as is the case in daydreaming or phantasms), but rather, the pleasure of thinking. But when we go on to politics, within a collectivity of autonomous adults, the transference element should tend toward zero. For as we know by the example of the exact opposite, that is, of a monarchy and even more, a totalitarian regime, the transference factor tends toward 100 percent in those cases: affects are directed toward the father figure who knows, who is capable, and who decides.

J.A.—Transference is massive, and "it is blind."

C.C.—And it is blind, of course. A 100 percent transference is necessarily blind, for the subject is faced with an omnipotent, omniscient, benevolent, and mysterious other. The God of monotheistic religions is obviously the extreme instance of this. The same cannot be the case in democratic politics. Even in a democracy there will of course always be political leaders, individuals who, at least on certain points, see farther than the others, are able to give more and better explanations. But even if relations with the leader can never be pure, they must be as devoid as possible of transference elements. This is another reason why true politics is even more "impossible" than psychoanalysis and pedagogy. In a sense, a pedagogue must arouse love in his pupils, sublimated love. The politician's role is not to arouse love in her partisans. If she does, she blinds them. It would of course be stupid to believe that these relations may ever be purified, rid of all affective vectors, but those vectors should be modeled after friendship rather than love. The subject would clearly merit a lengthy discussion.

J.A.—That raises a practical question, one that is not trivial but is actually central in terms of educating educators. That is, teacher training always focuses on initial training and overlooks continuing education. What you are saying means that it is very important to transmit that sensitivity, as a cultural fact, so as to alert teachers, still and all, without the framework of a psychoanalysis or of some therapy, to the fact that the teacher-student relationship is not simple, that it is not constituted uniquely of good intentions, that there are all sorts of problems, including, for example, for the teacher, the need to avoid a relationship where one is in the hold of the other. This brings us to the third theme of our talk, what we call multireferentiality. . . .

F.G.-D.—Before we go on, I would like to ask another question. I work on new schools and pedagogical innovation, in which the desire to develop the person, to develop the subject, is patent. And it is in fact successful: these children definitely become "more autonomous" than in other pedagogical contexts. But in every instance, there is really one point in common: that is, a deficit in the transmission of knowledge. It is as if to develop the individual person, the "political person," meant giving up on the transmission of knowledge. Whereas theoretically, I don't see any reason why this should be the case. Practical experience shows that developing the subject leads to a sort of disqualification of the transmission of factual knowledge and of knowledge in general! This would leave us with two opposing blocks: those who choose to teach subject matter, and the others tending more to develop the person and the citizen, and who would therefore be obliged to sacrifice knowledge and the transmission of knowledge.

c.c.—I, for one, reject that dilemma. If experience shows what you say it does, that means the experiments were conducted by people who didn't balance out the two components properly. In my opinion, to teach does of course mean to educate within the institutional framework, and therefore to help students to achieve personal autonomy. But it also means bringing them to love knowledge and the process by which it is acquired, and that cannot be done without learning things. Otherwise it would be a collective pseudopsychoanalysis for children or adolescents.

f.g.-d.—Of course, but why is it that . . . ?

c.c.—I don't know, I am not in education. I am not familiar with the experience of the schools you mention, but I am just as opposed to the excesses of pedagogues, rightly impugned by my friend Philippe Raynaud and others, as to the excesses of education qua formal instruction: Here is the way some Latin verbs are conjugated. Either you've learned your Latin verbs or you haven't. You get an A or you flunk, and that's it. Both attitudes are wrong. There is no reason for that dilemma to exist. I cannot see how you can form students as autonomous beings, in the true, full sense of the term, if those beings do not learn to love knowledge, and therefore do not learn. It's almost tautological.

j.a.—Can it be, to use your own terms, that this is one of the damaging effects of ensemblistic-identitary logic?

c.c.—It is, in any case, an excessive separation. Even more, a false antinomy is created, whereas, on the contrary, when properly understood the two terms entail each other. Before we go any further, I would like to go back to a word one of you used a while back: the word *sensitization*. Educators must be sensitized to all these problems, but also to something else: to the reciprocity of the pedagogical relationship. Not symmetry, reciprocity. Here too, we can take the example of psychoanalysis. As we know, it was not Freud who invented psychoanalysis; it was his women patients, so to speak. Freud was enough of a genius to understand what they were doing and to theorize it. He was capable of hearing the women who said to him, "Are you going to shut up at last, and let me speak?" That is where the crux of the psychoanalytic attitude comes from, and the same still holds. It is in fact one of the paradoxes that make the question of how to train analysts and how to define who is really an analyst impossible to solve. Because you don't learn psychoanalysis in seminars, you learn it by having people on your couch. "Transmission" is also, in one sense, re-creation of analysis by the patient. There are theoretical frameworks, of course, but they are enlightening half of the time, and the other half, they blind you. For you are almost unavoidably led to make a patient fit into a category, or to use some hackneyed key, so to speak, when interpreting dreams. It is through one's patients that one learns how the unconscious really functions, and also some modes of functioning of the unconscious of which one was not aware. I think the same thing is true for a parent. We forget that a child teaches his parents some things. And educators too must be aware that children can teach them many things about being-a-child that are not in the books—or not with that intensity, that pregnancy, that obviousness one finds in children's reactions. They can teach them things about how a child's mind and soul functions. Educators must be sensitized to that.

J.A.—To illustrate that reciprocity, along the same lines as what you have just said: I like to use a term that has helped me greatly, as both practitioner and research worker, which is what I call *negatricity*. It is the way I picture the capacity of the other to thwart the strategies he feels are directed against him, by means of his own counterstrategies. I think that is definitely connected with what you have just said?

C.C.—Absolutely.

J.A.—If I were to take a contemporary instance of negatricity, right now, perhaps one with some rather unfortunate effects, I would look at Saddam Hussein, among others.

C.C.—I agree, totally.

J.A.—What about the term *authorization*—we haven't gotten back to that topic. Do you see it as a useful notion?

C.C.—It is definitely important, and the whole question is to determine the limits to "authorizing oneself." To what point does one authorize oneself? That's the whole problem.

J.A.—The problem of the relation between the law and transgression.

C.C.—Exactly. Once again, autonomy, like democracy, means self-limitation and not a limitation imposed by someone else.

R.B.—Perhaps it would be interesting to go on to our third point now, to take a look at your understanding of the term *multireferentiality.*

C.C.—Before that, I would like you to explain what you mean by it.

J.A.—To begin with, we may contrast it with an expression that has become a commonplace nowadays: *multidimensionality,* which Gurvitch used for sociology. According to me, multireferentiality is characteristically not only plurality, but also heterogeneity. To use your language, it would be almost the same distinction as between the *different* and the *other.* To me, then, multireferentiality means a number of systems of reading and representation, but also different languages, accepted as plural. For instance, I cannot reduce the language of a psychological approach to that of a sociological approach. These frames of reference, necessarily differing from each other, imply that we relinquish unity, and they will serve as a means of accounting for the complexity of a phenomenon, and unraveling it somewhat. As I see it, there is already a degree of multireferentiality in the way the two imaginaries lean on each other and are articulated.

C.C.—This is an extremely vast question. It touches on just about everything. I will simply say a few words on it. I am in complete agreement on the principle, and I think that is visible in my work. Take the psychic and the social dimensions, for example. I have written, on several occasions, that the psyche cannot be reduced to society, just as society cannot be reduced to the psyche. Psychoanalysts commit the error of trying to deduce society from the functioning of the psyche, and sociologists commit a symmetrical error when they view the psyche as the mere product of society and socialization. The two are indissociable and irreducible. There is another, much broader indissociability and irreducibility, one that embraces everything that is; it involves the imaginary, strictly speaking, the poietic, and the ensemblistic-identitary, or ensidic, spheres. The immense ensidic, logical-mathematical sphere, in the broadest sense, is dense everywhere, throughout beings, dense precisely in the mathematical—more precisely, topological—sense. As close as we can come to any "point" of what is, we will find ensidic elements. The wildest delusion includes ensidic elements, without which it would not be a delusion—not even a noise. The same is true of the most sublime poem. Music is not mathematics, but it is pervaded by mathematics. To compose a fugue also means to calculate constantly: you have to transpose the theme into the dominant key, introduce a countertheme in a particular relationship, and so on. But it would be idiotic to say that music can be reduced to that. Conversely, in mathematics, everything that is not simple arithmetic has to do with the imaginary, the poietic. Those two dimensions are indissociable and irreducible to each other, and everything in existence, irrespective of its form, unfolds in both. But when we speak of multireferentiality, we have to try to define the limits. Because given the factors we talked about earlier, there are some fantastic confusions being made today, owing to outrageous eclecticism. Someone mentions Wittgenstein and "language games," and off we go, the sky's the limit: on page 14 we are in the Freudian play on language, page 15 in Dumézil's play on language, on page 16 it's the Palo Alto play on language, and so on. Now that will not do at all.

J.A.—That's the collector.

C.C.—The collector, the eclectic. We can't elude the demand for coherence. Of course the world isn't "coherent." It is fragmented, and we have to acknowledge those bits and pieces, that fragmentation of being, of which we ourselves are a manifestation since we are neither galaxies nor neutron stars, but something else entirely. Moreover, we cannot comprehend ourselves with the same categories, using the same concepts as for those other classes of being. But within any one sphere, we must attempt to be as coherent as possible, and we cannot establish articulations between the different spheres just any which way—supposing they do lend themselves to articulation. In psychoanalysis, for example, you cannot be both Freudian and Jungian, even if Jung did have some interesting ideas. Likewise, you cannot purely and simply mix psychoanalysis and thinking about society and history.

J.A.—The question you are raising is: can there be multireferentiality other than the New Age variety?

C.C.—It's exactly that. We must say no to the "spirit of Cordova" and everything that goes with it, that's it. I don't know if that will get René Barbier angry. . . .

R.B.—I never get angry. . . . (*Laughter*)

C.C.—Yes, that's your Krishnamurti side. There are unquestionably some admirable aspects to Oriental thinking, Buddhism and so on, but the idea that quantum physics has anything to do with that is mere confusion. It may be that Buddhism is much better and more worthwhile than quantum physics, but that's another question. All right, there you have it. I'm glad we agree.

R.B.—That does not mean that there are no parallels to be found.

C.C.—I think not, but that would require detailed discussion.

J.A.—We are not going to pursue this any further, but I would say that multireferentiality, when indeed it doesn't turn into confusion, or into syncretism, is a provisional instrument for the analysis of complex phenomena, which I in fact do not define ontologically, as a property of the object, but rather as an invention (it is also the fruit of the imaginary) in the subject's relation to the object. In other words, there is a first phase that consists of positing the complexity of the object. This is my representation of the object, which will enable me to apply appropriate alternative tools to it thereafter. The good side remains, precisely, the relinquishment of the imaginary unity coming from the monadic state. If we are to understand a certain number of phenomena, in the present state of our multiple understandings, we may not know any other way but to combine several types of discourse.

C.C.—What we call complexity is, to my way of thinking, one of the manifestations of what I call the magmatic nature of being, the fact that being is not a set or a well-ordered hierarchy of sets, but a magma. We can extract sets from it, we can construct sets within it, but those extractions and constructions will never exhaust it or cover it. The very relations between the different aspects that we succeed in conceiving as ensidic are not ensidic themselves. So that I am much less astonished, in a sense, by the complexity that seems to amaze the theoreticians of complexity. Take intertwined hierarchies, for instance (nonintertwined hierarchies are precisely specific to ensidic logic). There are the elements of a set, its parts, the set itself, unions of sets, etc.; and in the extreme cases, those hierarchies may be complicated and different depending on the viewpoint one adopts, but they are never intertwined. But outside of these ensidic hierarchies, there is no guarantee that any such beautiful hierarchies will exist. So relinquishing unification or ultimate simplification is neither provisional nor a rule of good conduct. We must say good-bye to them once and for all, without giving up our attempts to elucidate and make coherent whatever we are able to elucidate and make coherent. . . . And that is what distinguishes us from the Orientals, or at least from those Orientals we were talking about earlier. To put it bluntly, those Orientals have decided, once and for all, that behind appearances there is Nothing. First of all, I think that is not true—or more accurately, I think that statement is meaningless (or only has an anthropocentric meaning: behind appearances, there is not what we would like there to be). But above all, behind appearances there is, and there will always be, other appearances, and we cannot relinquish setting up an order of some sort in each of those strata of appearance, and in their mutual relations, with the awareness that this order is not an ensemblistic-identitary order, and perhaps—in fact, certainly—it is not an order at all. We don't jump to a final conclusion so as to withdraw into silence—and that is profoundly tied to our Greco-Western project.

Paris, February 7, 1991

§ 10   Psychoanalysis: Its Situation and Limits

The papers by Lawrence Jacobson and Philip Cushman raise a host of important and complex questions. I therefore feel it necessary to formulate my own views relative to the assumptions underlying today's discussion, touching as I go, explicitly or implicitly, on some of the points made by Lawrence Jacobson and Philip Cushman.

The Status of Psychoanalytic Theory

EPISTEMOLOGY

One of the reasons discussions around psychoanalysis give an impression of confusion probably without precedent in the modern world is the cloud surrounding its status both as a theory and as a practice.

As a theory, psychoanalysis is most often assessed according to whether it is a "successful" or "unsuccessful" science (or even, recently, whether or not it is viewed as a hoax). Behind this stands the dominant scientistic, positivistic, and technocratic ideology. Psychoanalysis would stand or fall according to whether or not it conforms to the criteria and standards of established science, by which it is meant "exact," i.e., essentially mathematical/physical science. In substance, these criteria boil down to cumulativeness, universal controllability (entailing some variety of verificationism or falsificationism), and predictive ability. The last two are easily seen as more or less equivalent. This amounts to the implicit requirement that psychoanalytic practice proceed along the lines of modern technology. Theory should lead to unambiguous practical prescriptions, the success (or failure) of which would serve as a check on its theoretical claims to validity.

This comparison and the resulting evaluations do not hold water. First, without for a moment disputing the tremendous successes of modern science (and of the corresponding technology), we cannot forget its huge theoretical limitations. Contrary to the prevailing vulgate, contemporary science is ridden with aporias and riddles, the solution of which is by no means at hand. To mention only the most important: mathematics, the backbone and the most secure part of modern science, is plagued by the well-known results (found by Gödel, Turing, and Church) on undecidability. For seventy years now, physics has been incapable of reconciling its two parts, general relativity and quantum theory, which are at the same time theoretically incompatible but "confirmed" experimentally, and each of which presents its own riddles. Biology, hailed as offering a universal explanation of evolution, does not in fact "explain" anything of the sort. Evolution is a massive and indisputable fact, but the neo-Darwinian (or "modern synthesis") conception has only a tautology to offer: the capacity for survival and the elimination of the "unfit" are a necessary but by no means sufficient condition for the emergence of new species. These are certainly due to (or correspond to) mutations of the genes, which, however, are essentially random, and nothing in the theory explains why there are some millions of different species on Earth instead of millions of varieties of bacteria, or why there is clearly a dominant trend toward ever more complex life.

Cumulativeness refers to results, not to the basic theories. The history of science moves forward by leaps and bounds, which the late Thomas Kuhn was the first to describe and stress.

There is a metaphysics underlying the contemporary scientistic/positivistic/technocratic view. Being, as a whole, would be a totally "rational" system, a rigorous structure dictated, through and through, by ensemblistic-identitary relationships and laws. This metaphysics is the necessary complementary assumption underlying the imaginary of capitalism, that is, the domination of the social imaginary signification of an unlimited expansion of "rational" mastery. In fact, there is indeed an ensemblistic-identitary (or "logical-mathematical") dimension, everywhere dense in everything existent. This elucidates the effectiveness and efficiency of the modern scientific outlook and the concomitant technical grasp of many aspects of the world.[1]

Briefly speaking, being is creation/destruction, and creation essentially means discontinuity, emergence of the radically new, and stratification of what there is—which corresponds to the big shifts in the scientific imaginary as scientific explanation moves from one layer of being to another. The human world—both psychical and social-historical—corresponds precisely to one such stratum in the layout of being, and to a break in its history. The type of existence, the type of being brought about by the emergence of the human world, is, first and foremost, that of *meaning,* which is why the claim that psychoanalysis should—but does not—offer "explanations" is strictly meaningless. Explanations have their place only relatively to the ensemblistic-identitary dimension, and it is only because physical being is for a large part reducible to ensemblistic-identitary relationships, as far as we know, that it is susceptible of explanation.

UNDERSTANDING AND INTERPRETATION

One of the main businesses of psychoanalysis is working with meaning, what is called understanding (*Verstehen*) and interpretation.

Despite an essential antinomy—or rather, a split (*Spaltung*) in his mind—Freud knew this very well. After all, he called his first major work "The Interpretation" and not "The Explanation of Dreams," *Traumdeutung* and not *Traumerklärung.* He knew that he was dealing with two layers of meaning, the manifest one—even if it appeared to be illogical, it was not meaningless, it was *sinnwidrig* but not *sinnlos*—and the latent one, supplied by interpretation. For this he had no need of Heidegger or Gadamer. He was a contemporary of Max Weber, the founder of "understanding sociology" (*verstehende Soziologie*), behind whom stand Dilthey, Windelband, Rickert, and, even further, Herder and Hegel. All these people knew that the human world is "the intermediate realm of immanent sense" (*die Zwischenwelt des immanenten Sinnes*), as Rickert put it. But Freud's tremendous innovation was to see that manifest sense and latent sense were two different things, and to make the fundamental theoretical decision that slips make sense, dreams make sense, delirium, delusions, and hallucinations make sense. This is what today's vulgar critics of psychoanalysis are unable to see. The truth of this decision is independent of the nature of the meaning he thought he found, or of the value of the ways in which he worked to establish it. It is also independent of the fact that Freud did not *name* the "hermeneutic circle"—which was not discovered by Gadamer et al. either, but is implicitly present in Nietzsche, Marx, and a number of classical German idealists, not to speak of Protagoras. This is what countertransference is about, and this is why he insisted on the need for "purification" of the analyst by means of a didactic analysis, perfectly aware as he was of the decisive role played by the interpreter and his preconceptions in the interpretive process. Of course this does not deal with *all* the parameters conditioning the interpreter's standpoint— his position in social-historical space-time, his belonging to a gender and to a social stratum. Those "discoveries" were made by Nietzsche, Marx, and Hegel. We must take them into account, and if Freud's "pansexualism" seems to stand in the way of this, this has to be discussed on grounds of content, not of principle.

METAPSYCHOLOGY AND THE QUESTION
OF ELUCIDATION

Understanding—or interpreting concrete psychical material—does not exhaust the theoretical tasks of psychoanalysis. We must also account for that which manifests itself as conscious and unconscious meaning, and for the grounds for this split. This is metapsychology, the inquiry into the structure and functioning of what Freud called the psychical apparatus. Here again we have to make some distinctions. There is the *theoretical decision* in itself: the psychical world is not just meaning, but the emergence, or as I would say, the *creation* of meaning, with a definite *organization*; that is, with constant, permanent, or enduring traits of structure and functioning, certain *determinations* and *laws*. And there are the particular findings of Freud as to what exactly this organization, this functioning, this enduring structure consist of, what the psychical apparatus is, and how it works.

But here too there is a specificity. Just as when we decide that the psychical world, and more generally the human world, is a world of meaning, we exclude ipso facto the possibility that it could be a world of quarks and gluons, or of cells, in the same way, when we decide that there is an organization, a structure, and a mode of functioning of the psyche, we rule out ipso facto the idea that this organization could be a physicochemical or a biological one. This does not of itself "solve" the mind-brain, or psyche-soma, question, but it certainly rules out the idea that psychical meaning and its embedding in enduring structures could be *determined* by physics or biology.

THE ROLE OF THE ENSEMBLISTIC-IDENTITARY (THE "LOGICAL") DIMENSION IN THE PSYCHICAL WORLD

As already said, the narrowly "logical"—ensemblistic-identitary—dimension is everywhere present in whatever there is. To use a topological metaphor, it is *everywhere* dense. But this does not mean that it exhausts what is. In the same way, the "logical" dimension is everywhere present in the psychical world without, by far, exhausting it. Indeed, in this case, as far as we know, the "residual" is more important than anywhere else. This is related, in my view, to the much stronger *poietic* element in humans. But in a sense, this is just another way of phrasing the same thing.

Let us take two examples. With respect to *content*, the interpretation of dreams strikes us by the fantastic amount of sheer logical work the interpretation deploys. What is even more striking, however, is the incredible quantity and quality of logic mobilized to construct and present the latent meaning—the dream work, in Freud's words. This process parallels the tremendous poetic creation found in all but the most trivial dreams.

In the field of metapsychology, we necessarily use notions such as force and intensity, economy, locus, permanent trends (e.g., the pleasure principle), etc. These notions have met with some discredit among contemporary psychoanalysts, especially in France, or have been treated with condescension as "metaphors" and so on. But these terms (granted, they cannot be taken in the sense they have in other fields—thermodynamics, for instance, despite some dangerous formulations by Freud[2]) cannot be viewed as mere images. For instance, Freud's topographical divisions and expressions may be correct or incorrect, but we cannot eliminate the question of the ordered, simultaneous coexistence of different entities, and this is exactly what space (*topos*) means. Again, the enigmatic character of the "economic" formulations does not obliterate the obvious fact of very different intensities among psychical cathexes.

The theoretical work of psychoanalysis—be it "concrete," i.e., psychological, or "abstract," i.e., metapsychological—contains an inescapable logical dimension. This is so not just because we cannot help but try to think logically, but because logic is immanent in the organization of the psyche—as, indeed, that very organization indicates—without, once again, being capable of exhausting it, as is shown for instance by the very fact that "the Unconscious knows no time and knows no contradiction."

The Status of Psychoanalytic Activity

"THERAPY" AND ITS AIMS

Historically speaking, psychoanalytic activity started as a sort of medical practice. It took a quarter of a century for Freud to decide (in *The Question of Lay Analysis)* that medical studies were less important for psychoanalytical practice than knowledge of literature, ethnology, history, and so forth (and, I would add, philosophy and political thinking). I don't know how much longer it took for the American Psychoanalytical Association to accept that being an M.D. was not a necessary requisite for practicing analysis.

Today we have reached the other end of the spectrum. Anything goes, and there is almost an unbroken continuity ranging from analysis to cartomancy and astrology, and including psychoanalytical counseling, transactional analysis, sexology, behavioral training, primal scream—you name it.

The constant, from the most rigid psychoanalytical treatment to the most degenerate and fanciful present-day varieties, is the idea of *therapy.* Now the meaning of therapy is either of the following: somebody is deviating from some kind of norm and has to be "set straight," or somebody is suffering and asks insistently for relief. Both ideas give rise to almost intractable questions. It is immediately evident that they are strongly tied to fathomless interrogations about the end and the ends of analysis.

To speak about a deviation from a norm implies we know what the norm is and *ought* to be and are ready to defend it. Now, setting aside Kant, whose norm is at any rate unattainable, a norm can be either biological or social. In our field, despite strenuous efforts to define "normal" development or "healthy" sexuality, a biological norm does not make sense. We do not have, nor could we have, a canonical model of what a "normal" psyche would be. Suffice it to recall that in one of his last writings, "Analysis Terminable and Interminable," Freud stops to ask himself and the reader why a bisexual life should be considered abnormal, and he bluntly states that he sees no reason why. But neither could we accept, uncritically and without further ado, the validity of existing social norms. A social norm is socially instituted, and it is hardly necessary to argue about the spatial and temporal relativity inherent in this status. The criminalization of homosexuality in many places until thirty years ago is well known, as are the cruel punishments inflicted on Oscar Wilde and Alan Turing (who was driven to suicide after coming out of prison). To this day, in the state of Georgia (and probably a number of others), sodomy and oral sex are punished by years in prison. More generally, and irrespective of any deeper critique, in view of our ethnological and historical knowledge, psychoanalysis cannot uphold the validity of social norms in the sexual field—and if it does, as it did for long decades, it draws on itself the fully justified accusation of adaptationism, on which more later. Here we find a necessary bridge between psychoanalytical and political questions, in the most radical sense of the word *political*: that is, pertaining to the institution of society and its contents.

But we are in no easier position with the idea of psychical suffering, however great the feelings of sympathy it arouses in us. Human life necessarily includes suffering, and who is to draw the line between "normal" and "abnormal" suffering, unless she is willing to champion a model of psychical "health"? Should we accept the demands for therapy of those who suffer because they have been abandoned by their boy- or girlfriend? Or condone the attitude of contemporary humans, rushing to take Valium, Temesta, or whatever, whenever they are confronted with a difficult situation? And in this case, why not abandon the whole field to neuropharmacologists?

Freud once gave an apparently irreproachable definition of the end and the ends of analysis: "to restore the capacity to love and to work." But to love *what*? And, much more problematical, to work *for what*? Are we keen to restore the capacity to work in a Taylor-Ford type of factory? Would slavish submission to circumstances be a valid indicator of psychical health? Work is valuable to the extent its own ends are valuable, and this is unquestionably a social, instituted valuation. Love raises other questions, owing especially to the vagueness of its content, the indefinable character of its object, and its enigmatic relation to time.

But Freud also spoke in a humbler fashion about analysis as aiming to lead from neurotic suffering to banal human unhappiness. The distinction is, I think, unmistakable for anyone in the least familiar with psychical life. But here again it would be fruitless to wait for a rigorous demarcation between the two. Lawrence Jacobson, in his beautiful and courageous paper, indicates what is the trouble with his two patients: their inauthentic attitude toward their own life. I have a deep sympathy with this idea. And, personally, I could never become friends with somebody who I feel is inauthentic. But the trouble is precisely with the word *feel.* I am perfectly sure as to what it intends, and as to my capacity to tell who is and who is not authentic. But I am absolutely unable to enclose it in abstract words. For me, it is of the same nature as the difference between Beethoven and, say, Saint-Saëns. The hollow men, the stuffed men of T. S. Eliot are a perfectly legitimate study for literature, and even there, who would assert with certainty that Madame Bovary was authentic or inauthentic? Perhaps the only authentic moment in her life was when she killed herself—but by then, it would be of no use to know it.

THE POLITICAL DIMENSION OF PSYCHOANALYSIS

Psychoanalysis contains an ineliminable *political* dimension. Political, of course, does not mean the professions of Mr. Clinton and Mr. Gingrich, but the questions and the activities pertaining to the institution of society. Thereby, it also becomes inevitably entangled with the controversies surrounding political ideas and activities. To this extent, psychoanalysis is a *practical* activity. It belongs to the domain of *doxa,* opinion, not of *epistēmē,* scientific knowledge.

This becomes evident whenever we consider the aims of analysis because they necessarily have to do with a *social* individual, including her relation with herself but just as much with the other and, beyond any particular other, with conditions determined by the social setup. (This is clearly the case with Lawrence Jacobson's two patients.) It is, by the way, totally inadequate to talk about the need for a "relational turn" in psychoanalysis. On the one hand, the relations of the patient with his environment have always been considered. Freud never stopped talking about the relations of his patients with the people surrounding them. But the problem with him was exactly the same as with today's "relational" analysts: the failure to properly realize that beyond any concrete other, psychoanalysis involves, both theoretically and practically, the whole network of impersonal, anonymous, social institutions and significations. Also, if we speak about "moral" or "ethical" parameters in analysis, we must realize that (contrary to the whole Christian and a great part of the philosophical

tradition) morals or ethics are simply a dimension of politics, and at any
rate, they are inseparable from it.

On this subject I can only dogmatically present my own opinions, of
course, but I beg you to bear in mind that in this field there can never
be a "foundation," a priori, but only a reasonable justification, down-
stream, of one's positions. The object of psychoanalysis is essentially the
same as that of politics: the autonomy of human beings. If we recognize
the fundamentally social character of human beings, this autonomy, this
freedom, has to be both individual and collective. I cannot live—I would
never have become a human being in the first place—alone, nor can I
eliminate the others. The question, therefore, is: how can I be free, if I
must live in a society where the law is determined by somebody else? The
only conceivable answer short of delirium à la Stirner, is: if I have the effective possibility of participating equally with everyone else in the formation and the implementation of the law. And this is the true meaning of
democracy. But also: how can I be free, if I am under the sway of my unconscious? Since I can neither eliminate nor isolate it, the only answer is:
I can be free if I establish another type of relation with my unconscious,
a relation whereby I know, as far as possible, what goes on in it and I am
able, as far as possible, to filter whatever of it passes into my external,
diurnal activity. This is what I call establishing a reflective, deliberative
subjectivity. And I think it can be easily shown that an autonomous society is only possible if it is formed by autonomous individuals, and that
autonomous individuals can exist only in and through an autonomous society. This is so because only the effective exercise of autonomy develops
autonomy, and an education geared toward the autonomy of individuals
can exist only in such a society.

IMPLICATIONS FOR PSYCHOANALYSIS: PSYCHOANALYSIS
AS A PRACTICOPOIETIC ACTIVITY

It is clear that autonomy cannot be imposed, nor can it be "taught."
The analysand can only be helped in his journey toward autonomy—and
this entails both knowledge and action. The sharing of knowledge is the
aim of interpretation, which can give insight into one's hidden and repressed motives and drives. But the analysand should be steered to this
interpretation so that he gradually becomes able to provide it himself.
Psychoanalysis is self-activity, reflection of oneself upon oneself; it is gain-

ing access to autonomy by effectively exercising autonomy, assisted by another person. The activity of this person—the limits of which can only be traced by considering the requirements of the development of the patient's self-activity—is not an application of a technique, but a *praxis:* that is, the action of a person aimed at helping another person to gain access to her potentialities for autonomy. And inasmuch as the concrete content of this aim is not and cannot be determined in advance, since it also entails the freeing of the creative capacities of the radical imagination of the analysand, it is creation: that is, *poiēsis.*

Thus, I define psychoanalysis as a practicopoietic activity, and this is also the defining character of Freud's two other "impossible professions." Psychoanalysis, like education and politics, is the action of one autonomy upon another—virtual autonomy—and like them, its aim is the creation of these new forms: autonomous persons and an autonomous society.

The Social-Historical Situation of Psychoanalysis

THE CONDITIONS UNDER WHICH FREUD WORKED

There is no need to recall the limitations and presuppositions imposed on Freud's work by his time, the cultural setting, and the dominant ideology of the period. Freud started as a scientistic positivist, an ideology dominant then as now, and he never stopped being one. But he was also (and perhaps became gradually more and more) ambiguous about this. He never forgot that the business of psychoanalysis was meaning, not molecules or chemical potentials. He was deeply steeped in the patriarchal culture of his milieu and his period (in fact, of some thousands of years of human history), and the scars this left on his work are numerous and well known. He never dared to uncover—or rather, to name—the fundamental role of radical imagination in psychical life. One of the most pathetic tragicomedies of intellectual history—where there is no dearth of such— is his initial belief in the "reality" of the traumatic event, followed by his gradual and reluctant admission that this "event" was a phantasmatic (that is, imaginary)—one. Then there were the accusations leveled against him eighty years later that he had consciously covered up his initial discovery of the seduction of infants by adults, and the recent reverse ones that he is supplying the American psychotherapeutic and legal industries with the alibi of scientific respectability in made-up seduction stories. But to my mind, the most damaging effect of the social-historical setting on psychoanalytic theory has been the total neglect of the fundamental role of society, institutions, and social imaginary significations on the formation of the individual, accompanied by the hopeless effort to "deduce" society from psyche, and the critical limitations this imposed on theory and practice. Society came to be seen as "reality" in the same sense as gravity is "reality," instead of seeing that the relevant reality here is society (despite an eloquent phrase in *Totem and Taboo,* lightheartedly ignored by successive generations of psychoanalysts). This is also why his unquestionable political radicalism became practically irrelevant with the years, and ended up with his ambiguous, even contradictory stance in *Civilization and Its Discontents* and *The Future of an Illusion.*

All of this does not cancel or diminish in any way his importance and the truth of what I would call the hard core of psychoanalytic theory, which I will address presently. To limit oneself to these points of criticism or other less important ones while forgetting or covering up the pathbreaking discoveries and insights of Freud is to behave like an inverted talmudist or, more to the point, a Stalinist or a Jdanovist. For this attitude implies that Freud's text has to be treated like the Torah or *Das Kapital:* not a word of it could ever be wrong, and if one finds points that have to be superseded, the whole should be thrown to the dustbins of history, or carried to the cemetery of dead white males, in the infamous company of Plato, Aristotle, Spinoza, Kant, and so on.

AFTER FREUD

As was already well known by Freud's time, but much better known after him, the mainstream of psychoanalytical theory and practice, both in America and in Europe, has taken a definitely adaptationist orientation, despite some well-meaning but unfortunate attempts (by Wilhelm Reich, for instance) to combine psychoanalysis and social critique. This has been one of the main conditions for the present "crisis"—a true crisis, sociologically speaking—which is manifested in a host of ways:

- First and foremost, in the almost undisputed domination of reductionism, either on traditional biological lines, or in the attempts to reduce the psyche to a more or less sophisticated version of a supercomputer.

- In the proliferation of all sorts of parapsychoanalytical varieties, as mentioned above.

- In the uncritical, wholesale rejection of psychoanalysis by various brands of feminists, "antiwesternizers," etc., and, clearly connected to this, the incredible vulnerability of the present epoch to every conceivable cultural fad: hermeneutics, constructivism, postmodernism, deconstructionism, and so on.

  For the most part, these phenomena express the huge ideological regression of the present epoch, manifest in almost all the domains of the humanities (e.g., economics, political theory, sociology). But a nonnegligible contribution is made by the theoretical necrosis—or psittacism—of mainstream psychoanalysis, and its incapacity to stand up to the problems of the time.

THE HARD CORE

Before I finish, I must briefly state the ideas that, to my mind, constitute the hard core of psychoanalytical theory and practice:

- The psychic domain is the domain of meaning, which must be considered as such.

- The human psyche is by necessity structurally divided, at least between a conscious and an unconscious level.

- On the unconscious level, the "omnipotence of thought" reigns supreme.

- The pleasure principle plays an essential role both in conscious and unconscious psychical life.

- Human sexuality is decisively dominated by imagination, and infantile sexuality is a central factor in psychical development.

- Projection and introjection are the channels through which the singular psyche relates to the "outside world."

- What we call the human individual is for the most part a product of society.

This is not a credo, and is certainly not sufficient to build a psychoanalytical theory. In particular, the functioning of human imagination and the process of socialization require lengthy elaboration. But those who attack psychoanalysis should be asked whether they dispute these premises.

Because if they do, it is to be feared that discussion with them would not be of great use.

The Nature of the Human Psyche and the Limits of Psychoanalysis

THEORETICAL AND PRACTICAL LIMITS

The human existence is undissociably a psychic and a social one. A nonsocialized human being does not and cannot exist. This is not an "external" but rather an essential condition: it impinges decisively on the organization and the content of psychic life. It is not enough to acknowledge this fact. One must recognize the limits it poses to both the practice and the theory of psychoanalysis.

From the practical point of view, we can help people work toward their autonomy, but we cannot, qua psychoanalysts, abolish or modify the social-historical factors, institutions, and significations that hinder and frustrate, often decisively, this work.

We must admit, both practically and theoretically, that phenomena such as psychosis present us with quite intractable problems. Interpretation—that is, understanding—encounters the walls of the full closure of the psychotic's world, and its possible effects are limited by the specific nature of the psychotic's transference, if and when transference is established.

Theoretically, and in a general way, the work of elucidation of the psychic world encounters a series of aporias. What, for instance, are psychic forces that are not *measurable*? And we cannot for a moment forget the abyss of the body/soul (or mind/brain) problem, with which we are also confronted almost daily in our practice, through psychosomatic diseases, effects of the interpretation on the analysand's physical state, and so on.

THE ULTIMATE LIMIT

The psyche is not a well-oiled, rational mechanism. The psyche is essentially radical imagination, a perpetually surging flux of representations, desires, and affects. As such, it is creative, which also means that this flow and its products are as often as not undetermined. This is already glaringly obvious—but not thematized—in the writings of Freud himself. *The Interpretation of Dreams* states clearly that not all dreams are interpretable, and no dream at all is fully interpretable. Freud does not say why this should be so, but his text gives the answer in part: the representations in a dream are *overdetermined*. They are also, obviously, *under*-determined. There is therefore no one-to-one correspondence between the images of the "dream content" and the various dream thoughts—of which Freud says that they branch out, or in—into the unknown. In a more radical and general way, the very idea of overdetermination reveals itself as insufficient in the "Drives" text of 1915. There, Freud speaks about the presentation of a drive by means of a representation (*Vorstellungsrepräsentanz des Triebes*). Now, clearly, in humans there is no canonical, "normal" representation for a drive. This role can be as well played by a bosom as by a stiletto-heeled shoe.

This creativity of the human imagination is at the root of the most severe psychical and political problems. Humans create their own distinctive world, different from that of other mammals. But also, within this generic framework, each singular human being creates his or her own distinctive world. This, however, is tantamount to saying that human beings are "solipsistic"; they are egocentric, self-centered not just "morally" but ontologically and epistemologically as well. In its deep layers—the Unconscious—the human psyche is amoral, but also asocial and acosmic. This also means that as such, left to itself, it is radically unfit for life. It only succeeds in living inasmuch as it is forcibly dragged out of its own world by society and its institutions, a process that carries a very heavy price, however. The psyche has to abandon—or better, to bury— what it identifies as meaning for itself, in exchange for the possibility, the quasi-necessity, of internalizing and cathecting that which society offers to it by way of meaning: its social imaginary significations. But this also means that henceforth an ineradicable *negativity* inhabits the psyche, against society, against the others, against reality, against the very social mask it has been forced to wear: that is, against itself as a social person. Hence the ineradicability, as far as the psychic core is concerned, of *hate,* of aggressive and destructive tendencies and/or of a fundamental masochism. Up to now, social institutions have dealt with this by creating intra- or extrasocial diversions, including competition and war. Other, more humane ways of accomplishing this function can and should be found. But we should never assume that human beings are "naturally good," corrupted only by the pernicious influences of society—a catastrophic illusion shared by anarchists, feminists, many of today's radicals, and some psychotherapists.

We should struggle for a change of society, for truly democratic institutions, for the expulsion of production and the economy from the central, dominant place they have come to occupy in today's world, for an education geared toward autonomy and not just toward professional skills. But we must face reality, and that is, essentially, psychical reality. A much more humane society is possible and desirable. But an angelic human being is neither.

July–September 1997

§ 11   The Psyche and Society Anew

The Psyche and the Radical Imagination

FERNANDO URRIBARRI—I would like to ask you, first, to define the radical imagination, that central notion of your theory of the psyche.

CORNELIUS CASTORIADIS—I believe the radical imagination is what distinguishes the human psyche from the animal psyche. What makes the psyche capable of producing those representations, those phantasms, which are not the outcome of perceptions? It is the radical imagination. That would be a first approach. The human psyche is characterized by an autonomous imagination, a radical imagination: I am not simply talking about seeing—or seeing oneself—in a mirror, but also about the ability to formulate what is not there, to perceive, in just anything, what is not there. In the human psyche there is a flux, a representational spontaneity that is not subordinated to any predetermined end.

Of course, if we take Freud's work, we encounter the problem of phantasms, of *Urphantasien,* or originary phantasms. The issue of whether these phantasms are transmitted genetically or produced by each individual in her psychic life is no longer of any concern to us. The only point is that they have no connection with reality. They are neither pictures nor photos of some reality, they are created by the psyche. And it is these creations that we encounter constantly in our clinical work when we analyze dreams, when we listen to a patient, with his own image of the world, distinctly different from other people's.

One crucial problem is the relation between these representations and drives. Many people think that drives impose a number of corresponding representations or phantasms on the psyche. That is only true for the animal psyche, in which we find canonical representations of instincts; for instance, the animal of the other sex when their sexuality is involved. For human beings, there is what Freud, in a text written in 1915 on "The Instincts and Their Vicissitudes,"[1] calls the *Vorstellungsrepräsentanz des Triebes*—that is, representation by delegation of the drive within the psyche. The process may be described as follows: according to Freud, drives [what he calls instincts—Trans.] originate in the soma, but to be able to act on the psyche, they must "speak the language" of the psyche. They must find a translation in the psychic sphere, and that translation is the *Repräsentanz* through a *Vorstellung,* a representation. It's like an embassy, a delegation, taking the form of a representation. This must be viewed as a manifestation of the radical imagination in human beings: there is no predetermined link or compulsory relationship between the drive and its psychical representative. That is absolutely clear in sexuality.

F.U.—What you are saying is that a drive can find a psychic expression, a representative that represents it, a representation, because the psyche is radical imagination, or in other words, it is the ability to create representations. . . .

C.C.—That's right. And there's more than that. . . .

F.U.— . . . which is that the specific representations created are not "canonical," universal for the species, predetermined.

C.C.—Exactly. In the animal psyche, there is reason to believe that representation is defined in a set manner, by the instinct. And it is functional. For an animal, sexual representation is functional; it is part of the process leading to reproduction. We can say all sorts of things about human representation, but not that it is determined by the reproductive function. That is in fact the essential characteristic of the human psyche, what I call its afunctionality: what a person imagines, or represents—be it consciously or on the unconscious level—is not determined by any biological functionality, even if the two may coincide from time to time: how many of the sexual acts of, say, a normal neurotic are aimed at reproduction over the course of an entire lifetime?

So we must accept that central feature of the human psyche, its "defunctionalization." And this characteristic is inseparably combined with the ability of the psyche to experience pleasure by means of representation, and by representation only. Moreover, this unbinding of the pleasure of representation and organ pleasure is possible in human beings only.

I call that imagination "radical" because the creation of representations, affects, and desires by the human imagination is subject to conditions, but never predetermined. There is no outside motor; it is a spontaneous force that creates phantasms, representations, and the corresponding affects, which is why they are defunctionalized. What is the biological functionality of religious passion? We cannot have the slightest understanding of the psyche if we don't recognize the essential presence of the radical imagination, of that spontaneous, creative, afunctional force, corresponding to the fact that representational pleasure is set above organ pleasure.

The radical imagination is also at the root of another extraordinary ability of human beings: the ability to symbolize. It is thanks to the radical imagination that human beings are able to see a thing in another thing. That is what quid pro quo is: taking one thing for another; seeing the word *dog* in writing and having it represent a dog, having a dog become present for me. As opposed to the animal level, at which there are only signals—the smell of a predator, for instance—attached to an object, for human beings, there are not only signals; there are, above all, symbols. And that is what makes language possible. It is the fact on which language rests.

F.U.—Your notion of the imagination implies that you reject both biologism and Lacanian structuralism?

C.C.—Lacan's notion of the imagination is ridiculous. To the Lacanian way of thinking, the imaginary is the same as the specular—that is, what can be seen in the mirror. "The image in the mirror is imaginary, it is not real." That lacks substance, it's vulgar reductionism. . . .

F.U.—Reducing the imaginary to the specular is the complementary reverse of the formalist reduction of the symbolic to the signifying combinatory.

C.C.—I agree. That's also what enables Lacanians to fail to recognize a whole series of essential aspects of human beings. For instance, they close their eyes to the creativity of the singular human being, as well as to creativity at the social-historical level. From the moment the imagination is reduced to the imaginary defined as a reflection in a mirror, all the imaginary can do is repeat/reflect what is already there. This takes us back to the most insubstantial notion of the imagination to be found in the history of philosophy and psychology, because if that is the case, how and out of where can anything new arise? It's impossible. In the Lacanian system, what is new—radically new—is "forclosed," to use his terminology. It is impossible then to conceive of such simple, fundamental things as, for example, why is it that at a certain point in time this new thing called psychoanalysis came into existence? The truth is that that is inconceivable, using Lacanian parameters.

F.U.—How do you relate your conception of the radical imagination to the Freudian notion of the unconscious?

C.C.—The unconscious is one of the realizations of the radical imagination, and undoubtedly the most important one for us psychoanalysts. But before going any further on the question of the unconscious, I would like to point out that the unconscious is not the only sphere in which the radical imagination manifests itself. It is to be seen in consciousness as well, in waking life, inasmuch as that life is not pure repetition. To the extent that we are capable of having new ideas, or of accepting new ideas coming from other people, that means that new representations are able to surge forth even on the conscious level. So conscious life is not condemned to be mere repetition. But for us psychoanalysts, the most important sphere is of course the unconscious.

F.U.—I would like to emphasize the need to spell out the relationship between the unconscious and the radical imagination. To go a step further, I would say that one "consequence" of the radical imagination is your understanding of the unconscious as something that is not defined by repetition only. The unconscious is also conceived as the capacity for new representations to emerge, as a source of creation, as if it were open, or at the limit, as if it had a "prospective" dimension, to be provocative, in line with your criticism of a one-sided comprehension of the unconscious as timeless. . . .

C.C.—That's true, but I don't know whether I would use the term "prospective," which may induce an opposite ambiguity, equivalent to what "timelessness" infers. The main point is that there is not simply repetition of the past. New things, new representations, and even new structures emerge.

F.U.—New structures? In what sense?

C.C.—Let's take the classical Freudian conception of individual development. We begin with the oral phase. Clinical experience tells us that in this first phase of its existence, the *infans* does not confine itself to relating to "one" essential object, the breast, and that it has "one" activity, sucking, which is also a source of pleasure, and of displeasure when the breast is absent. But that's not all. There is a whole oral psychic structure that unfolds during that phase. And in our clinical work with adults, we see the remains, or the traces of that structure, in their later life.

If we follow the Freudian schema, the subject then goes on to the anal phase. There is then another structuring of the psyche. These phases are not simply developmental phases; they also bring about other structures and psychic restructurings for the subject each time. I occasionally express this by saying that each phase creates a "world of its own," marked by its oral or anal character, for the subject. And those structures are not simply demolished or abolished by subsequent development. This too is clearly visible in clinical work.

One specific trait of the human psyche is precisely its stratification. The psyche is characterized by its many agencies and by the conflict between them. This is a product of the history of the psyche which always creates various strata, and these, far from disappearing, enter into various relationships. The history of the psyche turns into stratification of the psyche. The fact that the agencies—or types of processes—are constituted in and by that history and will not be "harmoniously integrated" or simply "outgrown" later is what distinguishes the evolution of the human psyche from any other "learning process." Let's say that in this history the subsequent phases do not cancel out the earlier ones, but rather, they coexist, conflictingly.

F.U.—In your conceptualization of the unconscious, in writings such as "The State of the Subject Today"[2] or in chapter 6 of *The Imaginary Institution of Society,* you define it as "a flux of representations, affects, and intentions" (or "desires" at other points). I would like to hear you expound that idea.

c.c.—Let's begin with the term *intention*. We have already alluded to
the animal psyche, but let's take living beings more generally: intention
implies a "being for itself." A living being possesses and pursues its own
ends, its objectives as "being for itself," such as self-preservation and reproduction. Each time, each living being creates a world of its own. It's
impossible to go into the details here; they refer more to philosophy than
to psychoanalysis. But as soon as a living being exists, we have a "being
for itself," which implies a "self-finality," the creation of a world of its
own and of objects or facts that this living being seeks out or avoids.
That is what I call *intention* at the level of the living being as a "being for
itself": the elementary tendency to seek some things and to avoid, to flee,
others. This is accompanied, as is clearly seen in animals, by an elementary affect, pleasure or displeasure, but which is only a simple biological
signal in this case, one on which they cannot elaborate. The main thing
is the vital function. When we talk about human beings, the situation
is different and more complex, although here too we have a "being for
itself," a living being. What makes it complex is the radical imagination
and its ability to elicit an upsurge of representations, affects, and desires.
On this level I no longer talk about *intention* but rather, about *desire,* to
point up the specificity of human beings. In human beings qua desiring
beings, intentions are not bound to biological functions. We might even
try to find different, specific terms for representation and affect, neither
of which exists exclusively in humans.

F.U.—You also take about unconscious affects. Freud's assertions are
contradictory on that point. Take, for example, the thesis of "repression"
and of the "unconscious" on the one hand, and such notions as the "unconscious guilt feeling" on the other.

c.c.—Your reference to Freud is fitting. If we look at his work as a
whole, we see that his position is not at all clear, even in the 1914 metapsychology writings. In "The Instincts and Their Vicissitudes,"[3] he speaks of
a representational representative of the drive and an affective representative of the drive. And what you point out is true: if we take Freud's last
writings, he obviously thinks that unconscious affects exist, and that it
could not be otherwise, since there are unconscious desires. An extremely
complex question arises here: the question of the relation between these
two psychic vectors. Freud occasionally expresses the idea that represen-

tation is shaped by desire. That is undeniably true most of the time, for example when we talk about wish-fulfillment dreams (I set aside how these differ from traumatic dreams, to avoid going astray). If we take that "princeps" case of the wish-fulfillment dream, what do we find? An unconscious desire seeking (unconscious) satisfaction by means of the dream. What are the implications of this? That the only way for desire to procure the affect of pleasure for itself in the unconscious is by means of representation. It is as if we had a stage director, the desire, ordering the unconscious to show it something that will satisfy that desire. And the function of the unconscious commanded by the stage director produces that representation in the latent content of the dream. But this is not the only case. Sometimes it's the representation that elicits the desire. We then have a complex relationship—between desire and representation in this case—involving a peculiar organization of the unconscious and of the psyche in general, one that is not conceivable using our usual, ensemblistic-identitary logic. We can't say that desire is always the cause and representation the outcome. Nor can we say the reverse. There is a mixture: it is impossible to conceive of a desire that would not be desire *of* something; of some thing evidenced, in at least some elementary way, by a representation. It is impossible to conceive of representations in the unconscious that would be indifferent.

F.U.—If they are not indifferent, it is because they are tied to affects in an inextricable flow of representations, affects, and desires. That metapsychological definition raises a philosophical, logical issue: the indissociability of components that cannot be carved into clear-cut, different units, separate from each other and from outside elements, implies a logic other than the ensemblistic-identitary one. A more complex logic, capable of going beyond the inherited ontology based on the notion of "being as determinacy" and also of making creation and imagination thinkable—which is what your elaboration of the "logic of magmas" attempts to do.

C.C.—That is accurate. This opens onto philosophical questions as well as onto psychoanalytic ones. That was what I was referring to. But if we go into those subjects now we run the risk, perhaps, of losing the thread of our discussion.

Structuring of the Psyche: The Monadic Psyche

F.U.—That thread—let's pick it up again—leads us to the question of how the psyche is structured. You speak of "stratification" as a metaphor of that process. You talk about the different phases leading from the monad, the "monadic psyche" to the "social individual," going through a "triadic phase" and resulting in the possibility—but simply the possibility—of an "autonomous, reflexive subjectivity." Before going into each stage in that process, I would like to ask you about the general meaning of this model, something like an overview.

C.C.—The general meaning, so to speak, of this perspective is based on the fact that all of the psychical phenomena known to us are comprehensible for us only if we refer them to a point of origin, what I call the "monadic psyche." For example, take what Freud calls the magical "omnipotence of thought." What does that mean? That in the unconscious, all a desire has to do is appear and it is fulfilled, and fulfilled in and through representation. Where does that come from? Or to put it another way, what is the origin of the fundamental egocentricity of human beings?

These questions lead us to discover one and the same reality: an initial state of the psyche—the exact chronological moment is quite unimportant—what I call the "monadic psyche." Now this designation attempts to account for its essential characteristic, namely, that nothing exists for the subject outside of the subject itself. Which subject experiences itself as the source of pleasure and as capable of achieving that pleasure; as the immediate satisfaction of any desire that might present itself.

Freud gave one of the best formulations of that monadic state in his notes from 1938.[4] He uses that concise, wonderful phrase: "I am the breast," about which he goes on to comment. Freud himself posits the existence of a first moment when the newborn babe "is the breast," obviously not for the observer, the wet nurse, the mother, or the little brother, but for itself. The object is not a separate object. The "good object" is the newborn baby for itself. "I am the breast" is not an attributive assertion, then, or a transitive one, like "I am blond." To try to represent that, we might complete the description: the baby experiences itself, at once the lip area, the oral cavity, and probably the upper portion of the digestive track, as undifferentiated from milk, that nice, warm liquid, and as having—being—a desire and being able to satisfy it pleasurably.

Here we may possibly have the root of absolute egocentricity, as well as of the magical "omnipotence of thought" and of the tendency for the unconscious to form representations that satisfy its desire, and so on. The monad "organizes" the experience of pleasure, not "with an object" but as the total—totalitarian, complete, absolute—experience of a state. The psyche will be magnetized by this experience forever, so that the "object of its desire," its search, will be to recover, to return to that state. It is more a "desire for a state" than for an object. In this sense, the alienation of the subject's desire to someone else's desire—such as it is seen in the triadic phase—is something secondary, coming later.

Obviously that state cannot last very long. It is continued through what Freud calls "hallucinatory wish fulfillment": the baby is capable of "making present" the object that is absent. And we can of course see this as an expression of the radical imagination: the breast is not there, but the baby hallucinates it, sometimes with the somatic support of thumb sucking. But after that stage, a break occurs. There is a pressing somatic need, and also there is the presence of the other that breaks into that closed circuit around the self. But it is not so much hunger as displeasure that will make a breach in the monad's closure. In other words, the need to give meaning to this displeasure—backed by somatic tension—makes it necessary for the psyche to create an outside to which to ascribe the source of displeasure; this need evidences the need for "making-meaningful" [*mise en sens*].

F.U.—Before "leaving" the monad, there is one crucial question in that respect: the predominance of the pleasure of representation over organ pleasure in human beings. The monadic stage is a founding, fundamental moment for that fact. . . .

C.C.—Of course. What is shown by the prolongation of the moment of "real," organic satisfaction by hallucination is the ability of human beings to experience pleasure by means of simple representation, irrespective of whether or not that representation is accompanied by organ pleasure. This is the nucleus. And it goes on developing in psychic life: we will see that the pleasure of representation takes ever-increasing predominance over organ pleasure. In the moment of hallucinatory satisfaction, we have the primal moment of that human capability in action—namely, the fact of being able to hallucinate, and of finding pleasure in hallucinating, by means of representation.

F.U.—What relationship can be established between the monadic phase and Freud's conception of primary narcissism?

C.C.—They are very similar, although Freud modified his position on narcissism considerably. Some writers contend that he dropped narcissism, or viewed it as less important, in the latter half of his work. This is untrue: that notion is still present in papers written in the 1920s and 1930s, even in phrases such as the one I quoted above. I think there is a genuine proximity between what I am saying and Freud's ideas, but I believe he never pursued them to their full implications. Or if he did, it was partially, in his "On Narcissism: An Introduction" and in some passages in which he speaks of newborn babies as being at a stage he doesn't call narcissism, but autism. I gave the exact quotation in the *Imaginary Institution*. . . .

F.U.—It's a quotation from "Two Principles . . . ,"[5] in a footnote in chapter 6: "This note should be quoted *in extenso,* for here Freud affirms . . . that the infant, including maternal care, constitutes a psychical system wholly under the domination of the 'pleasure principle,' and where he also states that a fine example 'of a psychical system shut off from the stimuli of the external world' and which even satisfies its needs for nourishment 'autistically' (to use Bleuler's term) is provided."[6]

C.C.—Yes, that's where Freud compares the psyche to a chick in its egg. What that means is not that the human subject is in a closed nutritive environment equivalent to an egg: if anything is shut in, it's the psyche shut into itself; it's the "self-enclosed" representation that the subject creates of himself and of the world. That is what closure is: it's the monadic psyche, the monadic stage, shut in within itself. And the human subject must break out of that closure in order to survive, except in the case—which "brings grist to my mill"—of infantile anorexia nervosa.

The Triadic Phase: The *Infans,* the Part Object, and the Mother

F.U.—But what place do you see for the libidinization of the human child, for his being cathected by an other as requisite, for example, for going from the functional, animal level to the level of the pleasure of representation?

c.c.—During the monadic stage there is no other and no object. "I am my object" or "I am the breast," as Freud puts it. And I believe that infantile anorexia nervosa shows that closure within the self, the total ignorance of the other. Now that other, as we know by observing the process from outside, is biologically and psychically essential for the subject. But it is not immediately inscribed in the psyche. That is an external vision of the infantile psyche. For the infant, the other does not exist as such. When the other appears, it is as if she disposed of the baby's crucial object: not crucial for its life—the baby does not think in those terms—but for its satisfaction, for its pleasure.

This is what I call the triadic phase, defined by the establishment of interplay, of interaction between the *infans,* the mother, and the breast. The mother is perceived as disposing of the breast, and the infant, on the basis of the only schema available to it—that of omnipotence—"projects" it onto the mother. In other words, the infant who "believed himself" to be all-powerful discovers it isn't and transfers that omnipotence to its mother. This will give rise to the baby's ambivalence toward the mother. In that sense, Melanie Klein is right with her idea that there is a good breast and a bad breast, corresponding—broadly speaking—to the breast when it is present or absent. This is the stage in which a three-term interrelation develops, in which the part object, the breast, is the crossroads, the area of intersection in the infant's relationship with its mother. But this is not yet an open world, although there are now three terms.

f.u.—In the triadic phase, the world is "closed" in one particular sense inasmuch as it does imply an opening up, an incipient differentiation and separation. I think this is a fundamental question, especially since the structuring of the psyche is simultaneously its socialization. Thus, the first separating operation characterizing the triadic phase implies an initial socializing moment.

c.c. Absolutely. The imposed socialization of the psyche is basically an imposed separation. And that is true in an immense, deep sense. For the monadic psyche it is tantamount to a violent break imposed by its "relationship" with others, by means of which a "reality," concomitantly external, independent, transformable, and participable, will be constituted. That violent break is what Piera Aulagnier called "primary violence," in her terminology. This means that whereas the monadic psyche constantly tends to close itself in, that breaking out is constitutive of what will be— or may possibly be—the social individual. The imposition of that relation to the other and thereafter to concrete others is a succession of ruptures inflicted on the monadic psyche, through which the social individual is constituted as a subject split between a monadic pole—which constantly tends toward reclosure—and that which was imposed on it and which it has gradually organized and integrated into varying syntheses.

F.U.—To return to the triadic phase, we may say that it breaks the monadic closure and brings a new "meaning-making," a "making sense" [*mise en sens*] of the world—a world made of three terms—in which omnipotence of meaning is ascribed to the mother. In the transition between these phases what is at work, and at stake, is the differentiation between inside/outside and the constitution of an outside world. Moreover, you point out that projection prevails over introjection in this process.

C.C.—To begin with, there is a fact: the baby experiences the mother according to its schema of omnipotence. That omnipotent mother is a projection. This process is crucial, for as we shall see, the other will be— at least potentially—a factor of alienation throughout life. It will always be possible to place some other person in the position of omnipotence. But at the same time, there are—and this is all-important—introjection processes. Without introjection the subject would remain enclosed in solipsism. Introjection is at the root of socialization; any communication between subjects involves the possibility of receiving and incorporating words, meanings, significations coming from an other. If I talked about the primacy of projection, however, it's because it is almost constantly present. Look at transference!

F.U.—You say that the triadic phase creates the pattern for the phantasm. Why is that?

C.C.—Because it is the first situation in which differentiation occurs. The other appears to be the master of the object of desire. In every phantasm, there is an underlying structure, and with it the presence of an object of desire. And the question is posed: "Who is the master of that object?"

F.U.—In this connection, it should be said then that the main element of this phase is the mother's function as "master of signification," as master of "meaning-making."

C.C.—That's exactly it. It is the mother who assigns a signification to each thing and to each situation—to begin with, as Piera Aulagnier showed, by naming the baby's affects. Also, it is the mother who says "that's good" and "that's bad."

F.U.—In your conceptualization, the structuring of the psyche is a socialization process as well, from the triadic phase on. This is therefore a key point in that double structuring/socializing process, at which the first separation takes place.

C.C.—Socialization begins in the triadic phase because the mother is the first person to say "no" to the infant. So the mother is construed as all-powerful, and simultaneously with the recognition that she has an existence and a desire, or will, foreign to the infant and that it does not control. This obliges the infant to recognize her as a separate entity.

Individual and Society: Meaning-Making Processes

F.U.—Let's talk about the exiting from the triadic phase, from that imaginary world still closed by the mother's omnipotence over meaning. So let's talk about opening up, not to the other but to others, to the father and the social sphere, which is to say, the transition to the "social individual."

C.C.—Exiting from that closed world begins as soon as the monad is fractured, with the obligation to forego omnipotence. But that first exit is a "sham exit" inasmuch as omnipotence is transferred to someone else— and to the extent to which the infant is able to remain shut in with its mother, which produces extremely severe, now well-known pathologies.

To proceed further, the baby must "depose" its mother from the locus of her omnipotence. And that actually takes place with the Oedipal function. The mother is no longer seen as all-powerful, as being the only one exerting any power. There is also the acknowledgment that she is incomplete, caught up in her desire by the other, which is to say, the father. She is obliged, then, to take the father's word into consideration. And it is at

that point, when the mother as all-powerful figure topples, that a socializing overture takes place.

The process must not stop here, however. The entry of the father does
not suffice to break the closure, to socialize and to fulfill the Oedipal
function. The father must also be recognized as one of many fathers, as
not being the source of Law in himself, but rather as spokesman for the
Law, with he himself subjected to the Law.

F.U.—What I retain as important in these developments is that the
structuring of the psyche is a socialization process as well. And the key to
that twofold perspective is unquestionably the notion of "meaning-making," of signification, as the essential characteristic of the psyche as well
as of society.

C.C.—Absolutely. The socialization process is at work and at stake in
and through the process of bestowing signification. Society is primarily a
magma of social imaginary significations that make collective and individual life meaningful. Consequently, socialization is nothing other than
entering—and functioning within—that instituted magma of social significations.

That is capital for the comprehension of the structuring of the psyche,
because without it one only sees the "negative" aspect of the process,
which is to say repression, what is denied or taken away from the subject,
whereas we must also perceive the "positive" side: society "gives" meaning
to the subject, its significations provide the meaning-making that satisfies
the psyche's compelling need. That wouldn't work otherwise.

It is, moreover, most important to acknowledge this, for our comprehension of the social sphere as well. The social sphere is locus and process
of creation. There could not be any history in the true sense of the term if
there were no change, rupture, and creation. The social-historical dimension is primarily the emergence of new social imaginary significations.
Its institution, the dynamic between the instituting agency—the radical
imagination—and what is instituted—the institutions already created—is
secondary with regard to that essential characteristic of human communities, the ability to create new significations, new meanings. The radical
imagination exists not only at the level of the individual psyche, but at the
social-historical level as well, in the form of the *radical imaginary.* Society
is not, nor is it constituted *purely and simply* by, prohibitions! In spite of

what one interpretation of *Totem and Taboo* may suggest to a few overly hasty psychoanalysts, and in spite of Freud's own ambiguities as well, society cannot be conceived as the outcome of two taboos—the taboo on incest and the taboo on murder. Prohibition alone can create nothing. It can just barely regulate some things. There is an almost infinite positive content in the creation and existence of societies, and not merely prohibitions.

So to return to the structuring of the psyche, let's say that if the psyche does not find a meaning susceptible of replacing the primal, monadic meaning within the social space, it will obviously be unable to come out of closure and survive. This is one of the requisites that the psyche "demands" of society: the psyche may be turned into almost anything, a Buddhist, a Christian, a bourgeois, a Nazi, etc., but what society cannot do is cease to provide it with meaning.

An Enlarged Conception of Sublimation

F.U.—One very important aspect of your work on the psyche—and the next logical step in our discussion—has to do with the sublimation process. I think this is a line of thought in which we can appreciate both the originality of your perspective and its profoundly Freudian roots. By elaborating on the classical notion and giving it its full import, you propose what we may call an "enlarged" conception of sublimation.

C.C.—That's true. But if I felt the need to advance what you rightly call an "enlarged" conception of sublimation, it is because there is that basic question: What is human life? What are we talking about? The satisfaction of drives? That's only a tiny part of human life. The human being is defined by the predominance of the pleasure of representation over organ pleasure, over the mere satisfaction of drives.

Any cathexis of objects that are not directly or indirectly—that is, immediately or in some mediated way—objects of a drive is what I define as sublimated activity. The prerequisite, the fulcrum, of such activity is the ability of the psyche to experience pleasure through representation. Of course, representational pleasure is also at work in phantasms and in waking phantasizing, but the main difference is that in the case of sublimation we are talking about the cathexis of socially valued objects.

What does psychoanalysis in general mean by sublimation nowadays?

When we read psychoanalytic writings, they give us the impression that the only model of sublimation is the one in which the child plays with colors instead of playing with her feces, and goes on to become a painter. That's absolutely ridiculous. The truth is that as soon as the child begins to speak she is involved in a sublimated activity; she is sublimating. She is not seeking any organ pleasure; she is trying to communicate and to do so has cathected—and is using—a social object, language. A child who wants to be first in his class or to excel at football does so because these are socially cathected objects that do not procure any organ pleasure or satisfy any drive.

F.U.—One of the most interesting consequences of your reconceptualization of sublimation is unquestionably that it makes it possible to conceive the articulation between the subject and the social imaginary.

C.C.—Sublimation is the subjective axis, or "side," of the functioning of the social institution.

F.U.—In *The Violence of Interpretation,*[7] Piera Aulagnier suggested the idea of a "narcissistic contract" and the notion of a "discourse of the whole" in order to think that necessary articulation between the psyche and the social dimension. Readers can be referred to chapter 6 of *The Imaginary Institution of Society* for a more detailed development. Nevertheless, I would like you to be more specific about the relationship between your own thinking and that of Piera Aulagnier on these questions.

C.C.—What Piera Aulagnier called "the discourse of the whole" is one aspect of the institution of society. It is the social discourse that says, "This is real, that isn't real, this is true or right and that isn't, and so on." With the notion of the "narcissistic contract," she was trying to theorize what the psyche expects of society as compensation for its abandoning its "monadic ultranarcissism." That's the "narcissistic contract": "If you behave in such and such a way, then you will get recognition from other people; you will be cathected by others, who will fill the narcissistic breach opened by your having abandoned primordial omnipotence." I think that these two ideas are entirely correct.

Subject and Autonomy

F.U.—Before we end our discussion, I would like us to talk about the notion of "reflective, deliberative subjectivity," which you suggest is a possible state of the social individual—a state that brings the signification and the very experience of autonomy into play.

C.C.—The social individual is a conscious individual. As such, his conscious ego is capable of reasoning and calculating. And we may stop at that. This is true for the major part of the history of humankind. Psychoanalytically speaking, and also from the social-historical standpoint, we can see that such individuals—although they are not psychotic, perverted, or neurotic—are alienated, that they are heteronomous. They do of course have criteria as to what is good or bad, right or wrong, and so forth, but they themselves did not produce those criteria. Those criteria were imposed on them by society through the socialization process. But if we stopped there, at submissiveness to social discourse, we would be unable to understand some facts and some historical processes, because human history is not just slavery and the Middle Ages.

For example, we could not comprehend how psychoanalysis could appear. Why wasn't Freud content with saying, "Yes, there are a lot of problems with sexuality" and things of the like? Why did he begin to say that when people repress their sexuality it makes them sick? Well, when Freud said all that, was he exclusively a "conscious ego"? No. I am saying that this is reflective subjectivity, meaning that a subject is capable of calling into question the imaginary significations of the society in which she lives, and even the institutions of that society. Whence my claim that there is creation in the history of humanity (which is not difficult for psychoanalysis to recognize, but should not be understood exclusively through psychoanalytic considerations). It is reflective subjectivity, which goes hand in hand with the birth of the project of autonomy, with the birth of autonomous, reflective, democratic political activity. The subject here is not simply conscious, but is capable of calling into question the significations and the rules handed down to him by his society.

F.U.—The psychoanalytic counterpart of that definition would be that autonomous subjectivity takes the form of a certain type of change in the relation between consciousness and the unconscious.

c.c.—You're quite right. In a psychoanalytic perspective, the autonomous subject is not simply carried away or driven by her unconscious, but is capable of being lucid about her desires, being in touch with them, being permeable to them and at the same time filtering them. This subject is capable of reflecting and deciding what she is going to achieve with her desires and what she is not going to do, and of acting accordingly.

f.u.—Which brings us directly to what you call the psychoanalytic project, which you see as tied to the emergence of the project of autonomy. It also leads us to understand the end of analysis in this perspective.

c.c.—Of course. The goal of analysis, at best, is to help the patient become an autonomous subject, which is to say a reflective, deliberative subjectivity. It is to help her develop a different relationship with her desires, so that she can channel and control them by means other than repression. This is an ideal objective. Minimally, the analyst tries to help the patient "go from neurotic suffering to a state of ordinary human unhappiness."

f.u.—Which is definitely in conflict with what Lacanians call the "ethic of desire." . . .

c.c.—The Lacanians talk a lot about ethics without ever saying anything specific. What does the "ethic of desire" mean? You can have the desire to kill someone. Should you fulfill it? At most, one might talk about "fulfilling some desires." But a key question arises then, which Lacanians avoid or simply ignore: which desires should be fulfilled? And here's another question, a necessarily social one: what is the criterion? Can the criterion arise exclusively out of psychoanalysis, as the Lacanians seem to hallucinate it doing? No. The decision will be singular and subjective, but it will also be tied to a collective, social-historical situation. For psychoanalysis, the project of autonomy is anything but a "privatized ethic of desire": it is brought into play as indissociably individual and social. This means that the question of subjective action and freedom, inasmuch as human beings are social beings, always brings into play the subject's relationship with other people's freedom. The free activity of a subject is necessarily activity directed toward the freedom of all.

Logos

§ 12   The Social-Historical: Mode of Being, Problems of Knowledge

The best a "positive" conception of history can offer is this: history is the sum total of actions of human beings through space and time. We may as well start with it. Immediately, though, questions arise. What are those human beings, and where do they come from? Can there be human beings without history, outside history? Are they not shaped into very different forms *within history*, and possibly *through the action of history*? Do these actions of human beings take place in a vacuum? Is there any possible meaningful human action outside an instituted society, the relations, the meanings, the purposes, the values posited by this instituted society? Unless by *history* we mean the mere unfolding of a sequence of any sort of events over time (as, e.g., in the phrase: "the history of the solar system"), have we ever encountered history without society? Should we then say that history, in the proper sense, is the product of societies? But can we forget that social forms, particular societies as defined by their specific institutions, are themselves "products" of history? Is society generating history, or the reverse? Or is this opposition meaningless?

Meaningless it is, indeed. And it would even be inadequate to say that society is the "product" of history, or that history is the "work" of society. History is the self-alteration of society—an alteration whose very forms are each time the creation of the society considered. Repetition itself—as, for instance, in primitive or traditional societies—is never, of course, strict repetition; in its actual occurrence, and in order to occur, repetition is heavily slanted by the basic orientation of the whole set of institutions of these societies. At a deeper level, it would still be inadequate to say that history is a *dimension* of society, the dimension by virtue of which the

past of a society is always immanent in its present, this present always being inhabited by a future of some unspecified content and form. History
is the self-deployment of society in time; but this time is, in its essential
characteristics, a creation of society, both as *historical* time—once and for
all—and in each particular case as *the* time of this particular society with
its particular tempo, significant articulations, anchorages, prospects, and
promises. In the same way, there is a self-deployment of society in space,
a topic that I will not dwell on here. By space I do not mean "geographical expansion" (or location), but the creation of a simultaneously ordered
"natural" and "social" multidimensionality proper to each and every society. As society cannot be without this self-deployment in time—as society
is, indeed, this self-deployment in time—we would better speak, in philosophical terms, of the *social-historical.*[1]

History does not happen to society; history is the self-deployment of
society. By this affirmation, we contradict the entire spectrum of existing
tenets: history as the product of the will of God; history as the result of
the action of ("natural" or "historical") "laws"; history as a "subjectless
process"; history as a purely random process. It is not my purpose, however, to discuss or to refute these tenets here.[2]

We posit history *in itself* as creation and destruction. We are speaking
at an ontological level here, for we are concerned with the creation and
destruction of *forms,* of *eidē.* Creation is not "production," the bringing
forth of an exemplar of a preexisting *eidos;* it is the *ab ovo* positing of such
an *eidos.* Even less would it be the random emergence of a numerically
singular combinatorial configuration. Destruction is, here, ontological destruction. When a star or a galaxy runs its course and eventually disappears
as this star or this galaxy, there is no destruction properly speaking. The
form "star" or "galaxy" is unaffected, and stars and galaxies of the same
type could be (and certainly are) produced again. And even if such were
not the case, the *eidos* would not be destroyed: an ideal scientist-observer
could, in principle, reconstitute this form. In a certain sense, nothing is
really "lost" with the explosion of a supernova or the disappearance of the
dinosaurs (whatever the empirical gaps and problems thereby created for
biologists); however, the destruction of the Athenian *polis,* of the Roman
religion, of Florence as it was from the twelfth to the sixteenth centuries,
is the destruction of the singular, unique *eidos* embodied in each of these
historical entities. It would be meaningless to say that this *eidos* is ideally preserved in the sense one may say the Pythagorean theorem would

be ideally "preserved" even after the disappearance of the Earth and the end of the human race. Because the being of a social-historical entity is not purely (not even essentially) "intelligible" or reducible to "intelligible" elements, it is in principle impossible to recover, after it is destroyed, the *eidos* it embodies and realizes. It is not only the glory that was Athens or Rome that has vanished. It is the whole world of meanings, of affects, and of intentions—of social imaginary significations—created by these societies and holding them together that cannot be recovered, but only approximated with the greatest difficulty, on which more later.

Even more than the creation of *eidos,* the *destruction* of *eidos* must remain wholly unthinkable for the inherited ontology. Just as the creation of social-historical *eidos* is not a combinatorial pasting together of "immutable elements" (e.g., the "pairs of opposites" of structuralist theories), destruction of *eidos* in history is not the decomposition of components, of "elements" that have been combined in this form and could be recombined in another. There are no such "elements" in the human domain. The "elements" of social-historical life are, each time, created *as* elements, in their relevancy, meaning, connections, etc., in and through the particular institution of society to which they "belong." Thus, each social-historical form is truly and genuinely singular; it possesses an essential, not numerical or combinatorial, singularity (strictly speaking, structuralism and poststructuralism assert that the singularity of a society—or indeed, for that matter, of an oeuvre ["a work"]—is, and must be of exactly the same character as the singularity of the numbers, say, 556, 632, and 413). Indeed, the "proof" that social-historical *eidos* is created is that it can be destroyed in a way that no other *eidos* can. For instance, any physical form (whether it be taken concretely or abstractly, as type) can have its elements "taken apart" and can subsequently, at least in principle, be recomposed. (That this may well *not* be the case even in physics, as might be inferred from some aspects of contemporary cosmology and quantum theory, is an indication that perhaps even sheer physical being cannot be fully captured in the ensemblistic-identitary categories of inherited ontology.)

The specificity of the social-historical is not just being-for-itself, "meaning for . . . ," "representation," "affect," "intention" (or "desire"): these are already creations of the living being as such—though, of course, they acquire completely different contents in the social-historical field.[3] The social-historical is, first of all, the phenomenological specificity of the forms it creates and through which it exists: institutions embodying so-

cial imaginary significations, and their concrete product, bearer and re-
producer, the living individual as social-historical form. More important,
however, the social-historical is the ontological form that *can put itself
into question* and, through self-reflective activity, *explicitly alter itself.* To
be sure, this is not a fated or necessary result, nor does it happen *hōs epi to
polu,* but rather as an exception. Nonetheless, it is only in the social-historical domain that we encounter an *eidos* that puts into question its own
laws of existence (politics in the proper sense) and that, more particularly,
puts into question the transmitted representations it has for itself of a
world and of itself (philosophy). We not talking about an "immanent" or
"essential possibility" of the social-historical. Democracy and philosophy
are not the outcome of natural or spontaneous tendencies of society and
history. They are themselves creations, and they entail a radical break with
the previously instituted state of affairs. Both are aspects of the project of
autonomy. But the emergence of this project (of which ontology and the
self-ontology of the social-historical as embodied in this very self-reflection are an aspect) has taken place at this level of being only.

This essential feature of the social-historical lays bare to our scrutiny
the abyssal question of social-historical knowledge. Of course it is not our
conception that produces the question. The question is there, manifest
in the innumerable substantive difficulties of social-historical knowledge
and hardly veiled by the various "theories" about society and history formulated by historical materialism, functionalism, structuralism, etc., as it
cries loudly for recognition over the Procrustean beds on which all these
theories lay their social-historical "material." Our conception simply allows us to gain, from the start, a clear vision of the infinitely enigmatic
character of the question.

Each and every society creates, within what must be called its cognitive
closure—or, even better, its *closure of meaning*—its own world, which is
both "natural" (and "supranatural") as well as "human." Our fountains
are inhabited by nymphs, our stars are palaces for our gods, only a young
virgin woman may marry honorably, and so on. In this world, other societies (other human groupings) have a (generally very poor) limited and
defined place, meaning, and role. Knowledge referring to them is scant,
mostly pragmatic (they trade salt, they use poisoned arrows) and religio-
mythical in character (they are heathen, under the curse of God, etc.).
As far as we know, only two societies, the ancient Greek and the Western

European, have developed a genuine interest in the others *as* others and attempted to attain a knowledge and an understanding of their ways of being. And this is the tradition in which we find ourselves.

The attempt to "know," as far as possible, other societies than our own, be they "present" or "past," immediately raises two questions: Why, and how? Let us eliminate facile answers to the first question. Of course, we may want to accumulate a knowledge of sorts about the others (in a sense, all societies do) in order, e.g., to exploit, conquer, dominate, or proselytize them. (*The Use of Geography Is to Make War* is the title of a recent French book.) I am asking, however, for a reasonable, defensible, arguable answer. This can only be found in the implications of our project of autonomy. In attempting to know, to understand the others irrespective of any "practical use" of this understanding, we go over and beyond the *closure of meaning* of our own institution. We stop dividing the human world between "us" and "them"—us: the only true human beings; the others: savages, barbarians, heathens, and so on. We stop considering our own institution of society as the only good, reasonable, truly human one and the institutions of the others as curiosities, aberrations, "primitive nonsense" (Engels), or divine punishment for their devilish nature. We also stop considering our representation of the world as the only meaningful one. Without necessarily abandoning our institutions—since, after all, *they* are the institutions that made this questioning possible—we can take a critical stand against them: we can discover, as did the Greeks in the sixth and fifth centuries, that institutions and representations belong to *nomos* and not to *physis,* that they are human creations and not "God given" or "nature given." This immediately opens up the possibility of questioning *our own* institution and of *acting* in regard to it. If its origin is *nomos* and not *physis,* then it could be changed through human action and human reflection, and this leads immediately to new questions: Ought we to change it? For what reasons? Up to what limits? How? This is why a genuine interest in the institutions of other peoples as such appears in fact only in the two social-historical formations, ancient Greece and Western Europe (which includes, of course, the United States), where true *politics*—in the sense of calling into question the existing institutions and of changing them through deliberate collective action—and true philosophy—in the sense of calling into question the instituted representations and meanings and of changing them through the self-reflective activity of thought—were created. What I have in mind here is not a "causal" or "chronological" sequence. Geography, historiography, and ethnology (as distinct from chronicles of priests and kings and accounts of marvelous/mythical voyages) were in fact born as part of philosophy in the largest (and truest) sense, which is itself a dimension of the democratic and emancipatory movement born in the Greek *poleis* and reborn—much later, following a long period of regression—in the cities of Western Europe after the height of the Middle Ages.

Of course, once born, this interest starts feeding on what becomes our unquenchable thirst for knowledge per se. This thirst is one of the manifestations of our freedom, or autonomy: we constantly put into question the inherited (be it "scientific" or "philosophical") representation of what there is; we constantly shake the walls of our own closure. Indeed, this is the very meaning of truth, as created in the Greco-Western world. Of course, in every society there must be some sort of "truth"—but we should rather call that *correctness*: the canonical correspondence of statements and representations with what the instituted and closed world of meanings of the society considered has once and for all established as the "real" state of affairs as well as the instituted criteria whereby this correspondence is, each time, judged. In the Greco-Western world, truth is created as the perpetual movement of doing away with the closure of meaning (the movement is perpetual because this closure can never be eliminated). In the particular case of social-historical knowledge, however, our interest also has another, equally strong motivation: to grasp human beings' essential possibilities. We consider their social-historical creations, and their, or our own, sublime or monstrous deeds, and we thereby enlarge the view of our own possibilities. If Socrates existed, this is something a human being can be. If Hitler existed, this too is something a human being can be. And so too can the social-historical formations that made these human exemplars possible.

But *how* can we know other societies and historical epochs? What we do know is heavily, perhaps exhaustively, conditioned by what we are as social individuals brought up in and fabricated by this particular society, our own. This goes far beyond "prejudices," and far beyond epistemology and theory of knowledge. The question has an ontological grounding. We are, and are what we are, because we share in a world that, far from being free-floating or neutral (assuming "humanization" or "socialization" in general), is created and instituted by our own society. Neither Kant nor

Husserl writes in a transcendental language. They both write in German. And the German language—as any other—conveys an entire world.

Therefore, the first presupposition is the calling into question of the institution that made us what we are and of the ways of thinking it has furnished us. This is of negative value only. We thereby avoid uncritically imputing to others motives, feelings, and value orientations that have currency and meaning among us, and even "rationality" in general. (And, by the way, who said that our "rationality" is rationality "*tout court*"?) The first task in this respect is indeed to start probing our so-called rationality—and this would be the first *rational* task. As we know, this task remains in fact incomplete and is, in principle, unable to be completed (except in trivial domains that exclude the infinite and exclude self-reference—that is, exclude by definition the self-reflective activity of thought). And we recognize, to begin with, that another society lives literally in another world—its own world (this was already known to Herodotus, as shown by his remarks about Cambyses and the Egyptians, or Darius and Greek and Hindu burial customs). How can we enter this other world, or, in fact, even approach it?

As I have done in the preceding pages, I offer these conclusions without benefit of "proofs" (i.e., without the necessary argumentation and empirical corroboration).[4] There are some scant and (unless they be trivial) always problematic social-historical universals. They fall into two broad classes. The first belongs to what I call the ensemblistic-identitary (*ensidic* for short) dimension of the institution of any society. Given what we are and what we know, we can deduce them almost a priori. For instance, if a society is to have language, it must be familiar with predication, and it must divide statements into correct and incorrect. It also must have some arithmetic and geometry as well as functionally adequate descriptions and classifications of the part of the physical world in which it is living (the "first natural stratum"), including human beings as "biological" entities. Now, it happens (*sumbainei*) that we share with all humans the same biological constitution and the same "physical world," and know something about its properties. If a society is to last, it has to "function adequately"—maintain and reproduce itself—and therefore it must, up to a point, construct its world in some correspondence with the given first natural stratum and in accordance with some requirements of ensidic logic—to which, we find, the first natural stratum also "corresponds." It would be easy, and tiresome, to multiply ad infinitum examples of the constraints thereby imposed on the creation of social institutions.

But this does not take us very far. It boils down to this: given the physical environment of the Earth and the biological properties of human beings, each and every society, if it is to maintain and reproduce itself (i.e., if it is to remain *observable*), will have to provide for its material and sexual reproduction. To this purpose, it will have to create some coherent fragments of ensidic logic and of "applied" knowledge of this world. Yet this would also be true of an "ape group"; and it would not in the least make intelligible the almost unlimited variety of societies and their corresponding institutions and social imaginary significations. Our knowledge of these constraints, and their particular character (geographical environment, inherited or borrowed techniques, and ensidic "knowledge"), only points, in each particular case, to some of the beams used and to some of their particularities that have helped and/or hindered a society in the building of its institutions. The plan, the form, the articulations, the purpose of the building are another matter, and they are what we are chiefly interested in. It is not the properties of stone that tell us the difference between the Pyramid of Cheops, the Parthenon, and the cathedral of Amiens. Neither is it the (problematic) sameness of their syntactic structures that will teach us anything about the difference between "the apple is a fruit borne by a tree" and "life is a tale told by an idiot."

The construction of its own world by each and every society is, in essence, the creation of a world of meanings, its social imaginary significations, which organize the (presocial, "biologically given") natural world, instaurate a social world proper to each society (with its articulations, rules, purposes, etc.), establish the ways in which socialized and humanized individuals are to be fabricated, and institute the motives, values, and hierarchies of social (human) life. Society leans on the first natural stratum, but only to erect a fantastically complex (and amazingly coherent) edifice of significations that vest any and every thing with *meaning* (think again of language). This is also a transhistorical universal, and, up to a point, we can elucidate it and some of its implications. Society socializes (humanizes) the wild, raw, antifunctionally mad psyche of the newborn and imposes on it a formidable complex of constraints and limitations (the psyche must renounce absolute egocentricity and omnipotence of imagination, recognize "reality" and the existence of others, subordinate desires to rules of behavior, and accept sublimated satisfactions and even death for the sake of "social" ends). Society thereby succeeds to an unbelievable degree (though never exhaustively) in diverting, orienting, and channeling the psyche's egotistic, asocial (and, of course, fully "arational") drives and impulses into coherent social activities, more or less "logical" diurnal thinking. But "in exchange," as it were, the psyche imposes on the social institution an essential requirement: the social institution has to provide the psyche with meaning. Viewed from the standpoint of the psyche, the process whereby the psyche abandons (although never fully) its initial ways and objects and invests (cathects) socially meaningful ways of behaving, motives, and objects is *sublimation*; viewed from the standpoint of society, it is the social fabrication (nurturing, rearing) of the individual. Thereby a new *eidos* (different in each particular society) is created: the social individual (you, me, and the others). The individual is, in fact, the effective concrete bearer of the institutions of its society, and it is, in principle, bound by construction, as it were, to maintain and reproduce them. That this binding is more or less broken with the appearance of societies containing the germ of autonomy and the corresponding type of individual raises a further question.

The substantive task of "knowing" another society is thereby brought back to the attempt to penetrate, make accessible, and reconstitute the world of its social imaginary significations. (And, insofar as the concrete bearer of the emerged parts of these significations is the individual, some degree of "methodological individualism" is legitimate, though by no means sufficient.) The term *social imaginary significations* should not, however, be given an "intellectualistic" or even simply "noematic" content. The imaginary significations construct (organize, articulate, vest with meaning) the world of the society considered (and lean each time on the "intrinsic" ensidic organization of the first natural stratum). Yet in the same stroke and indissociably, they also do much more than that. To borrow, metaphorically, the distinctions correctly made by ancient psychology, they determine at the same time the representations, the affects, and the intentions dominant in a society. In fact, one can show almost a priori that these distinctions necessarily correspond to the fundamental ways of being of any entity that is "for itself"—and, in their own way, both society and the social individual are "for themselves."[5] Not only is the "noematic" ("representational") construction of the natural and social world a creation, each time different, of each and every society, but also each society posits its own important and dominant intentions (to live calmly with music and dance, to worship God and be saintly, to be *kalos kagathos*, to conquer the world, to expand the "forces of production," to "build socialism," etc.); moreover, and this point is usually ignored, it creates its dominant and characteristic *affects*. Even the sheer characterization of these affects is extremely difficult and can drag us onto very slippery ground or into the swamps of pseudoliterary "*à peu près.*" One example may help to understand what I mean. After describing Thomas Aquinas' philosophy and his tremendous effort to import Aristotle into Christian philosophy, Etienne Gilson comments, "But for Thomas, faith remains primordial." Now, this sentence would be Chinese for Aristotle—or, indeed, for any Greek from the classical period. *Pistis* in classical Greek, *fides* in classical Latin, have only a homonymic relation to what *pistis* and *fides,* faith, became with Christianity. (The possible antecedents in Judaism need not detain us here.) Faith, as this complex of *Erlebnisse* that is centrally and decisively organized around an *affect,* is a historical creation of the Christian institution of religion (and, for fifteen centuries, of society itself). We can follow its instauration from Paul and the Greek fathers to Augustine; we can point to specific aspects of theological and mystical texts, of hymns, of church architecture, of paintings; we can force people to listen for hours to the *Matthäus Passion;* we can describe crusading, pious, or caritative behavior. But we can neither show nor demonstrate faith (neither exhibit nor define it); and without this, any description, let alone understanding, of a Christian society would be hopelessly mutilated.

Thus, after the "external description" of a society (of its ensidic and functional organization), we have to attempt to grasp its particular *eidos.* This leads us to the need to penetrate and understand the magma of its singular social imaginary significations. *Some* "constituent parts" of this magma, and some institutional forms, may be universal—and this may help (but also create illusions about) our work. What matters, however, is the singularity of this magma.[6] Of the three "vectors," so to speak, that characterize this magma, the least difficult to describe is that of the "intentions" of the society considered—since they can be read immediately in its effective actions. Even in this case, though, things are far from simple. It is relatively easy to "understand" the "intentions" (the "drive," the "push") of capitalist society (or of the capitalist component of today's Western societies). Let it be granted that they can be adequately described by the expression: "unlimited expansion of 'rational' mastery." (The innumerable problems conveyed by this expression and the actual facts to which it refers need not detain us here.) The relative facility of access, in this case, is not only due to our proximity to, or participation in, this society. The very nature of the "goals" of the capitalistic system and of the means it uses (as, more generally, of the world it constructs) makes it to a large extent amenable to considerations of ensidic logic (*Zweckrationalität*). How individuals in this society live the universal expansion of pseudorationality, and why on earth a society would aim at it, is another part of the story.

The situation is very different, however, in most other cases. Consider, for instance, Aztec society or even, much nearer to us, the "true" Christian societies (from the fifth to the twelfth centuries). Here the "intentions" are so intimately entangled with "meanings" (in the narrow sense) or "representations," on the one hand, with "affects," on the other (cf. what has been said earlier about faith) that, very often, one's understanding risks remaining external or simply verbal. Some aspects of Max Weber's considerations about "world religions" seem to me to exemplify this risk. To use an image: in music we always have rhythm, melody, and harmony. Of course there are monophonic melodies, but even in this case harmony is embedded in the melody, which melody cannot exist if it does not belong to a mode, which confers upon each note its potential harmonic value. Even bare rhythm, e.g., the monotonic banging of a tam-tam, contains a "melody" as a borderline case (here the "melody feature" is simply *a, a, a . . .*).

The situation is akin to that implied by having *full* possession of a "foreign" language (and the simile is not gratuitous because language bears and conveys virtually the whole of the life of a society and a substantial part of its "history"). Such possession is possible, although very difficult, and perhaps not easily accessible to all people. (We are not committed to the thesis that everybody must be able to understand each and every foreign language, even less than we are committed to the thesis that everybody must be able to master, with equal facility, all branches of contemporary mathematics, say.) But the knowledge thereby acquired is not readily "translatable" in the native language of the student. As in the case of language, the "translation" (the transposition of meaning) would entail the restitution of all the relevant connotations of the second culture in the first—which is, strictly speaking, impossible and can only be posited as a limit or an ideal. This by no means implies that all statements about a foreign society (or, for that matter, about our own) are equivalent, that "anything goes." The validity of the attempts to understand and reconstitute a foreign culture can be judged on the basis of the following criterion: To what extent are they capable of making sense of this other society, of encompassing as many as possible of its aspects and dimensions, and of plausibly (reasonably) showing that there is a magma of social imaginary significations, distinct from our own, that accounts for the specific organization of the society considered, holds it together, and stands behind the "observable" activities and works (*oeuvres*) of the individuals belonging to it?

One should not confuse this last criterion with Max Weber's conception of *Idealtypen* and their "comparison" to "actual" behavior. Not only is the *zweckrational* component of behavior (its "instrumental" or "functional" dimension) for us the least important one and itself, as such, only instrumental in character; it is, each and every time, a *creation* of the society considered and deeply permeated with the imaginary significations of that society. The universality of even purely instrumental "rational" determinations throughout different social-historical forms is both a datum (mostly in its trivial aspects) and a question (for the more important ones). But there is much more than that. Any reconstruction of "understandable" individual behavior starting from observable social realities has to recognize the fundamental constraints of coherence, complementarity, and (ideally speaking) completeness. Ideal types are not garments hanging on a coat rack. They have to be *internally* connected, and, by necessity, they refer to each other and all together to the institution of society and its social imaginary significations. The Roman *pater familias* refers from within—and not because the theoretician "constructs" it so—to the Roman spouse, the plebeian to the patrician, and all of them to the laws of the *urbs,* the Roman religion, etc. They must fit together in order to produce not only a society as a functionally going concern, but *a coherent world* of (what is to us) *alien meaning*—and there is the rub. To be able to proceed to such a reconstruction, we would therefore have to be able to penetrate, to a nontrivial degree, the Roman imaginary of, say, the first three centuries of the Republic, and to reconstitute it, more or less satisfactorily (through various types of circumlocutions), in our own idiom. The fundamental precondition for this endeavor is, of course, the philosophical one: to understand that nothing of this idiom of ours can be taken for universally granted (even, for instance, or perhaps particularly, "rational economic behavior"). As was hinted at earlier, the easiest part of this reconstitution concerns the "intentional" "vector"—the drive or push of a society—for it can be deciphered from its activities and its hierarchy of values. The difficulties of reconstructing the "representational" vector are larger, but once we have shaken open *our* world and partially broken its closure, our imagination allows us to invent different, even violently "exotic," world schemes and to compare them with the observable social-historical phenomena. The most difficult—and, in principle, inaccessible—task is the reconstruction of the "affective" vector. Nobody will ever be able to say how the Greeks lived their religion, nor what initiation into the *mysteria* of Eleusis meant for a newcomer.

And here the circle closes upon itself. Our inability to relive the *Stimmung* of an alien society, owing to the essential unity of the social space defined by these three "vectors," does not make social-historical knowledge vain, but instead stamps it with an essential lacunarity.

Tinos, August 1987–Paris, December 1987

§ 13 False and True Chaos

Before nonchalantly broaching my subject, I would like to ask us all to suspend the dialogue among ourselves for a few seconds and to reflect on the situation to which our Russian colleague was referring in his talk, and on that not-so-distant period when some psychiatrists and psychoanalysts in the West were fighting to get people to acknowledge the terrifying situation in Russia, and most often came up against the obstinate denials—not so much stupid as self-interested— of the international psychiatric establishment.

The term *chaos* was launched about twenty years ago, and there now seems to be a tendency to turn it into a catchall concept, the correlate of an allegedly more or less stringent method—nowadays, stringent means mathematical—that would embrace each and every discipline, and—why not?—renovate philosophy as well. I do not begrudge my admiration of the works and new feats of mathematical physicists (which work in fact mostly pertains to applied mathematics, a term that implies no contempt on my part). They provide the means of explaining, to some extent, and here again we would have to define what is meant by explanation, all sorts of phenomena, and of finding certain behavioral kinships crossing fields belonging to totally different registers, such as turbulence in fluids and clusters of asteroids in the solar system. But I have strong doubts, first about the essential novelty of the basic ideas underlying that work, second about their philosophical portent, and last about their claim to universality. I think—and I came to this realization as I listened to René Thom a moment ago—that what I have to say here coincides with or echoes the concerns he expressed earlier.

First of all, let us clarify the notion of chaotic phenomena. The situation has come to a point where chaos is used to designate anything and everything, any region in which there is a degree of disorder, where things are not simple. I know only one approximately rigorous definition of chaotic phenomena. It is given by D. Ruelle, and seems to be generally accepted: they are the processes of temporal evolution in which there is a sensitive (or appreciable, considerable) dependence on initial conditions and namely on what there was at the outset or on the conditions at the limits, as mathematicians put it—that is, on what surrounds the phenomenon.

If that is what we are talking about, there really is nothing new in it as an idea. Every one of us who has been in a car accident must have thought, at some point: "If I had left the house half a second earlier or half a second later I wouldn't have had that accident." Need I remind you of Pascal, or Cleopatra's nose? Had it been just a little shorter, the face of the world would have been different. But I defy anyone to write the equation that would tie up the nanometers of Cleopatra's nose to everything that has transpired since in world history; and yet that should be the upshot.

Thom very aptly cited Poincaré, Hadamard, and Ruelle, successively, a moment ago. We might add Maxwell—for his ideas, not for their mathematical elaboration, definitely taken much further by the thinkers mentioned by Thom. Maxwell speaks of that sensitive dependence on the initial conditions in *Science and Free Will,* written in 1870. I will simply quote a short passage, although the whole text is interesting. For example, he says, "The rock loosed by frost and balanced on a single point of the mountainside, the little spark which kindles the great forest, the little word which sets the world a-fighting, the little scruple which prevents a man from doing his will, the little spore which blights all the potatoes, the little gemmule which makes us philosophers or idiots. Every existence above a certain rank has its singular points: the higher the rank, the more of them. At these points, influences whose physical magnitude is too small to be taken account of by a finite being may produce results of the greatest importance."

After this historical reminder, let me return to the question at hand, the "sensitive dependence on the initial conditions." We should recall, first, René Thom's theory of catastrophes; he himself did not mention it, out of modesty I think. Thom shows how an infinitesimal shift in the basic variables can lead, precisely, to catastrophes, in his acceptation of the term, which is not the usual sense, in the domain of the phenomena observed. But really, "sensitive dependence" is too vague an expression. "Extreme dependence" would be more appropriate. What can be said about that notion of extreme dependence? To take a shortcut, I think it can only be understood as a discontinuity that would remain to be defined more accurately but about which we may already say one thing: that there is extreme dependence when a continuous variation of initial conditions leads to a discontinuous variation in the result. As we see, this puts us right in the middle of René Thom's catastrophe theory, in another form. Moreover, with this formulation, we discover that all modern sciences have been subsisting up to now on an implicit postulate: the postulate of the continuity of physical phenomena, and actually of extant phenomena in general. In fact, that continuity is not even mathematical continuity in the full sense of the term. It is simple linearity, which is to say that in order for that implicit postulate to be met, all effects would have to be proportionate to their causes. It suffices to state that idea clearly to realize how preposterous it is. But be that as it may, that idea was already demolished by turbulence, and by quantum physics. What have the last twenty years contributed in this respect? Simply, cases of discontinuity have become much more important; and they were discovered by accident. That reminds me of the story Henri Atlan tells about the drunkard who is looking for his key under the lamppost. Another fellow passes by, and asks: "What are you doing here?" "I'm looking for my key . . . " "You're sure it fell under the lamppost?" "Absolutely not. I'm sure it fell somewhere else!" "Then why are you looking under the lamppost?" "Because that's where the light is!"

"Positive" science only deals with those phenomena it knows more or less how to deal with, which is legitimate, and it proclaims that they exhaust everything that exists, which is aberrant.

Since there were no computers, and phenomena with very great discontinuities could not be treated, the subject was dropped, as Thom reminded us, and as Hadamard, Poincaré, and so on had already pointed out. Then computers arrived: so it became possible to treat those phenomena, and from then on the subject took on the importance we now see, with results that are far from negligible in the field of concrete research, but with nothing fundamentally new. And above all—and I come here to my second point—there is nothing new with respect to the ideas of determinism and indeterminism. The confusion is such, here, that the idea of chaos is used, on the one hand, by people who want to attack determinism, and on the other hand by those—and I believe they are the more serious ones—who want to show that some processes may be perfectly deterministic and nonetheless be unforeseeable or unpredictable.

Obviously forecasting may be taken much further than in the past, thanks to computers. But what is a computer? A computer is a deterministic machine par excellence. As the famous GIGO principle says, "garbage in, garbage out"; if the data are correct and the software is good, it will produce correct results. In any case, it's a deterministic machine.

Third, there is the question of universality, and I will be brief on that point. For chaos theories to be of universal portent, we would have to be able to write the nonlinear equations that governed, say, the collapse of the Roman Empire or the collapse of the Russian Empire. I don't think we have reached that point; I actually think we will never reach that point. I would even go further: I say that to postulate universalization, we would have to postulate that everything in existence, absolutely everything, is mathematizable and ensemblizable, that is, liable to set-theorization. That postulate is meaningless. I contend that neither mental nor social-historical phenomena, nor even the totality of biological phenomena, can be subsumed under algebraic or topological structures, or under ordering relations. My question is, simply: is Beethoven closer, topologically speaking, to Mozart or to Haydn? Did Romeo and Juliet love each other more or less than Tristan and Isolde? Is the Greco-Roman component of our Greco-Western culture heavier or lighter than its Judeo-Christian component? The day we begin to claim that these propositions are meaningful, we will be able to go back to discussing that universality.

Now, to take up our second point: contrary to what our Russian colleague said a moment ago, in the original Greek terminology, in Hesiod's *Theogony*—as Olof Gigon demonstrated in a book written in 1945[1]—chaos absolutely does not mean disorder and confusion. Chaos means the void; it is derived from the verb *chainō* or *chaskō*. What Hesiod says is that at the beginning there was emptiness, there was nothing, and starting from that there was the Earth, the Heavens, and Eros. The term *chaos,* with its present-day connotation of a jumbled mix-up, appears for the first time in the first century CE, in Latin literature. It is true, however, that the idea of chaos as, effectively, an initial state of formless confusion is already present in Hesiod, in a passage toward the end of the *Theogony* in which he describes the place where Zeus imprisoned the Titans, then the Giants, once he had defeated them: that is a chaotic place, and it is described as such. It is also present in Plato and Aristotle. It is not called chaos, but in the *Timaeus*, Plato's great cosmological dialogue, it is called *chōra*, which is to say space, in a sense. It is not an amorphous mixture of muddled elements. It is pure, absolute becoming as such, which is to say total indetermination. This is also what *hulē* (matter) means for Aristotle. Plato, like Aristotle in fact, conceives of that chaos as a component of the sublunar world, provided at least that forms and ideas are imposed on it. For Plato, those forms, those *eidē,* are imposed [on sublunar beings] by the demiurge who gazes at eternal forms. According to Aristotle, those forms have been there for all eternity and will persist for all eternity. I think those ideas (about *chōra* and matter) are extremely important. It is they, and not a deterministic chaos, that must be our starting point: we must start off with the idea of something completely indeterminate.

However, since we no longer want either a Platonic demiurge or the Aristotelian ideality of forms, and to the contrary, since everything pushes us toward accepting the idea of novelty within being itself and not simply as a subjective impression, I think we need to make an ontology—a new ontology in which chaos will be the fundamental "determination" of being. We may be more specific, speaking of inexhaustibility, for one thing, and for another, above all of the immanent ability to create, of a *vis formandi* of being; and we can maintain, and I will maintain, that this inexhaustibility of being comes from the immanence of its *vis formandi.*

Before going any further, I would like to justify this idea of creation, of immanent creation. Absolute novelty exists; novelty does not mean unforeseeability. If you play roulette, the 27 may come out. That's unforeseeable, but it is not new. It has already come out billions of times. It is not what is unforeseeable that is new, and it is not indetermination per se that produces novelty. Quantum phenomena are indeterminate, in a sense, when we get to the reduction of the light wave packet level. They can only yield probabilities, but they are not new; you will always find those same old protons and electrons. What is new is the indeducibility and improducibility, which is to say the inconstructibility of X on the basis of the whole prior situation. That whole of the prior situation always gives you some necessary conditions, but in the cases that interest us here, where there is something new, those conditions are not sufficient. Whence the novelty of what is created, qua form, qua *eidos.* Creation is *ex nihilo* but it is not *in nihilo* or *cum nihilo;* it arises somewhere and it surges forth by means of some things.

Chaos is the ultimate depth of being; more, it is the bottomless depth of being; it is the abyss behind everything that exists. And it is precisely through the creation of forms, qua determination, that chaos is always present also as cosmos, that is, as an organized world in the broadest sense of the term, as order. Simply, we are constantly discovering that the organization and the ultimate order of that cosmos escape us. They escape us precisely because the various strata of what presents itself as being cannot be reduced to other allegedly more fundamental or more elementary strata. I personally am convinced that the social-historical sphere cannot possibly be reduced to the psychic sphere, any more than the two can be reduced to something else, or the biological can be reduced to physics and chemistry, for the very simple reason that what already emerges with the biological sphere, for example, is a *meaning* of a kind that does not exist in the physical world, which is to say a meaning—a sense—for the self: a meaning directed toward self-preservation, for instance, or self-reproduction. A star or a galaxy could not care less about reproducing itself or preserving itself. Either they are preserved or they are not preserved; those are laws.

I think that what interests us most here is: to what extent can we speak of the psyche as chaos, and as chaos creating a cosmos or contributing to the creation of a cosmos—that is, of a bottomlessness, an abyss that is simultaneously formative potential, *vis formandi?* Why can we do so? First of all because there is emergence or creation of the human psyche in general as such, as a level of being that differs both from the central nervous system and even from the biological psyche. In comparison with the central nervous system, there is the emergence of meaning for the self [*pour soi*]; in comparison with the biological psyche, the meaning that the human psyche creates or that it is by creating is defunctionalized. This meaning within the human psyche is not compelled by the preservation of the individual, nor by the reproduction of the species. Men and women have been making love for thousands and tens of thousands of years, independently of their knowing whether or not they are going to procreate. A bitch, no. In human beings, sexuality is not functional, as it is in all known mammals and in other sexed creatures.

What does that defunctionalization mean? It means that the functionality of what was the animal psyche is shattered by the emergence of something that is constitutive of the human psyche, that is, the radical imagination as perpetual flux of representations, affects, and desires. Now, what emerges here, what is created in this way, is itself chaotic in the sense I have given to the term, which is, namely: it is perpetual creation, permanent surging from the abyss, from bottomlessness, but which can only be by giving itself, or by taking, form. This is true throughout a history I cannot relate here, one that is in fact extremely difficult to recount and totally unintelligible in many respects. I simply wish to emphasize one aspect, or rather, two. First, I would like to emphasize what is strange—indeed, more than strange—in the relation between psyche and soma, between the soul and the body, in human beings at any rate, perhaps in higher mammals and others, but it is human beings that matter for us. One of the thousand and one strange facts in that history, and that I think indicates why we will never succeed in ensemblizing all this, in mathematizing it, is the fact that psyche and soma are simultaneously inseparable and separable. What makes them inseparable? The fact that if I had a gun and if I were a bad guy, I would shoot a bullet into my friend Bourguignon's head, and if he had a hole in his skull there would no longer be any psyche of a man named Bourguignon. There are also other reasons why they are inseparable. People are given psychotropic substances and their mental functioning changes. Before that, people drank alcohol, or took peyote, and their mental functioning changed. Somewhere, the molecules of Largactil or alcohol meet that immaterial thing we call the psyche; where they encounter it, I don't know. At the same time, psyche and soma are separable because from birth on, the psyche is turned inward, and we have proof of this with infant anorexia, for example, and probably with autism, or more prosaically, with resistance to torture. Someone is cut to pieces and does not betray her comrades. Why? Biologically speaking, she should give them away, but she doesn't.

Throughout its history, with its ups and downs, this psyche forms a cosmos. It undergoes a long process resulting in an ordinary individual, you, me, anyone, an individual—a social creation but with the psyche in the backdrop—who is constantly plied, and haunted, by the underlying psyche which always comprises the possibility of creating something new. This psyche takes forms that are always more or less determinate. For example, what Freud calls the psychical agencies are determinate forms in some sense; nosological entities, or simply character formations, are determinate forms, more or less. The outcome of this history is an individual who is capable both of calculating and dreaming, and who can actually dream while he is calculating and calculate while dreaming, as Freud has taught us, since the numbers we dream of are analyzable, theoretically. That person walks and sings, loves and very often kills his loved ones, and his dreams, as Freud himself rightly says, are never completely analyzable. Freud does not use the term *chaos* when speaking about the psyche. Perhaps, being a self-proclaimed positivist, he would have been horrified by the term. But he was well aware of that reality, as shown in a passage in *The Interpretation of Dreams* (to which no one paid any attention fifteen years ago):

> There is often a passage in even the most thoroughly interpreted dream which has to be left obscure; this is because we become aware during the work of interpretation that at that point there is a tangle of dream-thoughts which cannot be unraveled and which moreover adds nothing to our knowledge of the content of the dream. This is the dream's navel, the spot where it reaches down into the unknown. The dream-thoughts to which we are led by interpretation must even obligatorily, and in an entirely universal fashion (for Freud no dream is fully interpretable), have no definite endings; they are bound to branch out in every direction into the intricate network of our world of thought. It is at some point where this meshwork is particularly dense that the dream-wish grows up, like a mushroom out of its mycelium.[2]

I think this quotation shows what psychical chaos is—and also that it is a far cry from the term in circulation today.

§ 14   Remarks on Space and Number

It remains, nonetheless, that mathematics (and, more generally, everything that we can conceive of as a formal system), within the limits sketched above, is wholly subject to ensemblist or identitary logic. The same is obviously true with respect to topology, which has recently become fashionable in the most unexpected places, due perhaps to the excessive attention paid to the signifier at the expense of the signified. Topology can provide striking metaphors or, in certain cases, allow the construction of models less rigid than those of other branches of mathematics. Doing topology, however, is basically no different than doing arithmetic: from a fundamental perspective, in both cases the logical operations and the mode of being of the object are the same.

The lines above are taken from *The Imaginary Institution of Society*.[1] I sent a copy of the book to René Thom when it was first published in 1975. Some time later I received a thank-you note from René Thom, assuring me that I was entirely wrong in assimilating topology to arithmetic.

At the time I had interpreted Thom's remark, coming from such a great topologist, as indicating that he was piqued. Since then, I have come to see it as the outcome of a philosophical stance increasingly clearly expressed in his writings of the last decade, in which he gives ontological primacy to the continuum (and to space, taken figuratively as much as literally) over numbers and discrete entities. Perhaps he would agree to define that philosophy as a reversal of Kronecker's famous saying: "God made the continuum, all the rest is man's creation"—the remainder including the natural numbers, of course.

Before I go on to discuss this position, I would like to explain the motivations and intentions behind what I wrote in 1975.

Ensidic Logic and Magmas

In philosophy, the idea that being exceeds habitual logic by far is strongly asserted in different forms from the first. This begins with Anaximander and Heraclitus, is clearly formulated by Plato and Aristotle, and goes on through Husserl and Bergson. When I was writing *The Imaginary Institution . . . ,* all sorts of rumors inferred that a more "modern" (and more rigorous) basis had been found for that exceeding of traditional logic, through the opposition between the "discrete"—the separate, inanimate or mechanical—and "continuity"—the unified, living or organic. Just at that time, Jacques Lacan was performing "topological" sleights of hand, at which his sheeplike followers from the rue d'Ulm[2] bleated and gaped in uncomprehending admiration.

My own work on the social imaginary and the social-historical sphere, as well as on the psyche and the radical imagination of singular human beings, had led me to the conclusion, since 1964, that something other than traditional (Aristotelian, "dialectical" or modern, formal) logic is at work in these spheres, although it was out of the question to assert, even for a second, that such logic had no hold on them. Whence the idea of a magmatic logic, encompassing traditional logic (what I then called ensemblistic-identitary logic [ensemblistic meaning set-theoretical.—Trans.] and now, to be brief, ensidic) but not reducible to it.[3]

What I understood of contemporary science had convinced me that logic of that type also corresponded to the mode of being of the physical as well as the biological world, finally meaning, then, to every being with the exception of human artifacts qua artifacts. An automobile is ensidic if we look at it as an automobile; otherwise it is an indescribable mass of "particles" constantly crossed by innumerable neutrinos, and perhaps also some quantity of "dark matter," the whole being partially governed by some rather incomprehensible "laws." An algorithm, viewed as such, without the axioms that found it, or a disembodied Turing machine, is purely ensidic, if we disregard the assumptions behind their existence as well as their possible consequences.

There is an ensidic logic underlying an infinite number of ineliminable propositions, such as 2 + 2 = 4, *a* is not *non-a, anthrōpos anthrōpon gennai,* you can't be at two places at the same time, and so forth. It is explicitly embodied in the *legein* and the *teukhein,* which activities are basic to any society.[4] It is dense throughout being. It is impossible to analyze a dream without resorting to it, impossible to confine one's analysis to it. Its basic presupposition is the existence of sets in the "naively" mathematical sense: the assertion of the existence of perfectly distinct, well-defined elements, separable and combinable at will, hereditarily transmitting their properties of "combinability" and separability to the sets (or "classes") that may be formed from them. Its most striking property is perhaps the possibility of partitioning, that is, of the exhaustive division of a set into nonoverlapping parts (the two-by-two intersections of which are empty), and the possibility of pursuing that partitioning down to well-defined "undividable" elements, ensidic atoms.

This latter aspect should be stressed in that it also shows why the usual (mathematical) idea of a continuum hardly helps us to go beyond ensidic logic. The set $\mathbb{R}$ of real numbers is supposed to be the very embodiment of the continuum, poles apart from the discrete. Yet every element of that set is assumed to be well defined and quite distinct from all others (and also, of course, from those that are "as close as we like" to it). The question of what becomes of that property when we discover that practically no element of $\mathbb{R}$ can be defined, and by the same token distinguished, will be dealt with later. Similarly, a (real) function in a space of functions, as such, is assumed to be perfectly distinct and well defined—independently, again, of the fact that its definition would demand the definition of a double, uncountable infinity of almost indefinable elements. "Fuzzy sets" belong in the ensidic realm because their definition is probabilistic: probabilities can only be defined ensidically (Borel tribes, etc.). For the same reason, quantum indeterminacy is determinist, and therefore ensidic, inasmuch as it assigns definite probabilities ("amplitudes") to the quantum elements.

Mathematical Continuum and Effective Continuity

If it is true that being exceeds the ensidic logic, then it exceeds (and at the same time contains) both the continuous and the discrete, space and number, geometry and arithmetic, topology and algebra, in the mathematical definition of those notions (and to top it, we should add ordering; if "quantification" cannot exhaust what is, then topology cannot do so either).

Let us delve further into this point. "Interesting" topology (setting aside trivial topology and discrete topology) works with the continuous.

Is the continuum in the realm of ensidic logic? A continuum is defined as any compact Hausdorff space. The definition of connexity posits the definition of partitioning, as the definition of compacity posits that of space conforming to the Hausdorff separation axiom, which is to say, distinct points possessing disjoint neighborhoods. In any case, the definition of a topological space involves a great many set-theoretic notions. If, then, the continuum is mathematizable—which certainly does not mean quantifiable—it is ensidic, meaning it is an animal of the same family as arithmetic (as number). It is not the same entity, but they have an ancestor in common: the set.

But can the same be said of the "intuitive" continuum or of the "real" continuum? We have an immediate representation (Kant would say a pure intuition) of space and time as continuous: neither has any holes. Living beings move, in reality, and we ourselves move in a continuous movement within a continuous space and a continuous time. That—tentatively, barring Zenonian objections—prevents us from considering continuity as a simple mathematical (ensidic[5]) artifact. But then, for exactly the same reasons, we are prohibited from giving any favor whatsoever to space over number, to geometry over arithmetic, to topology over algebra. Each of us pictures himself, perhaps wrongly, as one, with two arms and two legs. *The* living being tries to avoid *a* predator, *the* predator goes after *a* prey. The definite article, just as much and even more than the indefinite article, postulates unity. To speak of movement presupposes the one (and the fundamental schema of iteration, implicit in Peano's axioms), whereas the converse is not true, in the abstract. "One" is not simply a "category" as it is in Kant's table. It is presupposed by all the other categories, to an exorbitant extent. Moreover, if we cross over to the other side of the mirror, it is imposed on us by the existence of living beings. For the form "one," imposed on the simply physical being, certainly does postulate an ontological attribute in the latter: its unifi*ability*, just as the imposition of any other form on matter presupposes that it is form*able*. But we cannot say that it "comes out" of the object with the same strength as in the case of living beings. The unity of a galaxy, or even of a molecule, is not of the same order of intensity, if I may put it that way, as that of an oak tree or a snake. The unity of the living individual is not a matter of mere unifiability by the observer; it is in itself and for itself.

But a similar line of thought may be applied to the effective continuum. Because in the same way, the continuity of the living beings compels our recognition. We can even say that living beings are only discrete inasmuch as they are continuous, and they are only continuous inasmuch as they are discrete. *A* living being—a tree, a whale—is inasmuch it is continuous as life, as "movement" in the Aristotelian sense, and as "extension." Its parts are in constant interaction, both among themselves and with the whole of a "closed set" that is also in itself and for itself. Living beings as such are not divisible, as a rule. They do not retain their nature when partitioned. More about this later.

A Digression on Physics

The continuity of physical reality plunges us in other kinds of perplexity. Relativity, both special and general, postulates a continuous space-time. Quantum physics sets lower limits to the matter-energy units (Planck's constant) but also to space-time units (Planck's time, 10^{-43} of a second). If there is a lower limit to time units and an upper limit to speed (the speed of light, 3×10^8 meters per second), we would find a minimal spatial unit of 3×10^{-35} meters. Photons would make a tiny jump of 3×10^{-33} centimeters in "empty space" every 10^{-43} seconds. They cannot do any more or any less. As we know, quantum theory raises some formidable questions. Its compatibility with general relativity is one. Another, just as weighty to my way of thinking, is that of "dark matter." If, as is contended, that matter represents between 90 and 99 percent of the matter-energy in the universe, how can the existence of an inert matter of that sort, with no interaction other than gravitational with the rest, conceivably be reconcilable with quantum theories (quantum chromodynamics) on the interactions between particles (or "forces"), which are "curled," logically-mathematically speaking? But above all, we would have to admit that the space-time of physics cannot be assimilated to $\mathbb{R}^4$, but to a sort of $\mathbb{Z}^4$ (or rather, to a $\mathbb{Z}^3 \times \mathbb{Z}'$, with "units" of "1" = 3×10^{-35} meters and "1" = 3×10^{-43} seconds, respectively). Movement would then have to be broken down into an endless sequence of tiny jumps from one space-time "unit" to the next, and then on and on. In this case, we would be unable to distinguish between those tiny jumps and the disappearance of the particle at position (x, y, z, t) and its recreation in position (x', y', z', t'). The stability of everyday objects would then be the fruit of the crudeness of our perceptions. This may actually be the view most compatible with the spirit of quantum theory. Nonetheless, it would remain for it to justify the legitimacy of applying differential calculus to discontinuous variables[6] (but thermodynamics does not trouble itself with that).

Living Beings as Such

Can it be that this discontinuity also undermines the continuity of living beings through their purely physical substratum? Not if we accept a "metaphysical"—which is to say, ontological—distinction. As a *physical body,* the living being is (or is not) discontinuous, depending on the diktats of the prevailing doctrine in the physics of the moment. But as a *living being,* it achieves a temporal and spatial continuity unequaled in the physical world, a "strictly local" continuity in the case of a living individual, a "weak local" continuity for generations and for the species, and ultimately for the Earth's ecosystem. This continuity of the *vital,* of the *ti ēn einai,* of the *eidos* and of the *logos,* as Aristotle would say,[7] is constituted, in fact created, by the living being. (At another level, we find another sort of "continuity" in the psychical sphere, strictly speaking, and in the social-historical sphere, but that discussion would take us too far astray.) It is the continuity of all of the processes taken together (of the work of the "powers that resist death") that makes a living organism into something other than a collection of molecules, and they are transmitted hereditarily just as much as and even more than "inherited characteristics," the transmission of the latter being predicated on the former. Mutations, for instance, are mutations and act as such (even and especially when they are fatal) only because they occur in a living cell. It is this veritable *vis viva* that I unhesitatingly call the substance (the form, the *eidos*) of life.

Number

I have attempted to show that neither number nor effective space can be viewed as having priority over one another. I will now try to demonstrate something further: that neither number nor space may be viewed as purely ensidic. In both cases, the ensidic and poietic elements, difference and otherness, repetition and creativity, are intertwined, as they are intertwined in every effective being and in being as such.

First of all, we note that the entire set of natural numbers and any theory of that set are grounded in ultimate assumptions that cannot be deduced or produced out of anything else. In Peano's axioms they take the form of a first element or a distinguished element that is not the successor of any other, and of iteration (an indefinitely repeatable "successor" operation), as well as of identity or equality, implications between propositions and so on. Once this set is given, its successive extensions—which seem "natural" but took several dozen millennia to develop—lead to the sets of positive rational numbers, positive algebraic real numbers, rational integers, algebraic real numbers of all sorts, algebraic complexes and last, transcendental real and complex *computable numbers* (algebraic differentials, in É. Borel's terminology).

All these sets are effectively constructible (their elements may be calculated or computed) using well-defined, feasible operations and algorithms. Now, the set of all real numbers (and by the same token the set of all complex numbers, but I will not discuss these; for our purposes the set $\mathbb{C}$ of complex numbers is isomorphic with $\mathbb{R}^2$) is not effectively defined, because almost none of its elements is effectively calculable.

For the sake of simplicity, let us consider the set of numbers contained in the interval [0, 1]. We know it is equipotent to (that it has the same power, the same cardinal as) the set of positive real numbers, $\mathbb{R}_+$. All of these numbers may be written as an infinite sequence of digits such as 0, . . . (all possibly zeros from some point on). In binary notation, that gives us an endless sequence of 0 and 1. The set of those sequences is therefore equipotent to the set of positive real numbers, and we know (thanks to Cantor's demonstration by the diagonal argument that that set has the power of the continuum) that it is an uncountable infinite set. But we also know, following the work of Borel, von Mises, Wald, and above all Kolmogorov, Solomonov, Chaitin, and Martin-Löff, that almost all sequences of numbers are random. It is indeed legitimate and logical to call a sequence nonrandom when there is a law (in contemporary parlance, a program = an algorithm) capable of producing the succession of its terms. Thus, $\sqrt{2}$ may be calculated with as many decimals as we like by the use of a known algorithm. Likewise, the numbers called algebraic differentials by É. Borel, such as e or π, can effectively be calculated. For e one needs only push calculation of the sums of the terms of the form $1/n!$, $n \in \mathbb{N}$ to obtain as many decimals as desired. Similarly, π is approximated by 4 (1 - 1/3 + 1/5 - 1/7 + 1/9 - 1/11 + 1/13 . . .). But every law, every program, every algorithm must be susceptible of being written (formulated) by means of a finite number of signs. Therefore, the set of those "laws," programs, and algorithms would be countable, at best. But the set of sequences (and/or of real numbers) is not countable. There are "infinitely more." Almost none of the elements of $\mathbb{R}$ is effectively calculable, then; almost all of the elements of $\mathbb{R}$ are "random." Each of them could only be produced by an infinite series of "true" lot drawings (with the impossibility of proving that they effectively produce random elements because, for example, after an arbitrarily large number of drawings, the previous sequence *might* begin again). The calculable elements of $\mathbb{R}$ are countable, and their set is a negligible part of the set of all real numbers.

In mathematics, we are juggling with a set we do not know and for which we will never have any knowledge whatsoever (not even through an abstractly given inapplicable law) about practically any of its elements. It is abusive, I think, or ambiguous at the least, for us to call $\mathbb{R}$ complete, meaning, for example, that the $\mathbb{R}$ to which we have access contains the limits of all Cauchy sequences. It contains the limits of the Cauchy sequences *to which we have access,* that is, which we may be able to define, the set of which is obviously countable. Similarly, we can only specify a Dedekind cut by the two effectively given subsets of $\mathbb{R}$ defined by it, an operation that, I repeat, is only possible for a countable set of cases.

Let $\mathbb{R}_c$ be the set of real numbers calculable in the sense defined above, and $\mathbb{R}_a$ the set of "random" real numbers. The set $\mathbb{R}$ of all real numbers will then be the union of $\mathbb{R}_c$ and $\mathbb{R}_a$. The set $\mathbb{R}_c$ is not continuous in the mathematical sense (it is not connected, each element of $\mathbb{R}_a$ divides it into two open sets). To go even further, if Cantor's argument is valid, it has uncountably many holes. It is nothing but a succession of uncountably many holes held together by a succession of countable points. (The paradox, apparent or real, implied by this sentence cannot be discussed here.)

What, then, is $\mathbb{R}$, the set of real numbers, if the quasi-totality of its elements cannot be exhibited either in person or by a sequence of effective operations, be it an infinite sequence, or again by a generative law—a strictly demonstrable impossibility—whereas at the same time we can demonstrate with the same rigor that it "exists" (as Cantor did)? I suggest that we take $\mathbb{R}$ as a metaphor of Chaos and $\mathbb{R}_c$ as a metaphor of the Cosmos, that part of Chaos begot out of Chaos and continuing to plunge its roots therein, a more or less successfully defined part (more or less successfully because of Gödel et al.) and one evidencing many structures (laws). Certainly, neither 1 nor 0 is "generated by laws." They remain metaphors of *yes* and *no,* of *there is* and *there is not.* To go a step further, let us say that $\mathbb{R}$ is the metaphor of the poietic and $\mathbb{R}_c$ the metaphor of the ensidic *in materia.* (*In forma,* the poietic in mathematics is the positing of axioms and the creation of methods of proof; the ensidic, deductive, and computational algorithms.) We may also say that $\mathbb{R}$ yields an imperfect model of a magma: an indefinite number of set-theoretic (ensemblist) structures may be extracted from it or built within it; but it absolutely cannot be constructed using set-theoretical (ensemblistic) procedures.

Dedekind wrote to Cantor, saying that he visualized sets as bottomless bags. Cantor replied that he personally pictured them rather as an abyss.

Measuring Space

What is $\mathbb{R}$? One answer, as good as any other, is: the set of infinite arrangements with repetition of the signs (0, 1). Why are we obliged to think of this and to take it into account? Because of Cantor. What makes that more necessary than any other product of an unlimited combinatory logic? Because we have decided that a one-to-one correspondence may be established between its elements and the points on a "real" straight line. What is the justification for that decision? First of all, our intuition. It is impossible for us to conceive of a real straight line composed primarily of holes. We cannot "see" that straight line, and space in general, otherwise than as really complete, even if we are only able to specify the abscissae for a minute number of the points of which it is "composed."

Our intuition of continuity is intuition of the continuity of *kinēsis*, and within the latter, certainly mostly of local movement. Aristotle already gave it greater importance, although he was careful to differentiate the four kinds of movement. Since Galileo, local movement has eliminated all other ones. The continuity of *kinēsis* is, at once, continuity in both space and time. In ordinary life I cannot go from A to B without covering all the intermediate points. I cannot jump from now to later—to when I will have gone home, or when that pain I have will stop, when I will have had some appointment. The only place where this is not true is on the margins of our humdrum world, in magic, shamanism, seven-league boots, and cases of divine intervention, or godly omnipresence. But those aspects call for other reflections.

But how do we go from number to space, or vice versa, if numbers result in the set $\mathbb{R}$, almost no element of which can be "given"—whereas we intuit and "perceive" everyday, "phenomenological" space and time as a continuum?

Everyday space, the space of the first natural stratum, is locally quasi-Euclidean (see below). It "lends itself" to identity: changes of place preserve distances and effectuating congruences (superposabilities) is always a legitimate possibility. (Neither of these two properties is meaningful for time; however, through movement and spatial phenomena—the celestial sphere, the water clock—an ensidic, "measured" time is constituted that is sufficient both for primitive calendars and for quantum calculations.) This makes it liable to measurement: not to measurement in the mathematical sense—more about that later—but to elementary measurement, sufficiently satisfactory for our uses/needs (Aristotle would have said *pros tēn chreian hikanōs*). To this day, we are still indebted to some man or woman, back in the Paleolithic era, who first decided that a particular piece of wood = 1. A rather straight stick was needed (as straight as possible, convenient for many reasons) to level the piles of a lake dwelling, for example. Such thirteenth- and fourteenth-century philosophers of the Oxford school as Robert Grosseteste and Walter Burley were clear on that point: "Since the *continuum* is divisible to infinity, therefore in a *continuum* there is no primary and unique measure according to Nature, but only according to the institution of men."[8] Put in our parlance, this distant ancestor posits that some compact part of $\mathbb{R} = 1$—compact in a noncontinuous sense, because it is not connected. The branch is a closed set, and if I break it in half I have two closed sets (and I must be able to break it into two, three, or more pieces; otherwise it will not do as a measuring rod).

It is worth reminding phenomenologists that everyday space, the space of the first natural stratum, of "the world of life," is merely quasi-Euclidean, and even so, only locally. It is certainly not homogeneous, or even isotropic; it has an up and a down, railroad tracks converge in the distance; for people living in any Attic *dēme*, the direction leading from that *dēme* to Athens is uniquely special. We need only look at a map of the French railway system to see that French space is neither homogeneous nor isotropic. It is only quasi-continuous in the Aristotelian sense of being divisible since divisibility can never be pushed very far. As soon as we begin to reflect on it, the world of life turns out to be problematic.

Euclidean geometry, as has been said for a very long time (since Plato, at the least) is an outrageous idealization of this space. Moreover, it is constructed on the intuition of continuity, especially of the continuity of movements (drawing a straight line, rotation of a segment around a fixed extremity, and so on). Apart from its "arithmetization" by Hilbert, we find attempts, ranging from Pythagoras and Eudoxus to Cauchy, Weierstrass, Dedekind, and Cantor and including Descartes, to make algebraic entities coincide with the straight line. The first question, which I will not broach here, is why this idealization "works." Another question, particularly acute when we think of the previous one, is: by what right do we make algebraic and meta-algebraic entities ($\mathbb{R}$) correspond to the idealized space of Euclidean geometry (or non-Euclidean geometry, for that matter)? Transferring the properties of $\mathbb{N}$ to counting goats in a flock or individuals in a clan is not a problem, or not to the same extent. But what allows us to transfer the properties of $\mathbb{R}$ to a straight line?

This is not a vain question, as will be shown by a brief look back at Zeno's paradoxes.

A Digression on Zeno

Contrary to widespread belief, the paradoxes of Zeno are still alive and are still being discussed.[9] I shall confine myself here to the paradox of Achilles and the tortoise which, I think, is both the most fertile and the clearest, and contains the crux of the others, as we shall see. Note that the paradoxes are not solved by neo-Kantian refutations (such as Max Adler's). The contention that Zeno breaks space, but not time, into an infinity of pieces is blatantly a misinterpretation. The paradoxes are based, precisely, on the term-to-term correspondence between the "elements" on the spatial axis and those on the temporal axis. Nor can one contend that because space and time are pure forms of intuition, any attempt to grasp them by means of understanding can only produce paradoxes. To accept that argument would be to condemn both mathematics and mathematical physics to be nonsense.

In modern parlance, the aporia may be condensed into two propositions:

1. Whatever the tortoise's initial (finite) lead a may be, and whatever the ratio between the speed b of the tortoise and the speed c of Achilles, assuming $c > b$, there is always a time t such that $t(c - b) < a$, because $\mathbb{R}$ (and $\mathbb{Q}$) are Archimedean. That is why Achilles will get ahead of the tortoise.

2. There is always a bijective mapping between the segments $[a, a + bt - d]$[10] (with d small) and $[0, ct]$; in other words, those segments have the same power and similarly, they have the same power as the lapse of time t. In still other words, there are as many space-time "points" in any distance traveled by Achilles and by the tortoise, so that the latter maintains its ad-

vance d (no matter whether these segments are viewed as closed intervals of $\mathbb{R}$ or of $\mathbb{Q}$). That is why Achilles will never get ahead of the tortoise.

Today's reader will be jarred by the second proposition and will rightly view it as fallacious, for the same argument may be used to show that Achilles (or any other moving body) can never cover any more than an arbitrarily small segment, and taken to the limit, *none at all.* That in fact is what Zeno himself said with the paradox of the "dichotomy" (before arriving at point x on the abscissa, the moving body must arrive at the point $x/2$, and so forth). Zeno's argument may be said to confuse the *power* (the cardinals) of intervals of $\mathbb{R}$ (or of $\mathbb{Q}$) and measure of the segments. Measurement of distances on a line requires a "finite" unit of measurement, whereas "counting" elements of an infinite body ($\mathbb{R}$ or $\mathbb{Q}$) involves grasping those elements as "infinitely small," "evanescent," or "participating neither in space nor in time" (Euclid's definition of the "point"). At best, the reader will say, we come back to that old metaphysical saw: how can you produce an extended line using nonextended points, etc.?

Things are not that simple, however.

Every interval (open or closed) of $\mathbb{R}$ or $\mathbb{Q}$ has as many points as any other (and even as $\mathbb{R}$ or $\mathbb{Q}$ themselves, if the proper precautions are taken). That is what Zeno relies on, although his terminology is different, of course. In fact, I believe he should be credited with the first proof of that proposition (for the set of positive rational numbers) and implicitly with the first intuition of the idea of the power of an infinite set.

To this, Aristotle rightly responded: a segment is not composed of a "sum" of points. This is true. However, the question that arises is: *of what,* then, is a segment composed? Visibly, a segment is made of other segments since it is *dividable.* And it is infinitely dividable, in the sense that there is no lower limit to the size of a conceivable segment. (This is true in mathematics. The questions raised by quantum physics in this respect have been mentioned above. But if there is an "absolute" minimum for a unit of length—in other words, if space and time are made of indivisible units—we revert, as seen above, to the idea that movement is the outcome of a succession of immobilities, which is the meaning of the paradox of the arrow, motionless at each point in time.) Put otherwise, there is no absolute unit of length. There is no doubt that however far we push division, the number of minimal segments (of the same length) in two segments of different lengths will be different. It will only become identical if the limit is crossed and the very small segment becomes an "infinitesimal segment"—a point. That is what Zeno does and what Aristotle rightly says he cannot do. But the question remains, then: what gives us the right to identify the (real or rational) straight line with the algebraic field of real or rational numbers?[11]

The Measurement of Space (Continued)

The paradox of Achilles and the tortoise is "solved" if we accept the following distinction: the power of a set is not, generally speaking, the same thing as the measurement of that set. The fact that segment (a, b) is smaller than the segment $(a, b + c)$ provided the segment (b, c) has a strictly positive value has nothing to do with the power of the "corresponding" parts of $\mathbb{R}$ or $\mathbb{Q}$. There is noncongruency of the segments, which are of the same power. The relationship between space and number is strange.

This is seen, first, when we discover that this distinction does not always apply. In $\mathbb{N}$, for instance, the "distance" from n' to n (for $n' \leq n$) is equal to the cardinal (minus 1) of the part $\{0, 1, \ldots, n - n'\}$.[12] It is visible, above all, when we recall the difficulties entailed in the very notion of measurement, at least as soon as one leaves one-dimensional spaces.

According to one fundamental ontological proposition, space and time are nothing if they are not also determinate in one way or another, that is to say, ensidic (which does not necessarily mean measurable or quantifiable in some pertinent way). It turns out (*sumbainei*) that space and time may be made ensemblistic in several ways: they allow ordering and algebraic and topological structures. But it is not at all self-evident that space is algebraizable, which is to say numerable. Number must go through measurement. Primitively, you cut a piece of wood and use it as a unit of length, so as to "measure" the segments of a straight line. The operation is "squarable" and "cube-able" in physical space, whereas the same is not true of mathematical space. Hausdorff was the first to formulate the problem of universal measurement: for every bounded subset A of $\mathbb{R}$, is there a positive, real number $m(A)$, not equal to zero for $A \neq \emptyset$,[13] such that: first, $m(A \cup B) = m(A) + m(B)$ if A and B are disjoint; second, $m(A) = m(B)$ if A and B are derived from one another by translation or rotation.

He proved (in 1914) that the problem is insoluble when n equals 3 or more (which does not prevent us from continuing to measure volumes). Banach constructed a map m for $n = 1$ and $n = 2$ (but that map is not unique). But he also used the axiom of choice to construct what is known as the Banach-Tarski paradox (1923), equivalent to the assertion that one can always decompose two bounded subsets containing at least one point in their interior (for example, two balls with different radii) into a finite, equal number of mutually discontinuous, equal parts (that is, it is possible to cut up an orange and the visible universe into an equal number of equal, mutually disjoint pieces). This result, as counterintuitive as possible, does not seem to have given mathematicians too many sleepless nights, but Émile Borel viewed it as an additional reason for rejecting the axiom of choice.[14]

We should recall that all of the "measurements" used in topology (distances, pseudometrics, norms, seminorms, etc.) are essentially one-dimensional: mappings from $E \times E$ to $\mathbb{R}_+$, for couples of points, however strange the nature of those "points" (as in functions, sequences, etc.), or the mapping used (p-adic distance, etc.), may be.

Generalization of the Notion of Space

Is there an aspect by which space eludes the ensidic? Yes, but that aspect is not *immediately* topological. It is *qualitative nonhomogeneity,* itself generated by creation, which creation must be temporalized and spatialized, even if it deals in ideality. Platonic ideas coexist necessarily in a "supracelestial place," and "It is necessary that all being be somewhere, in some site and occupying a certain place, and . . . what is not on the earth or somewhere in Heaven is nothing" (*Timaeus,* 52b). Likewise, there is a space of mathematics in general, not a "mathematical space" but the space in which mathematics exists and that it brings into existence by existing, a receptacle for the partially organized coexistence of the multiple, created by the creations of mathematicians and altered by those creations. The space of mathematics is not the same before and after Pythagoras, before Descartes-Newton-Leibniz and after, before Cantor and after, before Gödel and after, and so forth. Today, natural integers and finite fields, regular polyhedrons and the Lowenheim-Skolem theorem, the set of prime numbers and Fréchet filters coexist within that space.

As Thom aptly writes, "every quality may be viewed, to some extent, as a spatial form, an extended form in an abstract space."[15] But it is not evident that such spaces are liable to topological treatment. He is talking about the most general idea of "space," not susceptible of mathematical treatment except perhaps in the trivial sense.

It is nonetheless true that in the "spatial" mathematizable domain—which happens to be multidimensional, in general; why "there must be" several dimensions is another matter—in its very spatiality, the link between quality and topology is obvious and primordial. (Suffice it to recall that algebraically, one- or two-dimensional spaces cannot really be distinguished and that their heterogeneity can only be established by resorting to topology.) *Eidos* takes on its original sense here: appearance, figure, form. That which is not trivial in spatial forms rapidly brings us to topology, just as, more specifically, the seizing of the transition from one form to another, inasmuch as it has to do with the emergence of a form, leads to the catastrophe theory. Topology and catastrophe theory definitely do work with ensidic, relatively rigid notions (closed sets, boundaries, etc.). But that is the consequence of the ensidic dimension, everywhere dense throughout being and particularly pertinent and rich here. It is absurd to accuse catastrophe theory of not being "explanatory." It is concerned with describing what is at work in the transition from one form to another. It does not aim at establishing a "dynamic of processes": such a dynamic depends on the temporal evolution of quantitative factors, and it would still remain to "explain" why those factors vary and to establish the law of their variation. Nor does it aim at "explaining" the creation of a form, which would be an absurd enterprise, let me say in passing. But to be able to speak of a new form we would have to be able to describe it rigorously, and this is where topology and catastrophe theory come in.

Would it be presumptuous of me to say that in 1975 I was not wrong, and neither was René Thom?

Closing Remarks

Being experiences the "discrete," since it *is* through breaks, creations, and heterogeneous strata. It also experiences continuity, inasmuch as those breaks and the forms that come out of them are conditioned, perforce, by what "precedes" them and what "surrounds" them—creation is *ex nihilo*, not *in nihilo* or *cum nihilo*—and inasmuch as each ontological level brings into being a specific "space" and "time." Although these terms are taken metaphorically, they are nonetheless imperative here. Also, they imply each other in the strangest way. The "order of coexistences" implies the *co-*, which is to say, simultaneity. The "order of successions," as an order, implies an "extension" along which there are succession and order within that succession. Leibniz may have thought he was giving a definition, but he was actually only giving an (admirable) circular clarification.

There is a "pure" idea of extension that cannot be eliminated. The fact is that multiplicity exists, and we can only conceive of the multiple, the many, as *in* a receptacle, or as *bringing into existence* the receptacle that will hold it. The multiple is in a continuity, or brings continuity into existence by being; the multiple is discrete; otherwise it would not be multiple. Multiplicity may consist of difference or of alterity (to be many may be to be different or to be other). In the former case we have an ensidic extension; in the latter a poietic (imaginary) extension.

Multiplicity cannot be deduced. Any deduction (or production) posits its existence, just as it posits the one, and to the same degree. To be more specific: if there were only being toward itself (*kath' auto*, Aristotle, *Metaphysics*, G, 1003 to 1021–22), the one alone would be conceivable (but for whom?). Yet being toward itself does manifest itself; it is also being for us. Or again: some beings appear, making being toward itself manifest itself to them, making it become being for them. We are something other than simply being toward itself, since we are those for whom there is being (toward itself and for us). As soon as we are, there is multiplicity owing to the very fact that we are. And that is not a "deduction," because "we are" is purely factual. Moreover, it turns out (*sumbainei*), unless we are mad, that even in the world without us, multiplicity was, is, and will be. That too is a pure fact.

The many is one (otherwise it would be nothing), and there are ones within the many. But multiplicity as such is not continuum. Multiplicity splits; it bifurcates into the discrete and the continuous—which are co-originary. The units of a cardinal (the "moments" of an ordinal) coexist in an "extension." Reflection forces us to concede that every "extension" includes (is made of?) uncountably many indivisible elements, the elements of the set of real (random and calculable) numbers, almost all of which will remain unspecifiable for all eternity. This is why there can be no quarrel between space and number; it is also why the relation between them elicits endless aporias, such as Zeno's paradoxes, and the paradox or the enigma of the measurability of space.

July–December 1993

Appendix

Books by Cornelius Castoriadis

IN ENGLISH

Crossroads in the Labyrinth (1978). Trans. Martin H. Ryle and Kate Soper. Cambridge, Mass.: MIT Press, and Brighton, England: Harvester Press, 1984.

The Imaginary Institution of Society (1975). Trans. Kathleen Blamey. Cambridge, Mass.: MIT Press, and Cambridge, England: Polity Press, 1987.

Political and Social Writings. Volume 1: 1946–1955. *From the Critique of Bureaucracy to the Positive Content of Socialism.* Trans. and ed. David Ames Curtis. Minneapolis: University of Minnesota Press, 1988.

Political and Social Writings. Volume 2: 1955–1960. *From the Workers' Struggle against Bureaucracy to Revolution in the Age of Modern Capitalism.* Trans. and ed. David Ames Curtis. Minneapolis: University of Minnesota Press, 1988.

Philosophy, Politics, Autonomy: Essays in Political Philosophy. Ed. David Ames Curtis. New York: Oxford University Press, 1991.

Political and Social Writings. Volume 3: 1961–1979. *Recommencing the Revolution: From Socialism to the Autonomous Society.* Trans. and ed. David Ames Curtis. Minneapolis: University of Minnesota Press, 1993.

The Castoriadis Reader. Ed. David Ames Curtis. Malden, Mass.: Basil Blackwell, 1997.

World in Fragments: Writings on Politics, Society, Psychoanalysis, and the Imagination. Trans. and ed. David Ames Curtis. Stanford, Calif.: Stanford University Press, 1997.

On Plato's Statesman (1999). Trans. David Ames Curtis. Stanford, Calif.: Stanford University Press, 2002.

IN FRENCH

Mai 68: la brèche. Premières réflexions sur les événements. Jean-Marc Coudray (pseudonym of C. Castoriadis), with Claude Lefort and Edgar Morin. Paris: Librairie Arthème Fayard, 1968. 2nd rev. ed. Paris: Éditions Complexe, 1988.

La Société bureaucratique. 1: Les rapports de production en Russie. Paris: 10/18, 1973.

La Société bureaucratique. 2: La révolution contre la bureaucratie. Paris: 10/18, 1973.

L'Expérience du mouvement ouvrier. 1: Comment lutter. Paris: 10/18, 1974.

L'Expérience du mouvement ouvrier. 2: Prolétariat et organisation. Paris: 10/18, 1974.

L'Institution imaginaire de la société. Paris: Éditions du Seuil, 1975.

Les Carrefours du labyrinthe. Paris: Éditions du Seuil, 1978.

Capitalisme moderne et révolution. 1: L'impérialisme et la guerre. Paris: 10/18, 1979.

Capitalisme moderne et révolution. 2: Le mouvement révolutionnaire sous le capitalisme moderne. Paris: 10/18, 1979.

Le Contenu du socialisme. Paris: 10/18, 1979.

La Société française. Paris: 10/18, 1979.

De l'écologie à l'autonomie. With Daniel Cohn-Bendit. Paris: Éditions du Seuil, 1981.

Devant la guerre. Tome 1: Les Réalités. Paris: Librairie Arthème Fayard, 1982. 2nd rev. ed. 1983.

Domaines de l'homme: Les carrefours du labyrinthe II. Paris: Éditions du Seuil, 1986.

Le Monde morcelé: Les carrefours du labyrinthe III. Paris: Éditions du Seuil, 1990.

La Société bureaucratique. 2nd rev. ed. in a single volume. Paris: Christian Bourgois, 1990

La Montée de l'insignifiance: Les carrefours du labyrinthe IV. Paris: Éditions du Seuil, 1996.

Fait et à faire: Les carrefours du labyrinthe V. Paris: Éditions du Seuil, 1997.

Dialogue. La Tour d'Aigues: Éditions de l'Aube, 1998.

Post-Scriptum sur l'insignifiance. Entretiens avec Daniel Mermet (novembre 1996). La Tour d'Aigues: Éditions de l'Aube, 1998.

Figures du pensable. Les carrefours du labyrinthe VI. Paris: Éditions du Seuil, 1999.

Sur Le Politique de Platon. Paris: Éditions du Seuil, 1999.

Sujet et vérité dans le monde social-historique. Séminaires 1986–1987. Paris: Éditions du Seuil, 2002.

La Création humaine, 1. Paris: Éditions du Seuil, 2002.
Ce qui fait la Grèce. 1. D'Homère à Héraclite. Séminaires 1982–1983. La Création humaine II. Paris: Éditions du Seuil, 2004.
Une Société à la dérive. Paris: Éditions du Seuil, 2005.

Note

A full bibliography of the writings of Cornelius Castoriadis, including texts written under various pseudonyms in the periodical *Socialisme ou Barbarie* between 1949 and 1965, may be found at the following Web site: http://www.agorainternational.org/.

Notes

Preface to the French Edition

1. Published in English as *Crossroads in the Labyrinth,* trans. Martin H. Ryle and Kate Soper (Cambridge, Mass.: MIT Press, 1984), henceforth *CL.*

2. Respectively, *Domaines de l'homme: Les carrefours du labyrinthe II* (Paris: Éditions du Seuil, 1986), henceforth *DH; Le Monde morcelé: Les carrefours du labyrinthe III* (Paris: Éditions du Seuil, 1990), henceforth *WIF; La Montée de l'insignifiance: Les carrefours du labyrinthe IV* (Paris: Éditions du Seuil, 1996); and *Fait et à faire: Les carrefours du labyrinthe V* (Paris: Éditions du Seuil, 1997).

3. *CL,* ix–x.

4. *CL,* xxii.

5. *La Montée de l'insignifiance.*

6. See below.

1. Aeschylean Anthropogony and Sophoclean Self-Creation of Anthrōpos

The original version of this text, in Greek, was first published in a volume of essays dedicated to the philosopher Konstantinos Despotopoulos, one of Castoriadis's oldest friends (*Afierōma ston Konstantino Despotopoulo* [Athens: Papazisis, 1991]) and reprinted in a volume of Castoriadis's recent essays in Greek titled *Anthrōpologia, Politikē, Philosophia* (Athens: Ypsilon, 1993). It was translated into English by Stathis Gourgouris and published in *Agon, Logos, Polis: The Greek Achievement and Its Aftermath,* ed. Johann P. Arnason and Peter Murphy (Stuttgart: Franz Steiner Verlag, 2001), 138–54. The original Greek was then translated into French by Zoe Castoriadis, taking into consideration Castoriadis's remarks at his 1993 seminar at the Ecole des Hautes Etudes en Sciences Sociales, and published in *Figures du Pensable.* The present text revisits the Gougouris translation in the light of the French version. In a translator's note, Gourgouris makes the following comments: "Translating Castoriadis directly from Greek, particularly insofar as his text pertains to ancient Greek material, demands that one remain faithful to the seamless transition from the ancient to the modern language, which in Castoriadis's hands takes a rare form of artistry and is deliberately exploited to enhance the philosophical point he is making. . . . Finally, risking a certain awkwardness, I have opted to retain the Greek *anthrōpos* instead of translating it into the usual 'man' in order to avoid, as much as possible, the gender strains inherent in the generic use. It is important to understand that although *anthrōpos* is a masculine noun in Greek (which is why in the possessive case I revert to 'his'), its use in the Sophoclean ode under discussion is not gender specific, unless one were to arbitrarily exclude Antigone from the ode's frame of reference."—Trans.

1. Although Castoriadis always made it very clear that "Greek tragedy does not exist. What exists is Athenian tragedy," he does use the term "Greek tragedy" here. Further on in the text, he makes it clear that he is talking about an "Athenian audience."—Trans.

2. Aside from the famous Cyclops passage in the *Odyssey,* what immediately comes to mind is Hesiod (*Theogony,* 507–616, and *Works and Days,* 41–121) and, of course, later than the tragedies discussed here, the *Mikros Diakosmos* by Democritus, as we know it from the commentary on Hesiod by Ioannes Tzetzes, as well as Plato's *Statesman* (268e–274e). Here, I shall discuss *Prometheus Bound* (lines 231–41; 248–54; 265–67; 436–507) and the famous stasimon in *Antigone* (lines 332–75). For both works, I am using the French bilingual "Budé" editions (*Prometheus Bound* edited by Paul Mazon and *Antigone* by Alphonse Dain). I take for granted that the reader is familiar with the tragedies and has immediate access to the text. [The original Greek mentions Plato's *Protagoras* (310d–323d) and *Gorgias* (523a–524a) as well. For the English translations, Gourgouris refers to Herbert Weir Smyth's translation of *Prometheus Bound* and Robert Fagles's and Richard Jebb's translations of *Antigone.* —Trans.]

3. For a compendium of contemporary discussions on *Antigone,* see George Steiner, *Antigones* (Oxford: Clarendon Press, 1984).

4. See Martin Heidegger, *Einführung in die Metaphysik* (Tübingen: Max Niemeyer Verlag, n.d.), 1952 edition of lectures first delivered in 1935. [Heidegger presented an expanded version of the same lectures on *Antigone* as part of a course on Hölderlin in the summer of 1942. Though more detailed, the crux of the interpretation and even the language itself remain the same. See Martin Heidegger, *Hölderlins Hymne "Der Ister"* (Frankfurt am Main: Vittorio Klostermann, 1984).—Trans.]

5. This translation follows Castoriadis's own French rendering of the phrase,

in which he enumerates three "capabilities" for a single word in Greek (*pantoporos*). See note 9.—Trans.

6. [Heidegger, *Einführung in die Metaphysik*, 154.] Note by S. Gourgouris: Here, I am directly translating Castoriadis's rendering in Greek of Heidegger's German version of the Sophoclean verse, which is "*überall hinausfahrend unterwegs erfahrungslos ohne Ausweg kommt er zum Nichts*," translated by Ralph Manheim as "everywhere journeying, inexperienced and without issue, he comes to nothingness" (*An Introduction to Metaphysics* [New Haven, Conn.: Yale University Press, 1959]) and by William McNeill and Julia Davis as "everywhere venturing forth and experienceless without any way out" (*Hölderlin's Hymn "The Ister"* [Bloomington: Indiana University Press, 1996]).

7. See Daniel Coppieters de Gibson, "Les Grecs et la question de l'homme. A propos d'une lecture de Sophocle par Heidegger" in *Qu'est-ce que l'homme? Philosophie/Psychanalyse* (Brussels: Publications des Facultés Universitaires Saint-Louis, 1982), 53–70.

8. Coppieters de Gibson, "Les Grecs et la question de l'homme," 65.

9. [The translation given here corresponds as literally as possible to the French version given by Castoriadis in his 1993 seminar.]

10. [See note 9.]

11. Aristotle, *Physics,* vol. D, 219b1–2; 220e3–4.

12. See my book *The Imaginary Institution of Society*, trans. Kathleen Blamey (Cambridge, Mass.: MIT Press, 1987), 273–339, henceforth *IIS*.

13. [See note 9.]

14. For example, in the "Budé" edition, Mazon translates: "I liberated humans from the obsession of death." It is not improbable that the usual interpretation is due to a retroactive application on Aeschylus' text of the Platonic version (*Gorgias* 523d): "First of all then, men must be stopped from foreknowing their deaths, for now they have knowledge beforehand. Prometheus has already been told to stop this foreknowledge" [translated by W. D. Woodhead in *Plato: The Collected Dialogues* (Princeton, N.J.: Princeton University Press, 1963)]. But the human beings described by Socrates in the myth of Gorgias have nothing to do with Prometheus' humans: those judged are clothed and may be of great lineage and wealth (523c). Evidently, Plato transforms Aeschylus' myth to fit the needs of his argumentation.

15. [For the translation, see note 9; for a discussion of this expression, see below.]

16. [Magistrate in charge of collecting contributions from the allied cities.]

17. Note by S. Gourgouris: These are the famous first lines of the stasimon from *Antigone* that Castoriadis examines here. The (mis)adventures of translation in regard to this particular verse—a translation that is impossible in essence—carry a long story of their own. In many ways, Castoriadis's entire analysis of the

stasimon is actually a meditation on the multifold and inexhaustible meaning of *deinon.* [For a complete discussion of the word *deinon,* the reader is referred to the essay entitled "Notes on Some Poetic Resources" in this volume.—Trans.]

18. ["Terrifying formidableness" (what Castoriadis formulated as *terribilité.*—Trans.); for a discussion of this word, see below.]

19. [In French in the original Greek text.]

20. For a more extensive presentation, the interested reader can consult "The Greek *Polis* and the Creation of Democracy," in *Philosophy, Politics, Autonomy: Essays in Political Philosophy,* ed. David Ames Curtis (New York: Oxford University Press, 1991), henceforth *PPA.*

21. [Which Castoriadis defined in his 1993 seminar as thinking correctly in concrete situations, but not in speculative thought.]

22. [See note 9.]

23. See "Notes on Some Poetic Resources."

24. [See note 9.]

25. [See note 9.]

26. Περὶ μὲν θεῶν οὐκ ἔχω εἰδέναι, οὔθ᾽ ὡς εἰσὶν οὔθ᾽ ὡς οὐκ εἰσὶν οὔθ᾽ ὁποῖοί τινες ἰδέαν Protagoras, H. Diels-Kranz (II, 80, 4). In English, *The Older Sophists,* trans. Michael J. O'Brien (Durham: University of South Carolina Press, 1972), 20. [See note 9.]

2. *Notes on Some Poetic Resources*

[This text, previously unpublished, had been in the writing for about twenty years, and is certainly not in as finished a form as Cornelius Castoriadis would have desired. These "Notes" do appear in the two Tables of Contents he projected, however. It seemed to us that the latter fact, as well as the originality of both the theme and the approach taken in the paper, justify its inclusion in this volume.] Original French title: "Notes sur quelques moyens de la poésie."—Trans.

1. [From here on, and aside from quotations of the poem itself, the word is spelled as it was in the Attic dialect, where it has an aspiration mark, as opposed to the Eolian used by Sappho.]

2. The word *root* is not used here in a technical sense, but rather as an image.—Trans.

3. Throughout this piece, Castoriadis refers to what are known in France as the "Budé" editions, which are bilingual Greek-French scholarly editions of numerous Greek texts. For English versions, see Herbert Weir Smyth's translation of *Prometheus Bound* and Robert Fagles's and Richard Jebb's translations of *Antigone.*—Trans.

4. [See lines 332–75, commented in "Aeschylean Anthropogony and Sopho-clean Self-Creation of *Anthrōpos.*"]

5. [See note 2.]

6. [Lines 781–800.]

7. Marcel Proust, *In Search of Lost Time,* trans. C. K. Scott Moncrieff and Terence Kilmartin, rev. by D. J. Enright (New York: Modern Library, 1999), vol. 4, *Sodom and Gomorrah,* part 2, chap. 1, p. 145.

8. Baudelaire, "Le voyage," in *Les Fleurs du Mal.* The English translation is taken from *Baudelaire's Complete Verse,* trans. Francis Scarfe (London: Anvil Press Poetry, 2004).

9. Victor Hugo, "Napoléon II," in *Les Chants du Crépuscule (The Songs of Twilight).* My translation.—Trans.

10. I have critically commented on the traditional opposition between deno-tation and connotation from another standpoint in *IIS,* 345–49.

11. The same obviously holds for prose, or at least for great prose. In point of fact, aside from the requirements of strict metrics, which are no longer required nowadays anyway, great prose always has "material" and semantic musicality. This might be illustrated by a great many passages from Thucydides, including of course the Funeral Oration, as well as by a host of quotations from Proust, including of course the death of Bergotte. [In *In Search of Lost Time,* vol. 3, *The Captive.*—Trans.] Zola, now unfairly disparaged as artist and prose writer, gives us some magnificent examples with the prostitutes' descent on the boulevards in *Nana,* the charge of the Marguerite division in *La Débâcle,* and the death of Catherine in *Germinal.* The fact that poetry and prose overlap to a large extent raises some difficult questions that cannot be discussed here.

12. This distinction is equivalent to the one formulated by Rémi Brague be-tween Greek culture, viewed as primary, and Latin, followed by European cul-tures, which may be called secondary in the sense that they explicitly presuppose and more or less always refer to that primary culture. The ideas contained in the present text were discussed in a seminar at the French EHESS [School of Higher Studies in the Social Sciences.—Trans.] on May 9, 1984. Rémi Brague, who was clearly unaware of that seminar, presented his distinction in his book, *Europe: la voie romaine* (Paris: Criterion, 1992).

13. See what Benveniste has to say in his *Indo-European Language and Soci-ety* on the supposed Indo-European root, the impossibility of establishing inde-pendently and enumerating the meanings attached to that root, and deciding whether it was not "already" polysemous.

14. See, for instance, the discussion of the expressive resources of ancient Greek in a book published by T. Zielinski a long time ago, *Wir und die Antike,* translated by H. A. Strong and Hugh Stewart as *Our Debt to Antiquity* (London: George Routledge & Sons, 1909), as well as various essays by Roman Jakobson.

15. On *phainesthai*, see my essay on "The Discovery of the Imagination," in *WIF.*

3. The "Rationality" of Capitalism

This essay was originally delivered as a lecture, entitled "Notes pour servir à une critique de la 'rationalité du capitalisme'" (Notes for a contribution to the criticism of the "rationality" of capitalism), at the October 1996 CIRFIP colloquium on "Instrumental Rationality and Society." The present version, considerably expanded and reworked, owes much to the critical comments of my friend Vassili Gondicas. It goes without saying that I take entire responsibility for any errors or weaknesses. [Previously published as "La Résistible emprise de la rationalité instrumentale" in *Revue internationale de psychosociologie* 4, no. 8 (1997): 31–51.]

1. See my 1974 paper, "Reflections on 'Rationality' and 'Development,'" now in *PPA,* and especially the section on the fiction of economic rationality.

2. See my essay on "Power, Politics, Autonomy" in *PPA.*

3. Stavisky was a swindler who sold worthless bonds with the complicity of many people in high places. His mysterious death, following public exposure, led to rioting, chiefly of royalists, in February 1934, triggered a government crisis, and discredited French parliamentary democracy in general.

Landru, famous as a serial killer of lonely, wealthy women, gained additional fame when Charlie Chaplin, on the suggestion of Orson Welles, used his life story as the basis for a film, *Monsieur Verdoux* (1947). A second film, *Landru* (*Bluebeard;* 1963) was later made by Claude Chabrol.—Trans.

4. This is already to be found in Adam Ferguson, *An Essay on the History of Civil Society* (1767), and in Benjamin Constant, "The Liberty of the Ancients Compared with that of the Moderns," in *Political Writings* (1819; Cambridge: Cambridge University Press, 1988).

5. Lord Robbins, *An Essay on the Nature and Significance of Economic Science* (1932; London: Palgrave Macmillan, 1984).—Trans.

6. See my 1965 text in *IIS* and my 1974 text (note 1).

7. See Aaron J. Gurevich's fundamental book, *Categories of Medieval Culture,* trans. G. L. Cambell (London: Routledge Kegan & Paul, 1985).

8. Another demonstration of this is provided in vivo (and *in anima vili*) in the truly Mafioso-style "primitive reaccumulation" brought about by the "privatization" process in the ex-communist countries.

9. The split between producers and means of production is absolutely not specific to capitalism; it is already present in slavery.

10. See William H. McNeill, *Keeping Together in Time* (Cambridge, Mass.:

Harvard University Press, 1996), and John Keegan's criticism of it in the *Times Literary Supplement,* July 12, 1996, 3; and September 6, 1996, 17.

11. In my 1974 text (referred to in note 1), I already remarked that officials in charge of "development policies" were beginning to understand that the "obstacles to development" were far deeper than the lack of capital or of technical qualifications. This was clearly stated in some official World Bank reports, for instance, but did not influence "theoretical economists." In fact, even "serious" political officials are still discovering the moon. In a speech, Alan Greenspan, the president of the U.S. Federal Reserve Board, advanced the idea that it was impossible to introduce capitalism in a country where certain "cultural" prerequisites were not present. In the July 14, 1997, edition of the *International Herald Tribune* William Pfaff quotes him as saying that he had discovered, after 1989 (!), that "much of what we took for granted in our free-market system and assumed to be human nature was not nature at all, but culture. The dismantling of the central planning function in an economy does not, as some had supposed, automatically establish 'market capitalism'" (8).

12. Joan Robinson, "Notes on the Economics of Technical Progress," in *The Rate of Interest and Other Essays* (London: Macmillan, 1952), 56. The same argument may be found in later writings by Karl Popper, also aimed at showing that technical progress is unforeseeable.

13. [Castoriadis is referring here to Kaldor's phrase about the Kaleckian theory of distribution.]

14. Keynes added the "cost" of investment measured by the interest rate. But for those brackets that count, variations in interest rates are less crucial than prospects for profit, and above all, their effects are asymmetric. The central banks may stifle expansion by raising their interest rates considerably, but it is much harder, if not to say impossible, for them to create it. This is visible in many instances since 1945, and is still true today in Germany, France, and especially Japan. Real rates in France and Germany have long been at an all-time low, whereas the discount rate in Japan is 0.5 percent and the return on bonds is under 2 percent.

15. See my 1958 essay "On the Content of Socialism III" in *Socialisme ou Barbarie,* 23, now in *Political and Social Writings,* vol. 2, henceforth *PSW2.*

16. I have developed this point repeatedly: in "Sur la dynamique du capitalisme," *Socialisme ou Barbarie,* 12; "Modern Capitalism and Revolution," *PSW2;* and "Value, Equality, Justice, Politics: From Marx to Aristotle and from Aristotle to Us," *CL.*

17. See my book, *Devant la guerre,* vol. 1, *Les Réalités.*

18. Joan Robinson, *Economic Philosophy* (Harmondsworth: Penguin, 1962), 130.

19. I was already talking about the foreseeable effects of the industrialization

of the "undeveloped" countries in 1974 (see my paper mentioned in note 1), and I was certainly not the first person to do so.

4. Imaginary and Imagination at the Crossroads

Lecture given in Abrantès, Portugal, in November 1996, at the invitation of the La Preia association.

1. [On the site of Foz Côa, on the upper Douro River.]
2. In *PSW2*.
3. In *PSW3*.

5. Primal Institution of Society and Second-Order Institutions

This paper was first given as a lecture, entitled "Imagination et imaginaire au carrefour," at a colloquium on "Psychanalyse et approche familiale systémique," held by the Centre d'Etudes de la Famille in Paris on December 15, 1985, then published in a pamphlet entitled "Y-a-t-il une théorie de l'institution?" (Is There a Theory of the Institution?). A first English-language version, "First Institution of Society and Second-Order Institutions," translated by David Ames Curtis, appeared in the periodical *Free Associations* 12 (1988): 39–51.

1. The term *institution,* as used by Castoriadis in his writings and in this text in particular, designates the instituting process, the "transhistorical requisite" (see his discussion of *nomos,* below), and the concrete institutions of a given society, all at once. For brevity, the term *institution* has been maintained in the English from here on whenever there is any ambiguity or polysemy in the French original.—Trans.

2. Readers interested in the reasoning behind these ideas and their further development are referred to my books: *IIS,* particularly chap. 6; *CL,* part 1, "Psyche," and "The Imaginary: Creation in the Social-Historical Domain"; and *WIF,* "Institution of Society and Religion."

6. Heritage and Revolution

[First published in English in *The Ancients and the Moderns*, ed. Reginald Lilly (Bloomington: Indiana University Press, 1996), 159–69. A first (unpublished) version of this essay was delivered in October 1985 at the Hannah Arendt Symposium organized by the New School for Social Research (New York). The French translation by Dominique Walter was published in *FP* as "Héritage et Révolution."]

1 [The Heritage Foundation.]

2. See Cornelius Castoriadis, "Institution de la société et religion" (1982), *DH,* 364–84.

3. Jean-Jacques Rousseau, *Du contrat social,* book 2, chap. 7, in *Oeuvres complètes* (Paris: Editions de la Pléiade, Gallimard, 1964), 3:381. A similar formulation may be found in the first version of the *Contrat,* book 2, chap. 2, p. 313.

4. See Montesquieu, *Considérations sur les causes de la grandeur des Romains,* chap. 1.

5. In particular, see *IIS.* See also François Furet, *Marx and the French Revolution,* trans. Deborah Kan Furet (Chicago: University of Chicago Press, 1988). A work on Marx's concrete analyses or other historical transitions, in the light of the problematic formulated here, would be helpful. His ambiguities concerning the French Revolution receive an excellent analysis from Furet.

6. I argued this point at length in "La question de l'histoire du mouvement ouvier," in *L'expérience du mouvement ouvrier* (Paris: Union Générale d'Éditions, 1974), 1:11–120. (An English translation appeared in *Telos* 30 [winter 1976–1977].) The text is included in my *Social and Political Writings* (Minneapolis: University of Minnesota Press, 1993).

7. What Democracy?

This paper was originally delivered at the Cerisy colloquium [devoted to the work of Cornelius Castoriadis] on July 5, 1990. It is transcribed here with some slight changes in style and the inclusion of the complete development on the economy that I had been obliged to abridge for the colloquium, for the sake of brevity. The footnotes, mostly references, are additions to the transcribed version. [French title, "Quelle Démocratie?"—Trans.]

1. Pierre Manent saw that clearly: "Democracy . . . [is] in the first place a *social state,* defined by *equality of conditions,* not an ensemble of political institutions" (emphasis in the original text). Pierre Manent, *Intellectual History of Liberalism* (1987), trans. Rebecca Balinski (Princeton, N.J.: Princeton University Press, 1994). See also Manent's *Tocqueville and the Nature of Democracy* (1982), trans. John Waggoner (Lanham, Md.: Rowman and Littlefield, 1996).

2. Published, respectively, in *PPA* and *Castoriadis Reader.*

3. My emphasis on how essential it is for relevant information to be circulated so that decisions may be made *knowledgeably,* as well as on the crucially political character (therefore implying responsibility and accountability) of collecting and circulating information, dates back to 1957 (see "On the Content of Socialism II" in *PSW2*).

4. Nouméa, French New Caledonia: in May 1988, between the two rounds

of the presidential election opposing Mitterand and Chirac, the gendarmes put a bloody end to a hostage situation; also in 1988, the French National Assembly voted a bill indirectly amnestying deputies (that is, themselves) for irregularities in campaign financing; the Urba-Technic scandal, uncovered in 1989, involved use of that company for illegal financing of Socialist Party election campaigns.

5. That actually did happen, fifteen months after this paper was delivered.

6. "Modern Capitalism and Revolution," in *PSW2*, first published in English as a Solidarity pamphlet and book, trans. Maurice Brinton (London: London Solidarity, 1963, 1965, 1974).

7. §C. The Universal Principle of Right: "Every action is right which [in] itself, or in the maxim on which it proceeds, is such that it can coexist along with the freedom of the will of each and all in action, according to a universal law" (Kant, *The Metaphysics of Morals,* part 1, "Metaphysical Foundations of the Theory of Right," introduction §C). See also the end of §B: "Right, therefore, comprehends the whole of the conditions under which the voluntary actions of any one person can be harmonized in reality with the voluntary actions of every other person, according to a universal law of freedom." In German, *recht* means both right (in every sense of the term), just, lawful, and straight (upright).

8. Various aspects of the above development have been discussed more fully in "Sur la dynamique du capitalisme," *Socialisme ou Barbarie* 12 (August 1953) and 13 (January 1954); "Modern Capitalism and Revolution," *PSW2*; "Technique" (1973), *CL*; "Reflections on 'Rationality' and 'Development'" (1985), *PPA*; "Value, Equality, Justice, Politics: From Marx to Aristotle, from Aristotle to Ourselves" (1975), *CL*; and *Devant la guerre,* vol. 1, *Les Réalités.*

9. See the collection of my writings in *La Société bureaucratique.* Also, and especially, "On the Content of Socialism III: The Workers' Struggle against the Organization of the Capitalist Enterprise," in *PSW2*.

10. I defended this principle and the ones that follow as early as 1957, in "On the Content of Socialism II," in *PSW2*.

8. The Psychical and Social Roots of Hate

The main ideas expounded in this text are to be found in lectures given at several conferences: "Psychoanalytic Perspectives on Neo-Fascism and Anti-Immigration Politics: Trends in Europe and the United States," San Francisco, May 8, 1995 (organized by the Psychoanalytical Institute of San Francisco and the University of California at Berkeley); "Guérir de la guerre et juger la paix," Paris, June 23, 1995 (organized by the University of Paris-VIII and the Collège International de Philosophie); and "Paysages de la pensée française," Rome, October 24, 1996 (organized by the French Embassy). It was considerably reworked for a lecture given as part of the "Die Konstruktion der 'Nation' gegen die Juden" symposium, Mülheim, November 26, 1996. [An English version, written by Castoriadis himself and edited by Fuyuki Kurasawa (La Trobe University, Australia) appeared in *Free Associations* 7:3, no. 43 (1999). The present text is a revised version of the latter, incorporating changes made by Castoriadis for the 1996 conference, as reflected in the French *Figures du Pensable* version.—Trans.]

1. What I have translated elsewhere as the "monadic psyche."—Trans.

2. Freud, "Formulations on the Two Principles of Mental Functioning," *Gesammelte Werke* 8:232n; *Standard Edition of the Complete Psychological Works of Sigmund Freud*, trans. James Strachey, rev. ed. (London: Hogarth, 1958), 12:220n, henceforth *SE*. Contrary to what is sometimes claimed, the theme of an originary narcissistic investment is present in Freud up to and including the *Outline* of 1938.

3. An algebraic field is said to be closed if all equations written with elements of the field find their solutions within the field itself. For instance, the field R of real numbers is not algebraically closed (the equation $x^2 + 1 = 0$ does not contain a solution), but the field C of complex numbers is closed (the preceding equation contains the solution $x = i$, where i is the square root of -1).

4. See my "Institution of Society and Religion," in *WIF*.

5. See "Communism in its Mythical Sense," in *IIS*.

6. See "Reflections on Racism," in *WIF*.

7. As is well known, this possibility is not absent from effective history. It corresponds to the different forms of acculturation, often imposed through violence (including economic violence), sometimes also adopted by the victors as partial acculturation compensated by effective domination. This was true of the Mongols in China, the Romans in relationship to Greece, etc. I am certain that detailed discussion of these various cases would demonstrate that the key to their understanding is contained in the ideas expressed here. The instances of massive "voluntary" conversion, notably religious conversion, call for different considerations. From the point of view adopted here, they are equivalent to "revolutions" during which an imaginary institution of the total society is subverted and replaced by another one.

8. Xenophon, *Constitution of the Spartans*, 14, 4.

9. Psyche and Education

This talk with Jacques Ardoino, René Barbier, and Florence Giust-Desprairie was held on February 7, 1991. It was published in *Pratiques de formation* (April 25–26, 1993): 43–63, under the title "Psyché et Education." [For reasons of space, the wording of the questions has been slightly abridged. Intertitles are by the French editors.]

1. *WIF.*

2. Henri Atlan, *Tout, Non, Peut-être: Education et vérité* (Paris: Éditions du Seuil, 1991).

3. Michel Serres, *Le Tiers-instruit* (Paris: François Bourin, 1991).

4. In *Speculations after Freud: Psychoanalysis, Philosophy and Culture,* ed. Sonu Shamdasani and Michael Münchow (New York: Routledge, 1994), 2–12, republished in *WIF.*

5. See note 4.

10. Psychoanalysis: Its Situation and Limits

[This paper was written by Cornelius Castoriadis for presentation at "Building Bridges: A Conference on Psychoanalysis and Culture," a conference organized in November 1997 by the William Allanson White Institute (New York), where it was read by Joel Whitebook. The present title was added by the French editors.] Castoriadis had originally given the paper another title: "On Psychoanalysis, Talmudism and Anything-Goesism." It is published here in a revised version.—Trans.

1. Heidegger's jeremiads about Western logocracy, the "forgetting of Being," and technicization of the world are unable to account for why this expansion and dominance "succeeds" to such an extent; i.e., how it would be possible if there were not "something" in Being itself that it encounters. The only elucidation possible within the Heideggerian perspective is that *Dasein* succeeds in "imposing" the *logos* on whatever there is—that is, on something bearing no relation whatsoever to it, thus finally "violating" what there is. Then, however, and despite all his rhetoric, Heidegger appears committed unconsciously to the credo of human "omnipotence." The same is of course true, mutatis mutandis, of postmodernist and deconstructionist relativism, even in its simplest, "pragmatist" forms, as in Richard Rorty. But deconstructionism is steeped in incoherence—the "anything goes" mentality, particularly flagrant when one looks at the practical/political level—to such a degree that discussion with it (deconstructionism) would in fact be impossible, were it worth our while.

2. Topography, the principle of constancy, and so on.

11. The Psyche and Society Anew

[This interview with Fernando Urribarri was first published in Spanish in *Zona Erogena, Revista abierta de psicoanâlisis y pensamiento contemporâneo* (Buenos Aires) 28 (May 1996): 4–6, 48–50. The title ("À nouveau sur la psyché et la société."—Trans), was added by the French editors.]

1. ["Instincts and Their Vicissitudes" (1915), *SE*, 14.]
2. *WIF.*
3. ["Instincts and Their Vicissitudes" (1915), *SE*, 14.]
4. ["Findings, Ideas, Problems" ([1938] 1941) in *SE*, 23:299.]
5. The *IIS* note gives the reference as follows: "Formulations on the Two Principles of Mental Functioning," *SE*, 12:219–20, note.—Trans.
6. *IIS.*
7. Piera Aulagnier, *The Violence of Interpretation: From Pictogram to Statement,* trans. Alan Sheridan (Hove, England: Brunner-Routledge, 2001).

12. The Social-Historical: Mode of Being, Problems of Knowledge

[Originally written in English for *Thought.* Published in *PPA,* ed. David Ames Curtis (New York: Oxford University Press, 1991), 33–46. Translated into French by Olivier Fressard. Published in *FP* as "Mode d'être et problèmes de connaissance du social-historique."—Trans.]

1. *IIS,* 167–220.
2. Cf. *IIS,* 9–70, 115–64.
3. "The State of the Subject Today" (1986), trans. David Ames Curtis, in *Thesis Eleven* 24 (1989): 5–43.
4. See *IIS,* passim, and *CL,* 119–44.
5. Cf. "Subject," passim.
6. Concerning this, see *IIS,* 340–44, and "The Logic of Magmas and the Question of Autonomy," trans. David Ames Curtis, *Philosophy and Social Criticism* 20 (1994): 123–54.

13. False and True Chaos

This lecture was given at the September 26, 1992, edition of the "Ville Evrard Nights," devoted to chaos, and published as "Faux et vrai chaos" in *La Nuit de Ville-Evrard, Temps, mémoire, chaos* (Paris: Descartes et Compagnie, 1993), 201–10. The present version contains some purely formal rectifications.

1. [*Der Ursprung der Griechischen Philosophie: von Hesiod bis Parmenides* (Basle: Schwabe, 1945).]
2. Freud, *GW,* 2:529–30; *SE,* 5:525. Castoriadis gave his own translation of this development in "Psychoanalysis and Philosophy" (*Castoriadis Reader*). He dif-

fers with Strachey on two points: the German *müssen ja ganz allgemein* is to be understood as "must even obligatorily, and in an entirely universal fashion have no definite endings" rather than "cannot, from the nature of things, have any definite endings," whereas he translates the German *dichteren* as "dense" rather than "close."—Trans.

14. Remarks on Space and Number

The French version of this previously unpublished text appeared in *Figures du Pensable* under the title "Remarques sur l'espace et le nombre." For the English version, I am greatly indebted to Daniel Ferrand, mathematician and professor of mathematics at the University of Rennes. Thanks to his advice and stringent rereading, this paper will, I hope, be comprehensible to specialists in the field. He also corrected several misformulations in the original French text. The original expressions are given in the notes.—Trans.

1. Page 242 of the English-language edition (*IIS*).
2. The rue d'Ulm is the location of Paris' prestigious Ecole Normale Supérieure. Many of France's outstanding thinkers have studied and/or taught there, and it is where Parisian intellectual fashions are made and undone.—Trans.
3. See "Modern Science and Philosophical Interrogation" in *CL*, and "The Logic of Magmas and the Question of Autonomy" in *Castoriadis Reader.*
4. See *IIS*, chap. 5.
5. I certainly would not have the reader take me wrongly. What is ensidic here is not the activity of the true mathematician, which is as poietic as any other activity, and may be one of the most imaginative of human activities. It is the *caput mortuum,* the dross of the resulting findings, that tends, ideally, toward the totally ensidic.
6. Original: "magnitudes."—Trans.
7. Aristotle, *De Anima,* II, 1, 412b16; 2, 414 a13.
8. Walter Burley, quoted by G. J. Whitrow, *The Natural Philosophy of Time* (1980; Oxford: Clarendon Press, 1990), 215.
9. Recent discussion of these paradoxes include Whitrow's solid, concise comments in *The Natural Philosophy of Time* (190–200). Alexandre Koyré's discussion in his "Remarques sur les paradoxes de Zénon" (1922, in *Etudes d'histoire de la pensée philosophique* [Paris: Gallimard, 1971], 9–55) is as relevant as ever. Suffice it to note that Peirce and Whitehead rejected the paradoxes (Peirce viewed Achilles and the tortoise as a "silly little catch," and Whitehead ascribed "Zeno's fallacy to his ignorance of infinite numerical series"), whereas Bertrand Russell thought they were "immeasurably subtle and profound" and William James felt

that refutations of the Achilles paradox "miss Zeno's point entirely." See also note 11.

10. Original: "[*a, a + b*]." The correct formula justifies the otherwise incomprehensible parenthetical "small *d.*"—Trans.

11. My intention here is not to discuss the paradoxes in themselves, and I agree, roughly, with Whitrow's conclusion that "definite logical antinomies result if we try to combine the hypothesis of continuity, and hence of infinite divisibility, with that of the transitional nature of time" (*Natural Philosophy of Time,* 200), except that I think that the root of the difficulties resides just as much with "continuity" as with the "transitional nature of time." Here, briefly, is why. It is impossible to divide the segment (0, 1) into an infinite number of equal segments. If the segments are equal, there will be a finite number in the segment (0, 1). But it is of course possible to divide the segment (0, 1) into an infinite number of *unequal* segments, of decreasing size for instance. This would produce segments defined by the points 0, 1/2, 3/4, 7/8 . . . $(2^n - 1)/2^n$ . . . The mathematician will say that the sum of those segments tends toward 1 and will go on to another problem. That is what Whitehead does when he reproaches Zeno for not knowing the sum of the series 2^{-n} ($n = 1, 2, 3 \ldots$), which is "equal to 1." But it is equal to 1 in the sense that the difference between the sum and 1 can be made as small as one likes. The mathematician says, "'As small as one likes' means nil," and he continues on his way. The philosopher (in this case, Zeno) says that there is absolutely nothing self-evident in the fact of identifying "as small as one likes" with 0. And he is right. The proof is the creation of nonstandard analysis, starting in 1960 (see A. Robinson, *Non-Standard Analysis* [Amsterdam: North-Holland Publishing, 1966], esp. chap. 10, "Concerning the History of the Calculus," 260–82).

12. Original: "from n to n' (for $n' \leq n$) is equal to the cardinal (minus 1) of the part $\{0, 1, \ldots, n' - n\}$."—Trans.

13. Original: "A $\neq$ 0."—Trans.

14. Émile Borel, *Éléments de la théorie des ensembles* (Paris: Albin Michel, 1949), 200, 201, 206–10, 226–29, 236–37, 239, 310.

15. R. Thom, *Prédire n'est pas expliquer* (Paris: Eschel, coll. "La question," 1991), 53; 2nd ed. (Paris: Flammarion, coll. "Champs," 1993).

MERIDIAN

Crossing Aesthetics